NEIL ZURCHE

"Neil Zurcher's One Tank Trips have fascinated Northern Ohioans for generations . . . [This] book is loaded to the brim with some of his most memorable excursions."
— *The Morning Journal*

"Sometimes humorous, sometimes touching, [Zurcher's] Channel 8 segments have made him something like Northeast Ohio's answer to the late Charles Kuralt."
— *The Plain Dealer*

"While an Ohio travel book is nothing new, Zurcher's everyman approach to travelling is what sets it apart from the rest. . . . [He's] Ohio's foremost expert on off-beat attractions"
— *Star Beacon*

"Zurcher writes as he speaks. Reading him, it's easy to think about jumping in the car with him to sample some new roadhouse and listening to his stories along the way."
— *Cleveland Enterprise*

"Famous for his 20-year run as WJW TV 8's travel reporter, Zurcher is known for locating little-known, interesting, and unusual destinations within a day's drive of the Greater Cleveland area." — *Stow Sentry*

"Keep a copy in your boat, your car, whatever you happen to drive. . . . Neil Zurcher is a very talented writer."
— WERE AM Radio

"The definitive guide for Ohio travelers."
— *Chesterland News*

"If a cross-country odyssey to the Gulf Coast or Rockies isn't within your budget, Neil offers hundreds of closer-to-home destinations."
— *Hudson Hub Times*

"If you can get there on a tank [of gas], Neil Zurcher has been there."
— *Canton Repository*

"The variety of places Zurcher has found makes you wonder why you would ever have to vacation outside of Ohio . . . Enough to provide Ohioans with [a] most comprehensive, practical and entertaining travel guide."
— *West Life*

Also by Neil Zurcher:

Ohio Oddities
Strange Tales from Ohio

.

OHIO ROAD TRIPS
– 2ND EDITION –

*52 TRIPS – HUNDREDS OF FUN AND
UNUSUAL GETAWAY IDEAS IN OHIO!*

Neil Zurcher

GRAY & COMPANY, PUBLISHERS
CLEVELAND

*This book is dedicated to my favorite traveling companion:
my wife, Bonnie Adamson Zurcher*

Gray & Company, Publishers
www.grayco.com

This guide was prepared on the basis of the author's best knowledge at the time of publication. However, because of constantly changing conditions beyond his control, the author disclaims any responsibility for the accuracy and completeness of the information in this guide. Users of this guide are cautioned not to place undue reliance upon the validity of the information contained herein and to use this guide at their own risk.

ISBN-13: 978-1-59851-057-7

Printed in the United States of America

10 9 8 7 6 5 4 3 2 1

Contents

Preface

For a quarter of a century I had the greatest job in television.

I was allowed to go anyplace I wanted to visit in Ohio, seven other states, and parts of Canada. It was for a television news segment called "One Tank Trips" of which I was the host. Each week a videographer and I would set out to discover a great family-friendly destination. We would then produce a television report in which I would try out various attractions—exploring, riding, shopping, eating, sleeping, whatever. It was like going on a new vacation each week, every week of the year. From a thrilling jet-boat ride to a romantic evening cruise on a sternwheeler down the Ohio River; from a parasail over Lake Erie to a moonlit winter's night ride in a one-horse open sleigh; from the wonder of a spring waterfall at Ash Cave in southern Ohio to stroll over a covered bridge on an autumn day in Ashtabula County, I got to do it all.

I hosted the show for 25 years, which reportedly makes it the longest running travel segment in television history. (Because of its success, it has since been emulated by many other TV stations.) In those 25 years I sampled things like edible worms and bugs, the world's biggest hamburgers, a five-pound omelet, and an ice cream sundae so big that it was served in a stainless steel kitchen sink. I spent the night in a fantasy hotel offering rooms decorated like a cave, an Egyptian temple, and even a drive-in movie theater (you slept in a 1955 Cadillac convertible). There were cabins in the woods and palatial hotels overlooking great natural wonders. We rode the world's tallest, fastest, and craziest roller coasters. We traveled into the earth in a coal mine and soared into the clouds in everything from a hot-air balloon to a world war two fighter plane. We had the chance to drive race cars, to ride on steam-driven trains and boats powered by jet motors. We spent quiet evenings at dinner with Amish families in their homes and watched sunsets from historic lighthouses. We visited the homes of presidents and walked the paths of pioneers.

I have gathered the best Ohio destinations from those trips in this book. They are places I hope will please every member of a family, from the youngest to the oldest. They're my personal favorites, and I'd like to share them with you.

When I travel Ohio, I don't think of it broken into five exact sections, Central, Northeast, Northwest, Southwest, and Southeast. Rather, I loosely imagine it as many overlapping regions. But to organize this book it was necessary to define some geographic areas. These groupings are meant to give a general idea of where the attractions are located, to make them easier to find on a map. This may mean, for example, that the town of Millersburg, in Holmes County, is listed in a grouping of trips in Central Ohio, while some consider it a part of Northeast Ohio. You've got to draw a line somewhere, but the lines are a bit arbitrary. Don't be afraid to mix and match some of the trips that are located in adjoining geographical areas.

The destinations listed in this book have been chosen by me on the basis of my own experience and from letters and phone calls I have received from my "One Tank Trips" viewers over the years. None of the destinations has paid a fee to be included in this book.

This is not intended to be a technical reference work. You won't find maps or detailed directions. Instead, this book is meant to encourage you to get out and sample some new places that might be fun, intriguing, and, hopefully, educational. Remember, half the fun of traveling is discovery. So, get out your map and plan your trip.

Lastly, I offer one bit of advice. When my wife and I are on one of our own Ohio road trips, and I suddenly find myself at the end of a dead-end road that wasn't on the map, and she says, "You're lost, aren't you?" I always reply, "I am not lost. I just don't know exactly where I am at this moment."

Happy travels.

Some Thoughts While Filling the Gas Tank

There is a very good reason why the U.S. Postal Service came up with ZIP codes for our mailing addresses: they had to deliver mail in Ohio.

My wife, Bonnie, who keeps track and cares about such things as where I have been, points to the problem the postal service must have had delivering mail to Ohioans before the ZIP code era.

There are 296 towns and villages in Ohio that share the same, exact name with another town or village in another county. And if that is not bad enough, there are 38 instances in Ohio where three towns all share the same name. Pity the poor postman who had to determine if a letter bound for Berlin, Ohio, was meant to go to the Berlin down in Williams County, or the Berlin up near Sandusky in Erie County, or the Berlin down in Holmes County where all the Amish live.

Some towns' names were so popular that they just multiplied like rabbits all over Ohio. For instance, take Avondale. There's Avondale down near the Ohio River in Belmont County, and there's Avondale over near Bellefontaine. There's Avondale near Canton in Stark County, and let's not forget the Avondale near Dayton, as well as another in Muskingum County, and the one near Cincinnati. Altogether there are six Avondales in Ohio.

And it gets worse. There are eight counties in Ohio with towns named Centerville. Now they are probably all near the center of something, which probably accounts for the name, but it makes me wonder, didn't anyone in town check the post office to see if there was another Centerville before they started painting signs at the corporate limits?

That brings us to Stringtown, Ohio, probably one of the stranger names. I can only speculate on how the name originated. Perhaps the pioneers laid out the town with bits of string to show where the various lots were. Who knows? In any event, there must have been a lot of string laid out in Ohio because Bonnie has discovered a total of 10 towns in Ohio that share the name of Stringtown.

And the postman's real nightmare was the town of Five Points. The name probably originated from the early Native American trails that intersected and became roads and places of settlement. No fewer than 11 towns, villages, and hamlets in Ohio bear the name Five Points.

What I am leading up to here is the importance of checking addresses and directions before starting out on a One Tank Trip anywhere in

Ohio, unless you like to find yourself in unexpected places and meet people who haven't the foggiest idea what you're looking for. For example, say you're heading for Boston, in Summit County, to visit the Blossom Music Center, and instead you end up at Boston down in Jefferson County. You'll probably get directions to someone's orchard if you ask anyone there how to get to Blossom.

Even if you're a seasoned Ohio traveler and think you know where everything is in the state, you may find yourself, like I did once, in the wrong Georgetown late at night, looking for a motel that doesn't exist in the Georgetown you are presently visiting. It is only then that you discover there are six Georgetowns, and the one that you want is at the other end of the state. At times like these you begin to develop a real affection for the postal service's ZIP codes and curse anyone who fails to include a zip code in their address.

The bottom line: use your phone. Call ahead. Get up-to-date directions, ask them to send you maps. I don't care whether you are using my travel book or someone else's, all things change with time, and if you are going to invest your family's time and money in a One Tank Trip, take a moment before you go to confirm times, places, costs, and, especially, just which Five Corners it's in.

CENTRAL
OHIO

Gateway to Amish Country

Baltic, Sugarcreek

Cheesmaking history at the Alpine Hills Museum

SUGARCREEK: GATEWAY TO OHIO'S AMISH COUNTRY

The town of Sugarcreek, the gateway to Ohio's Amish land, is known as the "Little Switzerland" of Ohio. You will find most buildings in this quaint village have façades that proclaim the strong Swiss heritage of many of its residents. It started in the 1950s when a local artist, Tom Miller, painted a mural of Switzerland on his downtown building. Miller was instrumental in starting the annual Swiss Festival that is held each autumn in the town. Today you will find many three-dimensional murals depicting scenes from Switzerland on many of the downtown structures. Even the local pay phone is housed in a small building that resembles a Swiss chalet.

Near this town is the world's largest Amish population. The *Budget*, a weekly newspaper that reports on the doings of the Amish, is published here and sent to Amish communities around the world.

A MUSEUM OF CHEESE

They celebrate cheese in this town because it is one of the staples of life here. This tiny museum on the main street shows, in specially prepared rooms, how early cheese-making was done. It also offers a peek into the past of this community with a nice display of local memorabilia and early vehicles.

▲ **Alpine Hills Museum**   ☎ 330-852-4113
106 W. Main St. · Sugarcreek

FOOD THE AMISH WAY

There are several Amish-style restaurants in and around Sugarcreek. This one is operated by the same firm that owns Der Dutchman in Walnut Creek. They serve the traditional Amish fare of beef, turkey, and ham with lots of mashed potatoes, gravy, and stuffing, as well as a large salad bar, homemade bread, and pies—all for a reasonable price. Most everything is made fresh each day in the kitchen. There is also a bakery in-house so you can take home some of those Amish goodies. Closed on Sundays.

▲ **Dutch Valley Restaurant**   ☎ 330-852-4627
1343 Old Route 39 NE · Sugarcreek

A MODERN INN

This is a luxurious place to stay while exploring Ohio's Little Switzerland or Amish country. Sitting high on a hillside overlooking State Route 39, the 69-room inn has a country look to it, but inside you'll find spacious rooms, some with fireplaces and balconies. All rooms have at least a queen-sized bed or larger and feature locally handcrafted furnishings made with oak and cherry wood. There is even an indoor swimming pool where you can relax after a day of exploring the countryside. The inn is located next to the Dutch Valley Restaurant and is only a short distance from two wineries.

▲ **Carlisle Inn, Sugarcreek**   ☎ 877-422-7547
1357 Old Rte. 39 · Sugarcreek

FLOUR POWER

This mill has operated for more than a hundred years. Owner Alvin Miller still grinds his flour daily from grain that he has dried in large tubs out behind the mill. My wife, Bonnie, insists this is the only flour she has ever found that makes the perfect loaf of bread in a bread-making machine. Closed on Sundays.

▲ **Baltic Mills**   ☎ 330-897-0522
111 Main St. · Baltic

THE OLDEST CHEESE FACTORY IN AMERICA

The Steiner Cheese Company in the sleepy little town of Baltic has a legitimate claim as the oldest manufacturer of Swiss Cheese in America. In 1833, Swiss cheese maker Jacob Steiner came to this area, bringing along his copper cheese-making kettle. The land reminded him of his

Carlisle Inn, with a hillside view in Sugarcrreek

native Switzerland, and soon he was joined by relatives and friends who were also immigrating to America. The lush pastures of Holmes and Tuscarawas Counties attracted farmers and herds of milk-producing cows. Steiner began making cheese just as he had in his native Switzerland, one small batch at a time.

The company continues that practice today, hand-crafting their cheese and still winning awards for some of the best Swiss cheese, not only in Ohio but across the country. You can watch them make the cheese each day at the factory through an observation window or make a reservation for a guided tour of the factory operation.

A retail store offers all the various types of their cheese, from classic Swiss cheese to more modern baby Swiss and even smoked cheese.

▲ **Steiner Cheese** ☎ 330-897-5505
201 Mill Street · Baltic

GUEST CABINS

These getaway cabins are operated by a Mennonite couple. Several modern cabins are located around a small lake behind their home. While not luxurious, the cabins are clean and have electricity and bathrooms, a gas-fired fireplace, two bedrooms, a small dining and living room, and a porch to sit on and watch the sunsets from. They welcome children (there is even a small playground near the edge of the lake and paddle boats with fishing). This is a nice family getaway spot, nestled on a quiet side road surrounded by Amish and Mennonite farms.

▲ **Mel and Mary Raber's Cabins** ☎ 330-893-2695
2972 Township Rd. 190 · Baltic

The Heart of Amish Country

Berlin

OHIO'S AMISH

Ohio is home to the largest population of Amish in the world. Forget what you have read about Pennsylvania; when it comes to the Amish, they are definitely number two.

If you are visiting the Amish country of Holmes-Wayne-Tuscarawas counties for the first or the fiftieth time, it's a good idea to start your visit at *Behalt* at the Amish and Mennonite Heritage Center in Berlin, Ohio. Here, a 265-foot mural of the history of the Amish and Mennonite people can be seen. It was the masterpiece of artist Heinz Gaugel, a former German soldier, who in the 1960s stumbled upon the Amish settlement in Holmes County and decided to stay and learn about the culture. He gained the trust of Amish community leaders and spent more than a dozen years creating his enormous canvas that depicts the development of the faith through several hundred years. Although Gaugel has died, you can still see his studio at the center and an unfinished painting, as well as his master work, *Behalt*, the story of a people.

The Heritage Center is a great place to learn about Amish customs, as well as where small cottage industries are located and directions to the many Amish-style restaurants in the area. They also offer some large and clean restrooms.

▲ **Amish and Mennonite Heritage Center**   ☎ 877-858-4634
5798 County Rd. 77 · Berlin
Follow signs east of Berlin on State Rte. 39

THE AMISH WAY OF LIFE

One of the best ways to get a better understanding of Ohio's Amish and their way of life is to visit one of the Amish homes that are open to the general public. The Schrock family in Berlin offers a different viewpoint, since many of the family were and some still are Amish. The home and its furnishings are authentic, and many of the possessions inside are things actually used by the Schrock family.

You can visit the barnyard and a petting zoo of some smaller animals. Real horse-drawn Amish buggies offer rides on a private road around the farm, and a miniature train carries passengers around the surrounding fields.

Heini's Bunker Hill Cheese Company, the first large maker of Swiss cheese in the area

If this is your first visit to Ohio's Amish Country, this would serve as a great introduction to Amish culture. For example, the Amish, for religious reasons, do not like to have their photograph taken. A stop here will help you to be a courteous tourist while visiting.

  ▲ **Schrock's Amish Farm**   ☎ 330-893-3232
    4363 State Rte. 39 · Berlin

THE FIRST CHEESE FACTORY

The area's cheese production began in the early 1930s with the opening of Heini's Bunker Hill Cheese Company, the first really large maker of Swiss cheese in the area. Today, the Dauwalder family still operates the business, which now ships cheese all over the world. They offer free tours of the cheese-making operation during the morning hours on weekdays, and they have a salesroom where you can have free samples from the more than 50 varieties of cheese that they make and sell here—everything from Swiss to chocolate cheese. That's right, chocolate. It tastes a little like fudge. Heini's also offers a series of shops in its complex that sell fudge, crafts, souvenirs, fresh baked goods, and many other things.

  ▲ **Heini's Bunker Hill Cheese Company**   ☎ 330-893-2131
    6005 County Rd. 77 · Berlin

MODERN AMENITIES IN AMISH COUNTRY

While you don't find many places to stay in Amish country that offer big-city amenities like swimming pools and exercise rooms, there are exceptions. Built on the rolling hills west of the town of Berlin is a motel complex that measures up to those in many big cities. Besides the basic rooms, they offer 20 suites with amenities like a 50-inch plasma TV,

Jacuzzi tubs and walk-in showers in the bathroom. It even has a small theater where groups can watch movies or use for meetings. There is a restaurant nearby, and on the other side of the motel is a fitness center that is open to motel guests. It includes exercise equipment, a spa, and an indoor swimming pool.

▲ **The Berlin Hotel and Suites**   ☎ 800-935-5218
5330 County Rd. 201 · Berlin
At the intersection of County Rd. 201 and State Rte. 39 west of Berlin.

CRAFTSMANSHIP IN OAK AND CHERRY

If you want to see Amish craftsmen at work making the beautiful oak and cherry furniture for which they are famous, you can do so in the salesroom at Schrock's Heritage Furniture. Through a large glass window you can look into the shop, where furniture is turned out one piece at a time. Inside you can choose from a fine selection of products ready for sale, or you can custom order your furniture.

▲ **Schrock's Heritage Furniture**   ☎ 330-893-2211
4760 E. Main St. · Berlin
Part of the Shrock's Amish Farm complex.

HANDMADE QUILTS

To see how some of the beautiful Amish-Mennonite quilts are made, watch the ladies sewing each day at this quilt shop. They will always answer questions and demonstrate how the intricately patterned quilts are made. There are hundreds of quilts on display and for sale.

▲ **Gramma Fannie's Quilt Barn**   ☎ 330-893-3232
4363 State Rte. 39 · Berlin
Part of the Shrock's Amish Farm complex, east of Berlin.

'TIS ALWAYS THE SEASON HERE

This landmark building was constructed long ago to house a cyclorama painting featuring Amish-Mennonite history. When the painting was finally finished, it was instead located in the Mennonite Information Center down the road. Since then this building has been used for a basketball court and an indoor arcade; now it is a year-round Christmas store. The main rotunda is filled with beautifully decorated Christmas trees. A small chapel in the center of the building contains all types of angels and other decorations. Upstairs, overlooking the rotunda, a series of shops sells unusual gift items and decorating ideas.

▲ **'Tis the Season Year Round Christmas Shoppe**   ☎ 330-893-3604
4363 State Rte. 39 · Berlin
Part of the Shrock's Amish Farm complex, east of Berlin.

Donna's Premier Lodging

A ROMANTIC HIDEAWAY

In Berlin, tucked away on a back street within walking distance of the main street, is a quaint bed and breakfast that offers a hideaway for honeymoons, anniversary celebrations, or any special occasion. There are two rooms in the main house and two small cottages that were once carriage barns. The cottages offer cathedral ceilings, floor-to-ceiling fireplaces, four-poster beds with Amish quilts, a whirlpool bath for two with lights, and even a small waterfall! In the morning, the owner discreetly places a tray with a large breakfast on it on a cart outside the door. Reservations are an absolute must here almost anytime.

△ **Donna's Premier Lodging**   ☎ (330) 893-3068
　 5523 East St. · Berlin

A REAL SODA JERK

If you are visiting Berlin and tire of everything Amish, you might want to make a stop here. The Catalpa Trading Company specializes in nostalgia and souvenirs, but in an attached room is a real gem: the 1940s-era working soda fountain, where the soda jerk still wears the paper hat and black bow tie. You can get a freshly made banana split or a phosphate (Remember those?). It's a pleasant way to take a break from seeing Amish country.

△ **Catalpa Trading Company and Old Fashioned Soda Fountain**
　 ☎ 330-893-3752
　 4846 E. Main St. · Berlin

IF I HAD A HAMMER

In a barn-like gift shop on the outskirts of Berlin, they sell hammered aluminum and copper plates, trays, dishes, and other metal products.

The forge, where the craftsmen do their work, is located in Pennsylvania, but they offer a video tour of the forge. There is also a small museum in the building with hammered aluminum products from the past and also the world's largest Amish buggy. Tour groups are welcome.

▲ **Wendell August Forge**   ☎ 866-354-5192
  7007 Dutch Country Ln. · Berlin

A craftsman at work in Wendell August Forge

Where Baby Swiss Was Born

Millersburg

WHEN YOU ROUGH IT, WATCH YOUR STEP

It was a foggy spring morning. It had rained almost all night, and now the mist of morning was just starting to burn away as the sun teased us with the promise of a balmy day.

Videographer Bill West and I had driven to this gravel road in the Doughty Valley, east of Millersburg, to do a report on what I called an "Amish motel": a collection of log cabins on a hillside operated as a campground by an Amish family. The cabins had just been completed a few weeks earlier, and we had convinced the publicity-shy Amish owners that it would be good for their business if we showed their new enterprise. We had also promised not to take any pictures of the owners.

The cabins were scattered down a hillside that overlooked the Doughty Creek, which flows through the valley. Across the valley, you could make out the stainless steel storage tanks at the Guggisberg Cheese Company, just now emerging from the morning fog.

I stepped out of our car and immediately noticed a strong odor of horse manure. But being in Amish Country, where horses are the main means of transportation, I gave it little thought. Bill was setting up his camera as I walked to the edge of the hillside to get a good look at the cabins. The wet ground seemed to be covered with straw. I stepped onto the steep path that lead toward the cabins, and I felt my feet start to slip. I threw up my arms to regain my balance, but then both feet went out from under me and I landed on my back and started to slide through the mud and straw down the hill.

When I finally came to a stop about 30 feet down the hillside, I realized where the smell of horse manure had been coming from. They had just seeded the hillside and spread fresh manure on it for fertilizer. I was now coated from the top of my head to the bottom of my heels with a mixture of horse dung, straw, and wet mud.

Videographer West and an Amish woman came skidding down the hill to help. They helped me to my feet, both trying—not too successfully—to smother their laughter as I stood up, mud and dung dripping from my hair, my back, and my legs.

"Where's the bathroom?" I asked the Amish lady.

She covered her mouth with one hand to disguise a smile and used the other to point to a small wooden building at the bottom of the hill.

"There it is," she said, "but there's no running water here."

"Where's the nearest place I can clean myself up?" I asked.

She pointed across the valley towards the Guggisberg Cheese Company's store.

I started walking up the hill towards our news cruiser. As I approached the door, Bill West jumped in front of me and said, "Where are you going?"

I explained that I was going to get in the car and have him drive me down to the cheese company so I could use their modern bathroom.

"You're not going to get in my news cruiser like that!" he said, refusing to budge. He pointed to the hood of his car.

A few minutes later, clinging to the hood of the news cruiser, spread-eagled across the car like a large animal bagged in a hunt, I was driven down the hill and across the valley, past startled Amish families in their buggies, to the cheese factory, where I was finally able to wash up.

As to how you rent those cabins, most of the Amish don't have telephones. But if you call on a Monday morning, they station one of the Amish youngsters at a pay telephone across the street from the cabins to take messages about reservations. Just let it ring a long time, in case he has decided to wander down the road to explore the ditch.

The cabins, while primitive, are quite nice. They offer a wood-burning stove, kerosene lamps, cookware and bedding for a family of at least four, and furniture for a very reasonable price. And, at the top of the hill, there is a non-electric bakery.

▲ **Countryside Campers' Paradise** ☎ 330-893-3002 (Mondays only, 8:30 a.m.–6 p.m.)
4280 Township Road 356 · Millersburg
South of Rte. 39 off State Rte. 557

GUGGISBERG CHEESE FACTORY

This is where baby Swiss cheese was created. Each day, Monday through Friday, they turn out about fourteen 200-pound blocks of Baby Swiss cheese to ship all over the world. In their cheese house you can watch the cheese being made early in the morning. There is a retail store, where you can buy the cheese and many gifts imported from Switzerland. There is also a fine restaurant across the street where they serve Swiss- and German-style foods, including their cheese. You can try it on sandwiches or even in fondue (melted cheese that you dip cubes of bread in). Next door is an inn operated by the family, in case you would like to spend the night.

▲ **Guggisberg Cheese** ☎ 800-262-2505
5060 State Rte. 557 · Millersburg

Guggisberg Cheese Factory, where baby Swiss cheese was born

SWISS, AUSTRIAN, AND AMISH

Across the street from the cheese factory is another of the Guggisberg family enterprises: an authentic Swiss chalet that serves Swiss, Austrian, and Amish foods. During tourist season this is a very busy place, and the wait for a table can be up to an hour at lunchtime.

▲ **Chalet in the Valley**   ☎ 330-893-2500
5060 State Rte. 557 · Millersburg

SLEIGH RIDES AND HAYRIDES

Another enterprise of the Guggisberg family is just up the road, where son Eric and his wife, Julie, have opened an inn. It offers whirl-pool bathtubs in some rooms and includes packages that give you and a loved one a horse-drawn sleigh ride when there is snow on the ground. In warmer weather, a horse-drawn Amish buggy takes you on a tour of the surrounding farms.

▲ **Guggisberg Swiss Inn/Amish Country Riding Stables**
☎ 877-467-9477
5025 State Rte. 557 · Millersburg

AN EXOTIC MIX OF ANIMALS

There's a place in Ohio's Amish country where you can really get up close and personal with wild animals.

Some of the Amish deal in exotic animals, raising and selling them to animal preserves, hunting preserves, or for their meat. But in Holmes County, one Amish family noticed how many tourists would slow down when passing their farm to gawk at the llamas, water buffalo, and other wild creatures waiting in their pastures until the next exotic animal auction. Idea became reality, and Rolling Ridge Ranch was born.

If you really want to get an up-close-and-personal look at the 500 exotic animals that call this home, like white elk, tiny pot-bellied pigs, African cattle with 12-foot-wide horns, seven-foot-tall ostriches, zebras, mountain goats, and even water buffalo, opt for a horse-drawn wagon ride through the 80-acre preserve. The wagon passes through forests and pastures and makes stops where the passengers can feed the animals, and as soon as they see the wagon, those animals come running. It is a bit disconcerting to be far back in a forest on a hillside road and suddenly see an eight-foot-tall elk plunging through the underbrush headed straight for you. But all he wants is his share of the grain that is on board the wagon. Goats even try to get on the wagon with you. At the conclusion of the ride, you are invited to the gift shop, where T-shirts and the usual souvenirs are on sale. There is also a petting zoo where baby animals and even camels and spider monkeys are waiting to for a visit. The ranch is open for tours from spring until late autumn. *[SEASONAL]*

▲ **Rolling Ridge Ranch**   ☎ 330-893-3777
3961 County Road 168 · Millersburg
Just north of the town of Berlin; watch for signs.

THE PEWTERWARE MAKER OF MILLERSBURG

There are only five places left in the entire United States where you can actually watch a master pewterware maker spin pewter. Millersburg is one of them. David N. Three Feathers Jones and his apprentice, Willa Hollingsworth, operate Three Feathers Pewter, across from the historic courthouse in downtown Millersburg.

Jones apprenticed himself to Master Pewterer Carl Steen to learn the rare art of spinning pewter. He opened his pewter business in 1984. He says he got the name "Three Feathers" when he was adopted by the Moon Society of the Shawnee Nation of Native Americans. Today in his gallery in downtown Millersburg, tourists can watch Jones and his apprentice spin pewter into fine pieces of jewelry or housewares that look like instant antiques.

▲ **Three Feathers Pewter**   ☎ 330-674-0404
12 E. Jackson St. · Millersburg

A LUXURY STAY AND HOMEMADE FOOD

If you would like to get away from the touristy area of Berlin for lunch or for even a night's stay, make a reservation at the Inn at Honey Run. It's tucked away on a hillside, far into the back roads of Holmes County. This unusual inn boasts several kinds of accommodations, from rooms burrowed into the hillside, to luxury cabins in the woods, to a rustic inn surrounded by trees. But it's the food that also brings the

The Honeycombs at the Inn at Honey Run

guests. The dining room is usually crowded, as folks line up for lunch or dinner. The menu is a break from the regular Amish-style cuisine of the area—plus they have a beer and wine license at the inn, while most of the Amish area is "dry."

🔺 **The Inn at Honey Run**   ☎ 800-468-6639
6920 County Rd. 203 · Millersburg

A MENNONITE GUEST HOUSE

A Mennonite couple and their children run this huge log home, which they built as a guest house. All the rooms have whirlpool baths, are decorated in different themes, and offer the solitude of a country back road. Some of the rooms have gas fireplaces. The front porch faces a pasture and a bend in the road; you can sit out here for hours watching horse-drawn buggies go by while listening to some classical music piped throughout the common rooms of the home. They have also added two log cabins with fully equipped kitchens, whirlpool tubs, and fireplaces.

🔺 **Fields of Home Lodge and Cabins**   ☎ 330-674-7152
7278 County Road 201 · Millersburg
On a side road north of Berlin. Ask for map when making reservations.

A LITTLE BIT OF EVERYTHING

Visitors have voted this one of their favorite attractions in Ohio's Amish Country. It's a little bit flea market, a little bit farmers' market, and a lot of crafts and tee shirts, along with Amish country foods and a view of the surrounding countryside that's one of the best in the state. It's open rain or shine because most of it is under cover in large, air-conditioned buildings equipped with elevators. The place is open from March to December on Thursdays, Fridays, and Saturdays, but not on holidays. From July to November it is also open on Wednesdays.

▲ **Holmes County Amish Flea Market**   ☎ 330-893-0900
3149 State Rte. 39 · Millersburg

SPIRITS AND TRADITION

You can find both at the Hotel Millersburg, built more than a century and a half ago. It has been modernized, and is one of the few places in Holmes County where you can have an alcoholic drink with your dinner. They have also added an elevator and some handicapped-accessible rooms. The governor of Ohio has stayed here, as have other celebrities. The rooms offer cable TV, Wi-Fi, modern bathrooms, and the convenience of being in downtown Millersburg. Enjoy outdoor dining and entertainment on the patio between Memorial Day and Labor Day. While the hotel does have the charm of being in the middle of a quaint small town where you can walk to just about everything, it is right on busy Route 39, the main street through Millersburg, and there can be a lot of truck traffic.

▲ **Hotel Millersburg**   ☎ 330-674-1457
35 W. Jackson St. · Millersburg

Hotel Millersburg (center of block) in downtown Millersburg

Peanut Clusters and Trail Bologna

Walnut Creek

PEANUT CLUSTERS!

This is a place where they still hand dip the chocolate candy, and you can watch them do it. Coblentz Chocolates has been around since 1987, when brothers Jason and Mark Coblentz decided some family candy recipes just might sell to all those tourists who were flocking to the Holmes County area. They were right, and the business has been growing ever since. If you're visiting Walnut Creek, they are located right next to the Carlisle Village Inn and within walking distance of Der Dutchman Restaurant. Candy always makes a good souvenir of Ohio's Amish country.

▲ **Coblentz Chocolate Company**   ☎ 800-338-9341
4917 State Rte. 515 · Walnut Creek

TRAIL BOLOGNA

One of the foods Ohio's Amish country is famous for is trail bologna, and you can't get it any fresher than at the factory in the tiny community of Trail, Ohio, where it was born. The Troyer family has been making the German-style bologna since 1912, and they have passed the recipe down through five generations of family. The general store in front of the plant sells the bologna, as well as locally produced cheeses and other products. There is also a small sandwich bar, if you can't wait to get home to make your own sandwich.

▲ **Troyer's Trail Bologna**   ☎ 330-893-2407
6552 State Rte. 515 N · Walnut Creek

A LOOK AT AN AMISH HOME

If you are curious about the lifestyle of these hardworking people who shun modern life, you can peek behind their curtains without invading their privacy at Yoder's Amish Home near Walnut Creek. Eli Yoder was raised Amish, and many of his family are still members of the community. The home and farm they have opened to the public was originally owned by another Amish family, and many of the guides who work at the farm today are Amish. You can see both an old-fashioned Amish home and a more modern one that includes many non-electric

Get a closeup look at Amish life at Yoder's Amish Home

appliances that may surprise you—including freezers and refrigerators. Rides in authentic Amish buggies are available, and locally made quilts and crafts are for sale.

   ▲ **Yoder's Amish Home**   ☎ 330-893-2541
     6050 State Rte. 515 · Walnut Creek

THE FIRST REALLY BIG AMISH-STYLE RESTAURANT

This is the hilltop restaurant that started it all when it came to Amish-style food in Ohio. Their family-style dinners of chicken, ham, and beef have become a tourist staple, and long lines form up every day they are open. But don't worry; they are accustomed to big crowds, and the lines move quickly. It's hard to decide whether the fresh, hot loaves of bread they serve or the homemade mashed potatoes are the main attraction. One thing is for sure: you won't leave here hungry. And don't forget those homemade pies for dessert.

   ▲ **Der Dutchman Restaurant**   ☎ 330-893-2981
     4967 Walnut St. · Walnut Creek

A REALLY BIG CONE

If someone in your family really likes ice cream, I mean lots of ice cream, then be sure to stop at this Mennonite-owned cheese house. For the most part, the Walnut Creek Cheese Company sells cheese, mostly brands made in Holmes County and its environs. But along with a lot of other goodies for the tourists, they also have a small ice cream and snack bar.

Folks who have been here before love to take new visitors to the ice cream counter and watch their faces when they order a "double-dipper."

The clerk starts to pile it on. First a large scoop of ice cream fills up the cone, and then they pile on the dips: one, two, three, sometimes four dips, until it looks like the whole creation is going to collapse. By this time, the customer usually is telling the clerk that all they ordered was a double-dipper. That's when they are informed that this is a Walnut Creek Cheese Company double-dip cone.

I guarantee it will be more ice cream than most people can eat. I have seen a family of four sit down and share one double-dip cone.

Here's a tip: be sure to ask for extra napkins because the ice cream will be melting long before you finish the cone.

Closed on Sundays.

▲ **Walnut Creek Cheese**   ☎ 877-852-2888
  2641 State Rte. 39 · Walnut Creek

A FOUR-DIAMOND INN

The Dutch Corporation, which owns the original Amish-style restaurant in town, has built a beautiful hilltop inn that received an automobile club's prestigious four diamond award. Some of the beautifully decorated suites have whirlpool baths for two, balconies overlooking Amish farms, and a country ambiance that is hard to describe until you stay there. The inn is very busy, and reservations are a must.

▲ **Carlisle Inn**   ☎ 330-893-3636
  4949 Walnut St. · Walnut Creek

Don't expect a small ice-cream cone at Walnut Creek Cheese

A Capitol Trip

Bexley, Columbus

TOUR OF THE GOVERNOR'S RESIDENCE

The governor's official residence is open to groups for tours by reservation. Each Tuesday, a member of the staff conducts tours of the lower floors of the 1920s-era mansion and the formal gardens behind the home. Every governor and his family since C. William O'Neill in the 1950s has lived here. All, that is, except James A. Rhodes, who chose to live in his own Columbus-area home. (He used the mansion only for formal entertaining.) You will get the opportunity to see, among other things, the silver service from the U.S.S. *Ohio*, on loan to the residence from the Ohio Historical Society, and the governor's personal office, where meetings are held with cabinet and staff members.

▲ **Governor's Residence**   ☎ 614-644-7644
    358 N. Parkview Ave. · Bexley

THE OHIO STATEHOUSE COMPLEX

Some critics say it looks like a wheel of cheese on a box. Others point to the Greek Doric structure with pride and claim it is unique among America's state capitol buildings. Tours of the Ohio statehouse are given seven days a week. Here you can see where Abraham Lincoln's body lay in state in April 1865 when his funeral train paused in town. The

The Ohio statehouse

The oldest Harley dealership in America, A. D. Farrow Harley-Davidson

rotunda has been restored to its former elegance, and you can peek in both chambers of the General Assembly, where Ohio's laws are enacted. Tours start about 9:00 A.M. and run throughout the day until about 3:00 P.M. Tours are free.

Inside the statehouse in Columbus is a great gift shop that specializes in all things Ohio. Here you will find things like Ohio-made pasta, Ohio arts and crafts, and a wonderful selection of award-winning Ohio-made wines.

▲ **The Ohio Statehouse** ☎ 614-752-6350
Corner of Broad and Third streets. Parking is available for a fee in the statehouse garage and at nearby City Center Mall.

Across the street from the statehouse, free tours of the Supreme Court are available. (Tours are unavailable between 11:00 A.M. and 1:00 P.M.)

▲ **Rhodes Tower Tours** ☎ 614-466-7361
30 E. Broad St. · Columbus

A free tour is offered of the General Assembly offices, also across the street from the statehouse. (Tours are unavailable between 11:00 A.M. and 1:00 P.M.)

▲ **Riffe Tower Tours** ☎ 614-644-5250
77 S. High St. · Columbus

OLDEST HARLEY DEALERSHIP IN AMERICA

It seems like Harley-Davidson dealers in Ohio try to really make themselves stand out. Take the dealership in Columbus, A. D. Farrow Harley-Davidson. It traces its history back to Nelsonville, Ohio, and 1912, when Farrow became the very first Harley dealer in America. You can see a replica of that tiny storefront dealership in today's modern salesroom in Columbus. A. D. Farrow is also home to a museum exhibit called "Heroes of Harley-Davidson." And, by the way, they also sell new and used motorcycles here.

   ▲ **A. D. Farrow Harley-Davidson** ☎ 614-228-6353
    491 W. Broad St. · Columbus

A QUIET SPOT OF HISTORY

Near bustling downtown Columbus is a quiet, historic spot, a cemetery where more than two thousand Confederate soldiers are buried. This was the site of Camp Chase, a prison for Confederate soldiers during the Civil War. The adjacent cemetery contains the earthly remains of 2,260 prisoners who never got to return to the South when the war ended. While many died of natural causes and diseases, some were killed while trying to escape and some died violently while imprisoned. Today their graves stand in ghostly formations of identical headstones, row after row. The cemetery is open daily from 8:00 A.M. to 5:00 P.M.

   ▲ **Camp Chase Confederate Cemetery**
    2900 Sullivant Ave. · Columbus

A SCIENCE MUSEUM MADE FOR KIDS

This is definitely a stop if you have kids in the car. COSI, or the Center of Science and Industry, offers a mind-boggling array of exhibits and hands-on activities for kids of every age, from a bicycle you ride high in the air across a steel cable, to flying a simulated space mission.

   ▲ **COSI** ☎ 888-819-2674
    333 W. Broad St. · Columbus

A JEWEL IN COLUMBUS

The Franklin Park Conservatory is rightly one of the gems of downtown Columbus. The nearly 100-acre site has been around for more than a hundred years. It was originally the site of the Ohio State Fairgrounds. It was here that Civil War General William Tecumseh Sherman made a speech in which he said, "War. It is all hell." The Victorian-style Conservatory building was modeled after the famous Glass Palace at the 1893 Columbian Exposition in Chicago. In the 1920s it was the home of the first animals for the Columbus Zoo. In 1992, Franklin Park hosted the world-wide floral exhibition called Ameriflora 92 that ran for six months. Today the conservatory offers many wonderful programs as well as being the only public botanical garden in the world to house a Dale Chihuly collection of glass artworks. Chihuly's work is found in many major museums. The conservatory and its surrounding park are beautiful any time of year. There is always something to see and do.

Franklin Park Conservatory and Botanical Garden, right in downtown Columbus

▲ Franklin Park Conservatory and Botanical Garden
☎ 800-214-7275
1777 E. Broad St. · Columbus

A GOLF MUSEUM

One of the greatest golfers of all time is honored at a sprawling 24,000-square-foot facility in the heart of Ohio State University. Jack Nicklaus—"The Golden Bear"—dominated the game during his career, which spanned 50 years and included victories in more than 100 events worldwide. Visitors to this museum can wander through galleries exploring Nicklaus's life and the history of golf. Replica clubhouse doorways open onto world-famous golf courses where Nicklaus played. His trophies, clubs, and personal mementoes are on display. The museum is open Tuesday through Saturday. There is an admission charge.

▲ Jack Nicklaus Museum   ☎ 614-247-5959
2355 Olentangy River Rd. · Columbus, Ohio

HENDERSON HOUSE BED AND BREAKFAST

This home was once an old farm, and there is a family legend that it was once owned by President Rutherford B. Hayes, although the Hayes Presidential Center in Fremont says it cannot substantiate this. The dining room furniture once belonged to President Andrew Jackson. In recent times, many internationally known celebrities and politicians have stayed here, including boxing champ Archie Moore and the cast of *Phantom of the Opera*. Lee Henderson, the owner, is a former nationally known model, appearing in *Life* magazine and *Playboy*. She says she is proud to be the first African-American operator of a bed and breakfast

The Topiary Garden reproduces a famous painting in 3D

in Ohio. There are several rooms on the second floor, but only one has a private bath. The others share a bathroom on the first floor.

▲ **Henderson House Bed and Breakfast**   ☎ 614-258-3463
1544 Atcheson St. · Columbus

IT'S A PAINTING. IT'S A PARK.

Here's something different and free to do in Columbus. Visit the park on the location of the old school for the deaf in the Capitol City. A wonderful topiary garden replicates Georges Seurat's post impressionist painting titled *A Sunday on the Island of La Grande Jatte*. The bushes and shrubs have been trimmed and trained into the shapes of 54 people, eight boats, three dogs, and even a monkey. The largest figure is 12 feet tall. It's a great place for a picnic or a place to take some unusual vacation or holiday pictures. There is a Topiary Park Museum Shop next to the park where you can learn more about the park as well as buy some souvenirs.

▲ **The Topiary Garden**   ☎ 614-645-0197
Old Deaf School Park, 480 E. Town St. · Columbus

SLEEP IN A WAREHOUSE

This is one of the nicest places you'll ever find to lay your head down for the night. The Carr Building was one of the last of the old warehouses in downtown Columbus, near the arena district. Instead of tearing it down, the building was converted into a small, exclusive hotel, called The Lofts. What you get for a night is a room with high ceilings but modern in every way, including massive bathrooms and bedrooms. They will bring breakfast to your room in the morning, if you desire,

and you can pick and choose from a large assortment of breakfast items.
This is one of those places you have to see to believe. I don't think you'll
be disappointed if you're looking for something very nice for a visit to
Columbus.

▲ **The Lofts**   ☎ 800-735-6387
   55 E. Nationwide Blvd. · Columbus

THE SANTA MARIA

A replica of Christopher Columbus's flagship, the Santa Maria, is
docked in downtown Columbus in the Scioto River. The wooden ship
is as close to being a copy of the original vessel as possible. Volunteers
wear costumes of the period and act out the roles of members of Columbus's crew when visitors are aboard. The ship is open from early
April through late October, with different hours in different seasons, so
it is a good idea to call for the operating schedule. *[SEASONAL]*

▲ **The Santa Maria**   ☎ 614-645-8760
   Battelle Riverfront Park, 25 Marconi Blvd. · Columbus

Replica of Christopher Columbus's Santa Maria *on the Scioto River*

Columbus Area: North

Columbus, Delaware, Powell

The "Muffins" baseball team plays at Ohio Historical Society's Ohio Village

THE ARCHIVE OF OHIO'S HISTORY

The Ohio Historical Society houses artifacts dating back to prehistoric times in Ohio; it also contains the state archives. The library is an invaluable resource for students, researchers, and writers. Next door is Ohio Village, a replica of a typical small Ohio community in the early nineteenth century. Costumed interpreters work as tinsmiths, cooks, bakers, and shopkeepers to bring that period alive to visitors. A nineteenth-century baseball team plays games against other classic teams from around the state using rules from that era. This is a way to learn about a lot of Ohio history in just one stop. Don't miss the bookstore in the museum; it contains many books on Ohio that are just not found in other bookstores.

▲ **Ohio Historical Society**   ☎ 614-297-2300
   1982 Velma Ave. · Columbus

THE LAST WHISTLE

A Columbus firm holds the distinction of being the last American manufacturer of metal whistles, the kind policemen, referees, and band directors use. They also make the 24-karat-gold-plated presentation whistles that are given each year to the officials in the Super Bowl game.

By the way, these presentation whistles are available to the public. They make a nice gift for a friend or relative who uses a whistle.

The factory is open for tours during working hours, but reservations are required. No reservations are required to visit the gift shop.

▲ **American Whistle Corporation**   ☎ 800-876-2918
6540 Huntley Rd. · Columbus

AN UNUSUAL CAMERA SHOP

This shop has always been a personal favorite of mine. Located in an old, abandoned church, the business was started by a group of Ohio State University students and advisors who were interested in photography. They began by buying out bankrupt camera stores, and also by picking up discontinued products and selling them by mail order. The business grew to the extent that today it fills every nook and cranny of the old church. Much of the merchandise is old, some outdated, and even rare. Prices are often negotiable, especially for the used merchandise and outdated film. This shop is a bit hard to find, but worth the effort. You can find photographic equipment here that cannot be located anywhere else.

▲ **Columbus Camera Shop**   ☎ 614-267-0686
55 E. Blake St. · Columbus

AN ETHNIC ADVENTURE

Take the family on a trip to Ethiopia tonight if you are in the Columbus area. A stop at the Blue Nile Restaurant will be a real adventure in dining. Gather around a *mosseb*, a tray that everyone eats from. The tray comes loaded with different foods. (You can opt for vegetarian or meat dishes, some spicy, some bland.) You eat with your hands, using a piece of *injera*, a sort of pancake-like bread that you fold over the meat or vegetables and then carry to your mouth. It's fun, and the food is wonderful and healthy.

▲ **Blue Nile Restaurant**   ☎ 614-421-2323
2361 N. High St. · Columbus

GOURMET PB&J SANDWICHES

The Krema Nut Company knows a lot about peanut butter. The oldest peanut butter company in America still in operation, they have been churning out chunky and smooth peanut butter since 1898.

They also operate perhaps the only sandwich shop anywhere dedicated to the peanut-butter-and-jelly sandwich. The shop offers a dozen "gourmet" PB&J combinations that really melt in your mouth. Manager Brian Giunta loads up homemade wheat or white bread with hearty sloshes of Krema's chunky or smooth peanut butter (all natural—no additives) and then spreads delicious preserves like strawberry jam or orange marmalade on top. If you can dream it and it contains PB&J, Brian will try to make it for you.

Group tours of the peanut butter making operations are available for adults (no children allowed) by appointment only from January through October.

▲ **Krema Nut Company Factory Store**   ☎ 800-222-4132
1000 W. Goodale Blvd. · Columbus

OLENTANGY INDIAN CAVERNS

These caverns, formed by an underground river, have been explored to a level of 150 feet below the surface. There are several levels, and some of the passages are believed to lead to the Olentangy River a half-mile away. The caverns were first used by the Wyandot Indians as a hiding place and for tribal ceremonies. The great Chief Leatherlips was killed by his own people at the entrance to the caverns. I like these caverns because they are roomy, reasonably easy to tour, and have smooth passageways and steps. *[SEASONAL]*

▲ **Olentangy Indian Caverns**   ☎ 740-548-7917
1779 Home Rd. · Delaware

RENT A CAMP

While in the Columbus area, you might want to turn your trip into a family adventure by camping out at one of the wonderful Ohio state parks. Alum Creek State Park is located near Delaware, just north of Columbus, and offers several ways to spend the night. They include cozy cedar cabins that offer all the amenities, like air conditioning and a full bathroom. For those that like a more rustic atmosphere they offer Camper Cabins that have just the bare necessities. Of course, these attractions are very popular, and you have to make reservations. Don't wait until the last minute to apply for one of these great getaways.

▲ **Alum Creek State Park**   ☎ 740-548-4631
3615 Old State Rd. · Delaware

THE ORIGINAL MERMAIDS

The U.S. Fish and Wildlife Service has named the Columbus Zoo a rehabilitation centers for injured manatees, giving the gentle aquatic mammals a home (and providing a great attraction) while they recover and prepare for return to the wild. An amphitheater has been built with a retractable roof to house the manatees.

▲ **The Columbus Zoo**   ☎ 614-645-3400
9990 Riverside Dr. · Powell

Manatee at the Columbus Zoo

SEE THE ZOO AND THE AMUSEMENT PARK, TOO

Just across the parking lot from the world-famous Columbus Zoo is a small amusement park. The beauty of its location is that when you visit the zoo, you can also take the kids to this neat park with dozens of water and amusement park rides.

Zoombezi Bay and Jungle Jack's Landing have taken the place of Wyandotte Lake Amusement Park, a fixture in central Ohio for many years. While it is not as big and flashy as, say, Cedar Point, it is just the right size for walking without wearing out the soles of your shoes. There are many upgraded rides and attractions now that the park belongs to the Columbus Zoo, including a roller coaster, the usual bumper cars, and Tilt-A-Whirl. The water rides include 15 state-of-the-art attractions, including a wave pool and an action river. All ages will find something to do here.

⛰ **Zoombezi Bay and Jungle Jack's Landing** ☎ 800-666-5397
4850 West Powell Rd. · Powell

Columbus Area: South

Ashville, Canal Winchester, Columbus, Groveport, Lancaster, Pickerington, Rockbridge

A GREAT SMALL TOWN MUSEUM

Let's face it. Many small-town museums can be pretty boring. Collections of bugs, some local dignitaries' Civil War uniforms and books from the one-room school that used to stand on the corner.

Not so in Ashville, Ohio.

Now, I realize they are asking us to take some of these exhibits on faith. There isn't much to substantiate claims like the dog that reportedly voted for the Republican party, or the rumor that Roy Rogers once worked in a local factory and was fired for singing on the job. But they make wonderful stories. Like Chic-Chic, the chicken that used to walk to a local restaurant every day (see "The Chicken Who Bought His Own Lunch" in my book *Ohio Oddities*), or the longest functioning traffic light in America. The museum is a blend of tongue-in-cheek displays, alongside some real pieces of Americana.

▲ **Ashville Museum** ☎ 740-983-9864
34 Long St. · Ashville

SLATE RUN FARM

I have long said that Ohio's greatest treasures are the metropark districts that abound in the state. These local parks get very little statewide publicity and many are almost unknown, yet they offer everything from caves, canyons, and scenic vistas to wonderful state-of-the-art nature exhibits and a host of other things to do for the entire family.

In Columbus, the Metropolitan Park District operates the Slate Run Farm, located in nearby Pickaway County. The farm is frozen in time at the turn of the twentieth century. Horses are still used to till the earth. The farmhouse still uses wood cookstoves. The workers here are all in period costumes and stay in character when responding to questions. Kids are allowed to help with chores like gathering eggs and cultivating the garden by hand, or they can use an old rope swing under a tree beside the farmhouse.

▲ **Slate Run Farm** ☎ 614-891-0700
9139 Marcy Rd. · Ashville

A BRUSH WITH FAME

Ohio has a lot of halls of fame. Rock and roll in Cleveland. Classical music in Cincinnati. Pro football in Canton. Trapshooters in Vandalia. There is even a bull from Ohio enshrined in a hall of fame in Plain City. Name a profession or a hobby, and chances are there's a hall of fame celebrating the best and the brightest of that field. Take barbering, for instance. In Canal Winchester, near Columbus, there is a barber museum and hall of fame. It's located upstairs over Zeke's Barber Shop. Here you will find barber memorabilia, like 58 different kinds of barber poles and barber chairs from six generations of barbers. All in all, the exhibit covers 150 years of barbering. It's open by appointment only. The man you want to call is Mike Ippolotti, and if he's around, you'll get a fascinating tour and learn a whole lot about the field of barbering.

▲ **Barber Museum and Hall of Fame**   ☎ 614-833-9931
2½ S. High St. · Canal Winchester

CATALOG BARGAINS

Have you have ever wondered what happens to that merchandise you sent back to J. C. Penney's catalog center? It ends up in a giant outlet store in Columbus.

The store is located right next to the catalog distribution center, and returned merchandise, along with discontinued items, is offered for sale. The merchandise is constantly changing, so there is always something new. A careful shopper can save up to 50 percent on some items.

▲ **J. C. Penney Outlet Store**   ☎ 614-868-0250
2361 Park Crescent Rd. · Columbus

A REALLY BIG BURGER

German Village in downtown Columbus is an example of what can be done with a deteriorating neighborhood. Private capital, over the years, has restored much of this ethnic community from a slum to an attractive residential neighborhood and popular dining area. One of my favorite spots is an old tavern that serves one of the largest hamburgers in Columbus. Called a "Thurmanburger," it contains nearly one pound of ground meat, cheese, ham, and condiments. It's more than a meal, all by itself.

▲ **Thurman Cafe**   ☎ 614-443-1570
183 Thurman Ave. · Columbus

MOTTS MILITARY MUSEUM

One of the finest military museums in Ohio is a privately owned operation just outside of Columbus. Warren Motts started the collection many years ago with a sword from the Civil War that he bought at a flea market. Today the collection fills several buildings and sprawls over several acres. Included in this collection is a full-size replica of the birthplace of Medal of Honor winner Eddie Rickenbacker, WWI flying ace. There are airplanes, tanks, guns, and uniforms from around the world here. It's an amazing collection and well worth the trip.

▲ **Motts Military Museum, Inc.**   ☎ 614-836-1500
    5075 Hamilton Rd. · Groveport

ZIPLINES IN OHIO

Canopy Tours was the first such attraction in the state of Ohio or the Midwest.

Quite simply, it is a ride for thrill seekers. Wearing a special harness, you are suspended by a small wheeled device from a single steel cable stretched high in century-old trees that line the edge of the Hocking River. On the signal of your guide, you zip from one treetop platform to another under the canopy of the forest—hence the name Canopy Tours.

First, just about anyone who does not have a fear of heights can ride the zip lines, including children ages 10 and up, as long as they weigh at least 70 pounds and are accompanied by an adult. As for grownups, they require that you not exceed 250 pounds and be physically able to pull yourself, if necessary, a few feet on the cable. Pregnant women and people with heart, leg, or back problems are not allowed on the zip line. All riders must sign a release form before starting the adventure.

Some of the treetop platforms are over seven stories high. The longest zip ride is 572 feet. That's like sailing over two and a half football fields.

It takes three hours to complete the course of 10 different zip lines, four adventure bridges, and a final rappel down the side of a stone wall.

The zip line tours go rain or shine. The only time they shut down is when there is lightning or high winds.

If you go, here are some things to remember: Wear comfortable clothes (obviously no dresses for the ladies). Be sure to wear shoes with covered toes (no flip-flops). Leave your dangly jewelry, scarves, and other valuables, like your cell phone, wallet, and anything loose that might fall out of your pocket, back in your car.

▲ **Canopy Tours**   ☎ 740-385-9477
    10714 Jackson St. · Rockbridge

THE HOMES OF LANCASTER, OHIO

The Fairfield Heritage Association in Lancaster has preserved two beautiful examples of early American architecture. One of them is the birthplace of the soldier who first said, "War is hell." William Tecum-

Motorcycle Hall of Fame and Museum

seh Sherman, hero of the Civil War, and his equally famous brother, John Sherman, who went on to become a U.S. senator from Ohio, were raised in this town. Their house today looks much as it did when the Shermans lived here. Besides the family antiques and other memorabilia, you can see an exhibit of General Sherman's Civil War field tent.

▲ **Sherman House**   ☎ 740-687-5891
137 E. Main St. · Lancaster

Just down the street from the Sherman House Museum is the nineteenth century mansion that once belonged to Lancaster resident Samuel McCracken. Today it is known as the Georgian Museum. Inside you will find some Elijah Pierce woodcarvings and an Erickson Glass exhibit. The home is filled with beautiful antiques and, like nearby Sherman House, is open for tours. The Fairfield Heritage Association operates both homes.

▲ **The Georgian Museum**   ☎ 740-654-9923
105 E. Wheeling St. · Lancaster

FOR MOTORCYCLE FANS
This hall of fame honors those who have made significant contributions to the world of motorcycling, including early pioneers and those who helped develop the cycles of today. You will find here some of the most famous racing machines in the world, as well as early examples of motorcycles and the gear that went with them. If you have ever had a motorcycle or wanted one, this is an interesting destination.

▲ **Motorcycle Hall of Fame and Museum**   ☎ 614-856-2222
13515 Yarmouth Dr. · Pickerington

A Tiskett, a Taskett...
a Heck of a Big Basket

Dresden, Frazeysburg, Granville, Newark, Utica

HOME OF THE GIANT BASKET

Imagine a basket 192 feet long and 126 feet wide at its base, widening to 208 feet by 142 feet at the top. A basket standing seven stories tall—now that's what I would call a heck of a big basket!

The late Dave Longaberger dreamed this all up and made it happen. Dave was the founder of the world-renowned Longaberger Basket Company in Newark. Back in the early 1990s the company had outgrown its existing home and was getting ready to build a new corporate headquarters. But what was it to look like? The architects came up with many different ideas, but one day Dave Longaberger walked in carrying one of the company's trademark market baskets. You know, the kind that you see in pictures of old ladies carrying with loaves of bread sticking out over the edges. Dave plunked down the basket on the table and told the architects to "make it look like this."

No one had ever built an office building that looked like a basket, but Dave Longaberger was the kind of a man who usually got what he wanted. So the contractors went to work, and ground was broken for the new basket-building on October 23, 1995. It took two years to build.

When it was finished, it was an exact replica of the market basket

Longaberger Headquarters is an exact replica of one of the company's products

Dave Longaberger had presented to the architects, only 160 times larger. The basket-building weighs 9,000 tons, has 7 stories and 84 windows hidden in the basketweave siding. It contains 180,000 square feet and holds 500 employees.

The building even comes with two huge basket handles that are attached to the top of the structure, with replica copper and wooden rivets. The handles are so big they have to be wired for heat to keep ice and snow from collecting on them. Just like the smaller basket, there are two Longaberger tags attached to the sides of the basket-building, but in this case each of the tags weigh 725 pounds and measure 25 feet long by 7 feet tall. They are covered with gold leaf.

The building has become a tourist attraction, and visitors are encouraged to stop in and tour the facility, which boasts a seven-story atrium in the lobby with a grand stairway that leads to some of the corporate offices. You can also see many of the new Longaberger products on display in the lobby.

   ▲ **Longaberger Headquarters**   ☎ 740-322-5588
     1500 E. Main St. · Newark

THE WORKS

This discovery center in Newark is aptly named "The Works." The purpose behind the complex is to stimulate analytical thinking and inspire an appreciation for the creative process in industry and innovation. An eclectic assortment of things are gathered into a row of storefront buildings near downtown, things like an art gallery, a child-friendly discovery center that offers education in basic science that is also fun. There is another lab where kids can learn by tearing apart old equipment. There seems to be something for just about every member of the family when it comes to art, history, or technology. Check their Web site for current special events: www.attheworks.org.

   ▲ **The Works: The Ohio Center of History, Art, and Technology**
     ☎ 740-349-9277
     55 S. First St. · Newark

PREHISTORIC MOUNDS AND FLINT

The Great Circle Earthworks in Newark is another mystery for residents of modern-day central Ohio. The Earthworks, an earthen wall, stretches for miles. No one is sure whether it was meant for defense or, perhaps, some religious rite. One thing is sure: the wall was built by prehistoric Hopewell people sometime between 100 B.C. and 400 A.D. Some bodies have been found in parts of the wall and in mounds nearby. Also nearby is Flint Ridge State Memorial, where early Native Americans came to get the flint they used for knives and arrow points. Many of the flint outcroppings are still visible, as are quarry holes dug

Great Circle Earthworks, built long ago by the Hopewell people

by prehistoric people searching for the flint. Interpretive centers at both memorials display artifacts found at the sites, and guides help give a better understanding of one of Ohio's most lasting mysteries. Open year-round. There is also a museum at 455 Hebron Road, Heath, Ohio.

   ▲ **The Great Circle Earthworks**   ☎ 800-600-7178
      99 Cooper Ave. · Newark

TEN ROOMS WITH A VIEW

The countryside around Dresden is some of the most beautiful in the Buckeye State. Hills and plains abound. If you're planning to spend the night, you can spend it in a famous dwelling with a panoramic view of the countryside. The hilltop home of the late Dave Longaberger, the founder of the Longaberger Basket Company, has been turned into a beautiful bed and breakfast. The inn is built on the crest of a hill just outside of town and contains 10 rooms on its various levels. Every level has a great view of the valley below. All the rooms offer many amenities; for instance, some have fireplaces, and others have whirlpool tubs.

   ▲ **Inn at Dresden**   ☎ 740-754-1122
      209 Ames Dr. · Dresden

THE TOWN THAT LONGABERGER BUILT

It isn't exactly a real town, but it's larger than some villages in Ohio. It's the Longaberger Homestead, a giant tourist complex built beside the sprawling Longaberger Basket Factory near Dresden. The "Farmhouse" includes shops that sell clothing, furniture, kitchen aids, flowers, and even one that sells a single style of basket that tourists may buy at the factory. There are several restaurants, including a tea room in a Victorian house on the property. In the barn, you can learn to make a basket and you can buy crafts from the area. Of course, you can go next door and watch the hundreds of basket makers turning out thousands of baskets every day to ship around the world.

▲ **Longaberger Homestead**   ☎ 740-322-5588
5563 Raiders Rd. · Frazeysburg

THE PRETTIEST ICE CREAM PLANT IN THE STATE

The Velvet Ice Cream Company of Utica has been around since 1914 and is still owned an operated by the Dager Family. They have turned this small town ice cream company into a major tourist attraction. The company headquarters is located in a historic old grist mill that today serves as the company logo on all their packaging. Inside the mill is the ice cream factory and an ice cream museum as well as a gift shop and soda fountain where you can sample some of the 500 flavors of ice cream that Velvet makes. (Would you believe they even make four different kinds of vanilla?). In the museum you can trace the history of ice cream (Many claim the Chinese were the first to discover the freezing capabilities of ice and salt, but it was the Italians who first added milk to the mixture that created today's modern ice cream.). There are interactive exhibits and you can even take a tour of the modern Velvet Ice Cream Factory and watch them make the frozen treat. Factory tours are available from May to October each year.

▲ **Velvet Ice Cream Company**   ☎ 800-589-5000
State Rte. 13 S · Utica

CANDLE-LIGHTING

I reported on a lot of holiday stories for television over the years, and I still believe that one of the best places to give yourself a holiday boost is in the restored canal town of Roscoe Village in Coshocton.

They begin the season with an outdoor candle-lighting ceremony about the first weekend in December. A special guest is usually asked to be the official candle lighter. One year I was invited, and I arrived on a very cold and dark December night. The town looked like a page from a Dickens novel. Frost painted the edges of windows. Guides from various attractions in the village were dressed in nineteenth century frock coats or hoop skirts. Streetlights illuminated the walks and roadways, where thousands of people milled about waiting for the ceremony to begin.

A stage had been placed halfway down the main street, Whitewoman Street. On one side of the street a steep hillside led up to the next street. On the other side were the stores that had serviced canal boats and their crews a hundred years before.

A brass ensemble was wandering the streets playing Christmas carols, while small groups of carolers strolled in front of the stores, singing the songs of the season.

My duties were simple. I was given a brief introduction, to polite applause, and as I stepped forward to the podium, the lights along the streets went out. I struck a match and lit a candle I was holding. For a moment, as I wished the crowd a Merry Christmas, I held in my hand the only light on the street. In the darkness several thousand people stood crowded around the stage.

I walked across the stage and, leaning forward, started to light candles held by the crowd. The light spread outward from my candle and, in moments, pinpoints of light had climbed the hill behind me and ignited a river of candles in the street around me. I led the crowd in the song "Silent Night." Never before had the song seemed so real, so personal, as it did this magical night in Roscoe Village as I stood bathed in the light of thousands of candles.

The restored canal town of Roscoe Village is open year-round to tourists. Many of the shops and stores have been re-created as living history museums, where you can watch long-ago crafts being practiced by experts. There are also antique stores and a host of places where you can eat and buy souvenirs and the crafts created in the village.

    ▲ **Historic Roscoe Village**   ☎ 800-877-1830
      381 Hill St. · Coshocton

RIDE A REAL CANAL BOAT

The *Monticello III* is a replica of boats that once traversed Ohio canals. Today, instead of hauling freight, it carries tourists on hourly runs over a mile-long stretch of the old canal. The boat is pulled by a pair of workhorses and follows the same towpath that was used over a century ago. The canal boat ride is only available during the summer months.

    ▲ *Monticello III* **Canal Boat Ride**   ☎ 740-622-7528
      Coschocton Lake Park, 23253 SR 83 · Coshocton

FOLK MUSIC INSTRUMENTS

Early musical instruments used by pioneers and canal workers can still be purchased here, including hammer dulcimers (or mountain dulcimers), banjos, and guitars. This small music store near the edge of the canal offers quality instruments and music.

    ▲ **Wildwood Music**   ☎ 740-622-4224
      Historic Roscoe Village, 672 Whitewoman St. · Coshocton

SPEND THE NIGHT ALONG THE CANAL

There are an assortment of bed and breakfasts in the Roscoe Village–Coshocton area and the nearby Amish country. But if you want

Monticello III *Canal Boat Ride*

to spend the night right in Coshocton, try the Coshocton Village Inn, which is operated by the Christopher Hotel chain that runs hotels and motels in several communities in central Ohio. The Inn offers 64 rooms, some with Jacuzzi tubs and the cost of your stay includes breakfast in the morning. It's located on the edge of Roscoe Village.

▲ **Coshocton Village Inn and Suites**   ☎ 740-622-9455
   115 N. Water St. · Coshocton

HAVE DINNER WITH A GHOST

Well, not really. But legend has it that the Buxton Inn in Granville is haunted. Many guests have reported strange sightings of a ghostly woman (believed to be a former owner of the inn) floating in and out of bedrooms on the second floor. True or not, it contributes to the charm of this beautiful inn that now stretches across a city block.

The Buxton Inn has been around since 1812, serving as a place of rest and refreshment all along. Neighboring homes have been purchased and are now part of the inn, giving owners Orville and Audrey Orr a chance to expand the number of rooms while leaving the original inn intact. The rooms are beautifully decorated, and each room has a private bath. The gardens surrounding the inn are truly spectacular, especially in the spring and fall.

The Buxton Inn offers lunch and dinner in the public dining room. If you are going to spend a night or are just visiting for the day, it's worth making a layover to stay for dinner. The large menu offers everything from steak to seafood, including such entrées as Louisiana chicken (cubed boneless chicken rolled in seasoned cornmeal and sautéed, served on a bed of rice with mushroom pimento cream sauce and a vegetable) and broiled Atlantic salmon with lobster butter. Vegetarians have several choices, including fettuccini alfredo and fresh ravioli with selected fillings and changing styles. The restaurant is closed on Mondays.

Beautiful inn, wonderful gardens, good food, and who knows, maybe even a ghost.

▲ **The Buxton Inn**   ☎ 740-587-0001
313 Broadway E · Granville

HOT SAUCE AND BRIDAL VEILS

Located not far from Roscoe Village is a most unusual junction. Actually, the name of the place is Unusual Junction. It's just an old railroad station with several railroad cars, both passenger and freight, on the siding beside the building. It's what's inside that's so interesting.

When you walk through the front door, you may be met by owner Jerry McKenna, a transplanted Clevelander, playing a badly mangled trombone, badly. But he's not the attraction here. It's the thousands, and I do mean thousands, of bottles of hot sauce that fill the delicatessen in the front of the building—everything from "Endorphin Sauce" to something labeled "XXXX Double Atomic." Jerry specializes in having some of the hottest hot sauces in the world. But that's not the only attraction here. Just behind the aisles and aisles of hot sauce is Jerry's bridal shop!

That's right, bridal shop. Now, to you and me it may seem a strange mixture of businesses: hot sauce, deli items, bridal gowns and veils. Jerry says it just makes sense. He points out that brides-to-be are often accompanied by male members of the wedding party—father, brothers, ushers, even sometimes the prospective bridegroom. While the women are trying on dresses, the men tend to drift toward the front of the store to look over the hot sauces. Some end up buying several. If it's a particularly long fitting, Jerry may even sell sandwiches and ice cream to the bridal party.

Jerry admits that some people are slightly taken aback when they first enter his shop, but he says by the time they leave, they are usually chewing on a sandwich and packing a couple of bottles of "Louisiana Sunshine" into the bag with the bridal veil.

Unusual Junction is open seven days a week. In the summer, there are crafts in some of the railway cars. There's also a small wedding chapel, and Jerry, a licensed minister, can not only sell you a wedding dress but also can officiate at your wedding in his own chapel right here at Unusual Junction.

▲ **Unusual Junction Bridals and Delicatessen**   ☎ 740-545-6007
56310 U.S. Rte. 36 · West Lafayette

Ohio Drama and History

Dennison, Dover, Gnadenhutten, New Philadelphia

TRUMPET IN THE LAND

This distinguished outdoor drama was among the first outdoor theater presentations in Ohio when it started in 1969. Each season since then, thousands have come to an amphitheater just on the outskirts of New Philadelphia to see the story of Moravian missionary David Zeisberger and his attempts to keep peaceful Native Americans out of the fighting between the British and the American colonists during the Revolutionary War. His efforts ended in a tragic massacre of the Native Americans. The play runs from mid-June through late August each summer. *[SEASONAL]*

> ▲ **Trumpet in the Land Outdoor Dramas**   ☎ 330-364-5111
> 1994 High St. (State Rte. 259) · New Philadelphia

OHIO'S OTHER LARGEST ANTIQUE MALL

This place also claims to be the biggest antique mall in Ohio, and in sheer size, it may be. Located in an abandoned discount store, it spills over 70,000 square feet! It's so big the aisles have street names, just like a small city. More than 300 dealers have their merchandise on display—everything from complete glassware sets from various years to petroleum collections to the usual furniture and silver collectibles. Delivery can be arranged for large items. A back room houses scratch-and-dent antiques that are on sale. There are restrooms and a snack bar. Open seven days a week.

> ▲ **Riverfront Antique Mall**   ☎ 800-926-9806
> 1203 Front Ave. SW · New Philadelphia
> At the edge of the Tuscarawas River.

SCHOENBRUNN VILLAGE

After you see *Trumpet in the Land*, you may want to see some of the places that figured prominently in the drama. One of them, Schoenbrunn Village, is nearby. This was the village founded by David Zeisberger and his Christian Indians. The homes, the school, and the church have been re-created. Costumed interpreters tell the village's story. It is open from Memorial Day to Labor Day. *[SEASONAL]*

> ▲ **Schoenbrunn Village**   ☎ 800-752-2711
> 1984 E. High Ave. · New Philadelphia

A GREAT OLD PARK

This is one of my favorite Ohio secrets, a tiny, community-operated amusement park tucked away in a city park that offers what must be the longest merry-go-round ride in America.

Tuscora Park in New Philadelphia has had a tradition for generations of giving youngsters their money's worth when they climb aboard the carousel at the park. The ride usually lasts several minutes. It used to last longer, but the folks who operate it say they had to shorten the ride because so many youngsters got dizzy and became sick to their stomachs.

The carousel is a Spillman, made in New York, and it has been in continual use at Tuscora Park since 1940.

In addition to the merry-go-round, the park also offers several other attractions, including a Ferris wheel, miniature train, small roller coaster, and kiddie rides. The park also holds the city's swimming pool and picnic area. Open from May through Labor Day. *[SEASONAL]*

▲ **Tuscora Park** ☎ 330-343-4644
161 Tuscora Ave. NW · New Philadelphia

DANDELION WINE

This was the first winery in the Amish country. The Bixler family specializes in award-winning berry, fruit, and sparkling wines. One of their specialties is dandelion wine. The wines, considered some of the best in Ohio as evidenced by the number of awards they have won, are made in the fruity German style. The winery operates a gift shop that offers wine tasting, locally produced cheeses, and gift items. The family also operates a bed and breakfast in Sugarcreek.

▲ **Breitenbach Wine Cellars** ☎ 800-843-9463
5934 Old Rte. 39 NW · Dover
Just off State Rte. 39, east of Sugarcreek; watch for the signs

SWISS CHEESE AND WINE

Since the 1930s, the Broad Run Cheese Factory has been turning out Swiss cheese that the area is famous for. They also still welcome visitors to watch them make the cheese early each workday. In the gift shop they sell cheese and various crafts, many locally made, and are known for their selection of lace curtains. They also have a winery and now produce their own wines to go along with the award-winning cheese they make.

▲ **Broad Run Cheese Factory and Swiss Heritage Winery**
☎ 800-332-3358
6011 Old State Rte. 39 NW · Dover

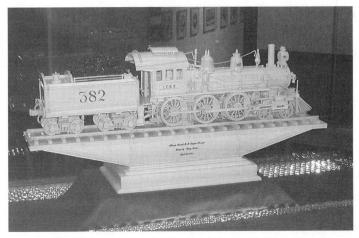

One of the works of the "Master Carver" at Warther Carving Museum

THE WARTHER LEGACY

In the 87 years of his life, Ernest "Moony" Warther left more than 60 intricate wood carvings as his legacy. Warther, who went no further than the second grade in school, did the carvings with no formal training, yet some of the foremost carvers in the world have proclaimed him "the Master Carver."

He carved many things, but his most famous carvings show the history of steam engines, including a made-to-scale, eight-foot-long replica of Abraham Lincoln's funeral train done entirely in ebony and ivory. He was working on his sixty-fourth carving when he died in 1973.

Today, Warther's sons and grandsons carry on the tradition he started, and his carvings are still on display in the family museum.

⛰ **Warther's Carving Museum**　☎ 330-343-7513
331 Karl Ave. · Dover

MOTORCYCLES AND PORK RIBS

The hogs they're talking about here are Harley-Davidson motorcycles, but they also specialize in barbecued hog or pork ribs. It was started by a father and son who turned their love for motorcycles and flame-kissed barbecue into a string of three restaurants between Canton and Dover. You can also get salads, steaks, chicken, and other foods for those who don't want to do the barbecue bit.

Other locations include:

6557 Columbia Rd., Dover

2730 Cleveland Ave. NW, Canton

1290 West High Ave., New Philadelphia

⛰ **Hog Heaven**　☎ 330-878-0038
6567 Columbia Rd. · Dover

GNADENHUTTEN

This is probably the town with the most-often-mispronounced name in the state. It was in Gnadenhutten that the tragic incident happened on which the play *Trumpet in the Land* was based. In 1782, an American militia massacred 96 Christian Indians because they refused to take sides in the Revolutionary War. Today, you can see the mass grave and a replica of the cabin where the killing occurred.

▲ **Gnadenhutten Historical Society**   ☎ 740-254-4143
352 S. Cherry St. · Gnadenhutten

DREAMSVILLE, USA

To thousands of GIs in World War II, Dennison was known as "Dreamsville, USA." It was just a watering stop, like dozens of other small towns along the railroad, for the steam locomotives that hauled the long troop trains carrying soldiers on their way to war. What made Dennison different was the people who lived there. They decided to show the GIs that they cared, and for the duration of the war, 24 hours a day, seven days a week, volunteers manned the small railroad station. When the trains arrived, the volunteers would have hot coffee, sandwiches, doughnuts, magazines, and other goodies ready and free for the men on board. Dennison became known by word of mouth as a place where a GI could get a smile from a pretty girl and a cup of hot coffee from a woman who reminded him of his mother. It was just a small thing, but it meant very much to the soldiers, some barely out of their teens, who were headed off to a dangerous war. By the end of the war, volunteers from the Salvation Army and citizens from Dennison and its neighboring town of Urichsville had served over one and a half million soldiers.

Today the depot is a museum (the 1873 building underwent a million-dollar renovation in 1989) and also tells the story of the WWII effort. The depot, the starting place for special railroad excursions, is a station for the popular "Polar Express" Christmas excursion train each November and December.

▲ **Dennison Railroad Depot Museum**   ☎ 877-278-8020
400 Center St. · Dennison

NORTHEAST
OHIO

Full Cleveland

Cleveland

SCIENCE ON THE LAKE

The Great Lakes Science Center, which is next door to the Rock and Roll Hall of Fame, is great place to visit with kids. It makes science fun. There is an eight-foot-tall exhibit that creates an actual tornado that you can see whirling and dancing inside the exhibit. You can even reach out and touch the tornado, something you can't do with the real thing. There is what they call The Bridge of Fire where you can stand while a static electricity generator creates 200,000 volts of electricity that makes your hair stand on end! And where else can you go to actually pilot a lighter-than-air blimp? They have one inside the hall here in which kids of all ages can take the controls and send the blimp soaring inside the building. For kids age seven and under there is the Polymer Funhouse with dozens of interactive exhibits, including air cannons and water toys.

Be sure to check their website for current travelling exhibits that are spotlighted every few months: www.glsc.org.

▲ **Great Lakes Science Center** ☎ 216-694-2000
601 Erieside Ave. · Cleveland

IT'S ONLY ROCK AND ROLL

Cleveland is home to the Rock and Roll Hall of Fame in part because disc jockey Allen Freed (whose remains are located within the Hall of Fame) coined the term "Rock and Roll" here back in the 1950s. Yet the music industry still does not hold the annual enshrinement ceremonies in Cleveland—a sore point with many northern Ohioans. Nevertheless, this is the repository of such artifacts as Jimi Hendrix's 1968 Stratocaster guitar, Al Green's white leather jacket, and Jim Morisson's Cub Scout uniform. There are thousands of items here, along with interactive audio exhibits and the hall of fame itself, all inside a beautiful I. M. Pei building on the lakefront. Anyone who grew up listening to music since the 1950s will find things to reminisce about here. If you have some extra bucks to spare and would like to really impress your family, how about a personal tour of the facility conducted by the president or the curator of the museum? It's by appointment only, and costs a cool $1,000. That could make a real gift for a rabid rock-and-roll fan. The rest of us will pay the regular admission costs.

▲ **Rock and Roll Hall of Fame and Museum**   ☎ 216-781-7625
One Key Plaza, 751 Erieside Ave. · Cleveland
E. 9th St. at Lake Erie

ANOTHER HALL OF FAME ON THE LAKEFRONT

Burke Lakefront Airport is the official home of the International Women's Air and Space Museum. The museum, which operated for several years in Centerville, honors women's contributions to space and air travel. Exhibits feature such women as Amelia Earhart (one of her flying suits will be on display) and Sally Ride, the first American woman in space.

▲ **International Women's Air and Space Museum**   ☎ 216-623-1111
1501 N. Marginal Rd. · Cleveland

THE FIGHTING *COD*

Few Great Lakes states have a submarine parked on their waterfront. The U.S.S. *Cod* was a fighting ship in World War II. After her wartime service, she was brought to Cleveland to be used by the Naval Reserve for training. When she was declared surplus and it looked like the submarine would be scrapped, a citizens group was formed, and funds were raised to have her made into a floating museum with a permanent home on Cleveland's lakefront.

The sub has been kept in her original World War II condition. That means to get in and out you have to squeeze through hatches and climb up and down ladders, just like the crew did in 1945. (It's not an ideal place for skirts and high-heeled shoes.) *[SEASONAL]*

▲ **U.S.S. *Cod***   ☎ 216-566-8770
1089 E. 9th St. · Cleveland

The U.S.S. Cod has been kept in her original W.W. II condition

A *GOODTIME* IN CLEVELAND

The grande dame of the Cleveland waterfront is the *Goodtime III*, the latest and biggest version of cruise boats bearing that name that have been carrying tourists on Lake Erie since the 1920s. It is the largest quadruple-deck passenger ship on the Great Lakes, with room for 1,000 passengers. She sails the Cuyahoga River and near-shore waters of Lake Erie. Besides sightseeing, the *Goodtime III* also offers dinner and dance cruises with live bands during the summer season.

▲ **Goodtime III Cruise Ship**   ☎ 216-861-5110
Voinovich Park, 825 E. 9th St. · Cleveland

EDGEWATER STATE PARK

The 100-acre park that sits on Cleveland's front step is one of my favorite spots to take visitors for a view of the Cleveland skyline. From an outlook called Perkins Beach on the western end of the park (accessible from the shoreway), you can see one of most impressive views of Cleveland, with tall buildings spiking into the sky. In the foreground, rolling waves hit the shore of Edgewater State Park. The park offers swimming, boating, exercise trails, fishing, and even kite-flying areas. It's one of the city's favorite playgrounds.

▲ **Edgewater State Park**   ☎ 216-881-8141
6700 Memorial Shoreway · Cleveland

THE CUYAHOGA COUNTY ARCHIVES

In this interesting old building you can find a description of Eliot Ness's apartment when he lived on Lake Avenue and a copy of George Burns and Gracie Allen's marriage license (they were married here while appearing at Playhouse Square). There are gruesome pictures of Kingsbury Run murder victims from the coroner's old files. If you are looking into your family's history, they have records dating back to the founding of the city—back when a bounty was paid by the county commissioners for killing wolves. It's a fun place to spend a rainy day.

▲ **Cuyahoga County Archives**   ☎ 216-443-7250
2905 Franklin Ave. · Cleveland

A BIG CORNED BEEF SANDWICH

At this workingman's diner on St. Clair Avenue, you'll find laborers sitting beside office workers in suits and ties during the lunch hour. The attraction here is primarily their huge corned beef and roast beef sandwiches. They carve it thin and pile it high on fresh rye bread—almost four inches high. You can nearly make two meals out of one sandwich. While it is always crowded, the service is fast.

▲ **Danny's Deli**   ☎ 216-696-1761
1658 St. Clair Ave. · Cleveland

PLEASANT UNDER GLASS

You can spend the night in the very first Cleveland building to be listed on the National Register of Historic Places. Built in 1889, the Arcade was one of the first enclosed shopping malls in the U.S. The five-story, glass-topped Arcade stretches 300 feet and connects Euclid and Superior avenues. With its huge skylights and open galleries, it became a popular Cleveland landmark. In 2001, the Hyatt Corporation took over the building and turned the former offices into 293 guest rooms. The rooms, which overlook the Arcade from four levels of balconies, have all the modern amenities mixed with the charm of the old Arcade's 1890 look.

▲ **Hyatt Regency Cleveland at the Arcade**   ☎ 216-575-1234
420 Superior Ave. · Cleveland

Hyatt Regency Cleveland at the Arcade

University Circle

Cleveland, Cleveland Heights

The spiny desert of Madagascar is reproduced in the Cleveland Botanical Garden

EXOTIC ENVIRONMENTS CLOSE TO HOME

You can visit some very exotic landscapes without leaving Ohio. The Cleveland Botanical Gardens offers two distinct ecosystems in their magnificent Glasshouse near University Circle. As you enter the Glasshouse, it's like arriving in the desert of Madagascar. There are cliffs, rock outcroppings and even trees that seem to be growing upside down, and there is also the Great Baobab Tree, a 40-foot-tall specimen right out of the spiny desert of Madagascar. From the desert you cross into the lush Cloud Forest of Costa Rica with 350 species of exotic plants, butterflies, insects, birds, and other animals. Madagascar and Costa Rica were both chosen to be represented in the Glasshouse because they represent ecosystems that are two of the most fragile and fascinating in the world. It's a place of beauty and tranquility and much more. There are also many outdoor gardens and a terrific children's garden with a pond, a treehouse, and hands-on activities for younger kids.

▲ **Cleveland Botanical Garden**   ☎ 216-721-1600
11030 East Blvd. · Cleveland

GREAT FOR LITTLE KIDS

Most major cities have children's museums—places where kids can explore the world in a safe and fun way. Cleveland is no exception. Permanent exhibits in its children's museum include Splish! Splash! exploring the world of water and weather; Bridges to Our Community is a miniature Cleveland designed for interactive, imaginary role-playing, including a two-story house and replica Rainbow Babies & Children's Hospital; and Big Red Barn, designed specifically for children ages four and under. Additional seasonal exhibits change every three to four months.

▲ **Cleveland Children's Museum**   ☎ 216-791-5437
   10730 Euclid Ave. · Cleveland

WHERE HISTORY COMES NATURALLY

It was a passion for the natural sciences among a handful of prominent Clevelanders back in 1830 that led to the wonderful Cleveland Museum of Natural History, today one of the gems of University Circle.

The 200,000-square-foot building now houses a range of displays from skeletons of dinosaurs to live mammals, an observatory, and a courtyard that features native Ohio fauna—including an otter habitat in which you can watch the otters above ground and under water. You can also see Balto, the famous dog (now stuffed and mounted) that once saved lives in the Alaskan wilderness and whose story has been told on the screen and television. (See "Balto the Wonder Dog" in my book, *Ohio Oddities*.)

There are hands-on exhibits for big and little kids and programs that will tell you much about the natural history of our great state.

▲ **Cleveland Museum of Natural History**   ☎ 800-317-9155
   1 Wade Oval Dr. · Cleveland

The otter exhibit at the Cleveland Museum of Natural History

The Crawford Auto-Aviation Museum has one of the best auto collections in Ohio

THE BEST CAR COLLECTION IN OHIO

This is probably one of the best automobile collections in Ohio, if not the whole United States. It offers some of the best examples of the earliest cars, as well as a cross-section of the cars of the 1920s and 1930s, and even muscle cars from the 1950s and 1960s. There is something here for every member of the family. Now if they would only add a Nash Metropolitan to the collection, it would be complete.

▲ **Crawford Auto-Aviation Museum**   ☎ 216-721-5722
   10825 East Blvd. · Cleveland

LOOKING FOR YOUR FAMILY?

The Western Reserve Historical Society is so much more than just a museum. It is a complex of many museums, libraries, and attractions in several northeast Ohio communities. The main complex is located in Cleveland's University Circle neighborhood.

If you have ever wanted to research your family tree, this is a good place to start (especially if you have roots anywhere in northeastern Ohio): one of the finest genealogy libraries in the country is located here. There are also archives of many other papers and books (like famed crime-fighter Eliot Ness's personal scrapbooks). The History Museum offers tours of a mansion built in 1911. The Chisholm Halle Costume Wing has one of the best costume collections in America. There are other revolving exhibits, too.

Next door is the Crawford Auto-Aviation Museum (see separate listing).

▲ **Western Reserve Historical Society Museum**   ☎ 216-721-5722
   10825 East Blvd. · Cleveland

LAKE VIEW CEMETERY

Friends are usually taken aback when I suggest we visit a cemetery. But this cemetery isn't your average burial ground. It started out as an arboretum and still has an impressive display of trees (and flowers in the spring). It is also the final resting spot of President James A. Garfield, tycoon John D. Rockefeller, inventor Charles Brush, famed lawman Eliot Ness, and many other notables of Cleveland's—and the nation's—past. Cemetery officials encourage visitors to walk, hike, and even picnic in the cemetery.

▲ **Lake View Cemetery**   ☎ 216-421-2665
   12316 Euclid Ave. · Cleveland

LITTLE DINER ON CAMPUS

I love diners, especially when they're located in unusual places. This one is tucked away among a grove of trees right on the edge of the campus of Case Western Reserve University. (In fact, the diner is owned by

The Silver Spartan Diner, on the campus of Case Western Reserve University

the University.) The food is just what you want in a diner: hearty plate meals, big sandwiches, and even homemade potato chips. Another interesting feature: When you come in the door, the first thing you see on the counter is four or five daily specials wrapped in clear plastic so you can see the size and exactly what you get when you order a special. The hours change with the school year, so call first to be sure they are open.

▲ **The Silver Spartan Diner** ☎ 216-368-0634
   11419 Bellflower Rd. · Cleveland

BOB HOPE SLEPT HERE

It's true. Bob Hope used to have an apartment in this historic hotel. Legendary songwriter Cole Porter was also among the many famous guests who stayed here. The Alcazar Hotel, a residential hotel built in 1923 and once one of the most exclusive addresses in Cleveland, now serves mainly as an apartment building but also offers five rooms as a bed and breakfast. It's a Cleveland landmark and a very special place for a special night.

▲ **Alcazar Hotel Bed and Breakfast** ☎ 216-321-5400
   2450 Derbyshire Rd. · Cleveland Heights

Cleveland: West

Brooklyn, Cleveland, Rocky River

A world of flavors can be found at the West Side Market

OLD-WORLD FLAVOR

This place has been the favorite food-shopping spot of thousands of Clevelanders since it opened in 1912. The huge European-style market hall and additional food stalls outside house almost 200 vendors of every delicacy imaginable. Fresh fruit from around the world, ethnic meats and cheeses, baked goods and spices . . . a visit to the West Side Market is a cultural experience. There are the smells of different foods and spices and a medley of a dozen foreign languages all being spoken at the same time. Here you will often find the rich and famous rubbing elbows with the poor and even the homeless as they search for good, fresh food. It can get crowded, especially on Saturdays, when there can be near gridlock in the aisles. Open Mondays, Wednesdays, Fridays, and Saturdays, year-round.

▲ **West Side Market** ☎ 216-664-3386
1979 W. 25th Street · Cleveland

INDOOR MOUNTAIN BIKE COURSE

The first indoor mountain bike course in the world (according to the owner) is located in Cleveland. Ray's MTB Indoor Park is a dream come true for biker Ray Petro, who lived for good weather each year when

At Ray's MTB Indoor Park you can mountain bike even in a February blizzard

he could take his mountain bike into the surrounding countryside and across the back country trails. The problem was that when winter came, all he could do was sit and look at videos of the warm summer day trips he had taken. Then he spotted an abandoned warehouse on Walford Avenue in Cleveland and took a chance and built an indoor park just for mountain bikers. Let history note: They came. Today, during the winter months, bikers from all over the Midwest travel to Cleveland to ride Ray's indoor course (the layout changes from year to year). This is not for beginners: if you are unsure of your abilities, call before you make the trip.

   ▲ **Ray's MTB Indoor Park** ☎ 216-631-7433
     9801 Walford Ave. · Cleveland

LARGEST INDOOR FERRIS WHEEL

The huge, sprawling I-X Center was built at the edge of Cleveland Hopkins International Airport during World War II. At times it has served as a bomber and tank plant, turning out weapons of war for World War II and Korea. More recently, it was turned into the largest exhibition hall in the country, with 20 acres under one roof. One of the more unusual ways this space is used is as an indoor amusement park each spring. The 10-story-high Ferris wheel popping through the roof stays year round and is used even when other shows are running at the center. It is the largest indoor Ferris wheel in the world. The amusement park is open for a short season, usually sometime between late March and the end of April, but check the schedule. *[SEASONAL]*

   ▲ **I-X Indoor Amusement Park** ☎ 216-676-6000
     6200 Riverside Dr. · Cleveland

MIDDLE EASTERN ON THE WEST SIDE

On West 25th Street, in the same block as the historic West Side Market, you'll find Nate's Deli. Folks who know Middle Eastern food say this is the place for the very best fatoosh salad or shish kabob.

▲ **Nate's Deli and Restaurant**   ☎ 216-696-7529
1923 W. 25th St. · Cleveland

SLEEP ON THE EDGE OF THE VALLEY

You can spend the night sleeping on the edge of Cleveland's famed "Emerald Necklace," the metropark system that surrounds the city with a string of beautiful parks with all kinds of recreation, only minutes from downtown. The Emerald Necklace Inn Bed and Breakfast is located in Fairview Park overlooking the Rocky River Reservation portion of the park system.

The inn has three rooms with private baths and amenities like fluffy robes, air conditioning, a fireplace, and tubs that accommodate two people.

▲ **Emerald Necklace Inn Bed and Breakfast**   ☎ 440-333-9100
18840 Lorain Rd. · Cleveland

ICE CREAM WITH A BIT O' HONEY

In 1974 Frank Page, a Cleveland fireman, had a sweet idea: he mixed honey into his ice cream. He started with one modest ice cream shop on State Road in Cleveland's Old Brooklyn neighborhood. Now he has four locations in the southwestern suburbs of Cleveland. Just how popular is Honey Hut? Just try to get up to the window on a warm day. The lines can sometimes be intimidating, but the taste is worth the wait. Honey Pecan seems to be a favorite, although I prefer Orange Blossom. Other flavors are offered, all with honey. All are made with natural ingredients and have no preservatives or artificial ingredients.

▲ **Honey Hut Ice Cream Shoppe**   ☎ 216-749-7077
4674 State Rd. · Cleveland

Other locations:
28624 Lake Rd. · Bay Village
7304 Chippewa Rd. · Brecksville
6250 State Rd. · Parma
15831 Pearl Rd. · Strongsville

MEMPHIS KIDDIE PARK

If you were a youngster growing up in the 1950s on the west side of Cleveland, chances are you probably spent some of your summer days at Memphis Kiddie Park in Brooklyn. And almost nothing has changed there since then. The very same rides, the tiny merry-go-round, the mini–roller coaster, the little Ferris wheel, and the kiddie train that passes Snow White and the seven concrete dwarfs are all just as they were back in 1950, though perhaps a different color. In 2006, the Little Dipper roller coaster was recognized by the American Coaster Enthusiasts organization as the oldest operating steel roller coaster still standing in its original location. *[SEASONAL]*

▲ **Memphis Kiddie Park**   ☎ 216-941-5995
   10340 Memphis Ave. · Brooklyn

SQUEEZE BOX HEAVEN

If there is a musical instrument most closely associated with Ohio, it has to be the accordion, from the Polka Hall of Fame in Cleveland to the Octoberfest in Cincinnati. The accordion has provided music for dancing, singing, and for a way of life.

There is even an accordion museum in Cleveland.

Jack and Kathy White have turned the basement of their suburban home into a museum for over 300 accordions. There are also sheet music, pictures of famous accordion players, and accordion memorabilia.

Visitors here learn that accordions are not just for polka bands; they have even been used in symphony orchestras. Also, they are one of the oldest musical instruments in the world. Although keyboards and computerized instruments have largely pushed them aside in recent years, Jack and Kathy White think nothing else sounds like the real thing, and at the drop of a hat Jack will strap one on and play a tune.

The Cleveland Accordion Museum is open only by appointment. Call first to make sure someone is at home.

▲ **Cleveland Accordion Museum**   ☎ 440-895-9223
   18974 Story Rd. · Rocky River

Cleveland Accordion Museum

The Queen's Underwear

Aurora, Boston Township, Kent, Northfield, Peninsula, Sagamore Hills

One of the "changing" exhibits at the Kent State University Museum

THE QUEEN'S UNDERPANTS

Kent State University in Kent offers an unusual attraction: a clothing museum. In 1985, the former university library was turned into a museum to house the huge collection of fashion and decorative arts that Shannon Rodgers and Jerry Silverman gave to the university. Since then, the mostly twentieth-century collection has been augmented by other donations and acquisitions that now include garments from the eighteenth and nineteenth centuries. It's a fun place to visit—I've seen everything from Tom Mix's cowboy hat to bloomers once reportedly worn by Queen Victoria of England. I'll let the museum folks tell you how the queen's unmentionables ended up in Kent. (They're not on permanent display; rather, the museum hosts changing exhibits.)

▲ **Kent State University Museum** ☎ 330-672-3450
   5190 Rockwell Hall, Kent State University · Kent
   Corner of E. Main St. and S. Lincoln St.

DOWN BY THE STATION

A lot of folks and college students head for the station when it's time to eat in Kent. The historic old railroad station is home to Pufferbelly Restaurant and Bar, and it offers some interesting surroundings for a dinner. (A freight train still pounds by every so often.) As for the food, most everything is prepared fresh here, no shortcuts. From pizza to pastas, to sandwich wraps, to sit-down dinners, there is a wide variety of choices. One of my favorites is their Jamaican chicken and shrimp entrée, served with rice pilaf and a loaf of hot, fresh French bread, but it is not on the menu anymore. You have to ask for it. They do advertise a Jamaican steak and shrimp dish.

▲ **Pufferbelly Restaurant and Bar**   ☎ 330-673-1771
152 Franklin Ave. · Kent

AN INN WITH STABLES

Would you like to stay at an inn where you wake up in the morning and look out the window, only to find a horse staring back at you? If that happens, you're probably at the Walden Country Inn and Stables in Aurora, Ohio. It's a luxurious place to spend a night on a special occasion or just a wonderful getaway destination when you want to unwind. They offer 25 suites with cedar-paneled ceilings and slate-tiled showers and whirlpools. There are fireplaces and telephones in six different languages! If you would like to go riding, horses are available from the stables next door for a slight additional charge. Overnight guests get a full breakfast for two and complimentary afternoon tea and evening snacks.

▲ **Walden Country Inn and Stables**   ☎ 888-808-5003
1119 Aurora-Hudson Rd. · Aurora

Walden Country Inn and Stables

AN AMUSEMENT PARK WITH HISTORY

Lots of water-soaked fun can still be had alongside historic Geauga Lake. The historic Geauga Lake amusement park, which entertained Ohioans for more than a century, was closed in 2007, and most of its rides were shipped off to other parks by the parks' owner, Cedar Fair. But Wildwater Kingdom remains. The park has 17 acres of outdoor water fun, including Tidal Wave Bay, a gigantic 390,000-gallon wave action pool, and Thunder Falls, Ohio's tallest waterslide complex, which stretches 10 stories into the air with seven different slides. It's a great place to cool off on a hot summer day. Coral Cove is a section of the park just for little kids, with bubble jets, shallow pools, and games. *[SEASONAL]*

▲ **Wildwater Kingdom**   ☎ 330-562-7131
1060 Aurora Rd. · Aurora

A WINTER SPORTS PARADISE

If you like sledding, cross-country skiing, or snowshoeing, you can find all three and more at the Kendall Lake Winter Sports Center, operated by the National Park Service. This is the main area within the national park for winter sports activities. All are available when the weather permits. Sledding is available at Kendall Hills on Quick Road; bring your own sled. For cross-country skiing, when the snow depth is greater than six inches, you can rent skis at the Winter Sports Center on Truxell Road. You'll need to bring along a driver's license or credit card for a deposit on the skis. Snow shoes also can be rented at the Winter Sports Center. *[SEASONAL]*

▲ **Kendall Lake Winter Sports Center**   ☎ 800-445-9667
Truxell Rd. · Boston Township

A TRAIN RIDE THROUGH OHIO'S NATIONAL PARK

This scenic railroad runs 12 months between Independence (just south of Cleveland) and downtown Akron through the Cuyahoga Valley National Park, offering an incredible way to experience the area's beauty and wildlife. In addition to the main stations (listed below), there are also special-event boarding stations, including a stop at the Western Reserve Historical Society's Hale Farm and Village in Bath. Train rides are also offered with package deals including a ticket to visit one of several area attractions.

Other main stations:
Rockside Station: 7900 Old Rockside Rd, Independence
Akron Northside Station: 27 Ridge Street, Akron
Canton Lincoln Highway Station: 1315 Tuscarawas St. W., Canton

▲ **The Cuyahoga Valley Scenic Railroad**   ☎ 800-468-4070
1630 W. Mill St. · Peninsula

Cuyahoga Valley Scenic Railroad

A QUIET GETAWAY BY THE FALLS

This historic old home next to the beautiful Brandywine Falls on the edge of the Cuyahoga Valley National Park is a bed and breakfast that offers three rooms and three suites (all rooms are non-smoking). It's filled with antiques and some rustic furnishings. It's a quiet place to get away to, and the nearby falls, especially in the spring and winter, are a great place for some unforgettable vacation pictures.

▲ **Inn at Brandywine Falls**   ☎ 330-467-1812
   8230 Brandywine Rd. · Sagamore Hills

Rubber City Favorites

Akron

"AMERICA'S BEST CHEESEBURGER"

When the 1950s left us, it seemed that the icon of that age, the drive-in restaurant, left us, too. But a smattering of drive-ins survived. A few did more than survive—they have prospered.

There is a school of thought that when Ray Krock bought out the McDonald Brothers and launched a new concept—people getting out of their cars and walking up to the window to get their food—he not only saved restaurants money by doing away with carhops, he homogenized America by creating just one standard menu. The day of the hand-sliced potato fries and eclectic menus slowly faded away, and national chains of burger restaurants arrived. But those well-run local drive-ins that offered good food and good service were able to compete, and some did survive.

First off, for those who have never experienced a drive-in restaurant, there is no restaurant per se—it's just a carryout place, where if you want to eat there you do it in your car. Clerks run out to your car to take your order, bring the food to your car, and, when you are done, come and take away the tray and the garbage. And they do it efficiently, like at Swensons in Akron, which over the years has grown to seven locations. Swensons built their business on good food and fast service that continues today. In fact, part of the entertainment is watching the carhops

At Swensons Drive-In Restaurants, the curb-servers actually run to your car

(they call them "curb-servers") literally run to take your order and then run the order into the kitchen. These guys and girls have to be in great physical condition for all of the running they do here.

Incidentally, some very prominent local and nationally known folks have worked as "curb-servers" here, including probably their best-known alumnus, Dick Jacobs, former owner of the Cleveland Indians, who apparently helped put himself through school back in the 1940s by hustling to wait on people. LeBron James, the restaurant says, is a frequent customer.

The big seller here is the cheeseburger, once declared by a writer for *Forbes* magazine to be "America's best cheeseburger." They buy their rolls from a private baker, and the sauces and the meat here are prepared, Swenson employees say, with a "secret recipe" hammered out by the founder, "Pop" Swenson. That same recipe is still in use.

▲ **Swensons Drive-In Restaurant**   ☎ 330-864-8416
40 S. Hawkins Ave. · Akron

Other Swensons locations include:
Akron: 658 E. Cuyahoga Falls Ave.; 330-928-8515
Montrose: 40 Brookmont Rd.; 330-665-1858
Seven Hills: 7635 Broadview Rd.; 216-986-1934
Stow: 4466 Kent Rd.; 330-678-7775
Jackson: 5815 Wales Road NW; 330-833-5454
North Canton: 1558 N. Main St.; 330-499-9494

COP HISTORY

The Akron Police Department has made police history at least twice. First, in 1899, they were the first police department in the nation to use a motorized police vehicle. And in the 1920s they scored another first when they used an airplane to make an arrest. You will learn about this and other fascinating police-connected activities including one special exhibit of confiscated weapons of all sorts, each tagged with a story about what crime was committed with the weapon and what happened to the perpetrator of the crime. You will also see confiscated drug paraphernalia, counterfeit money, and tables full of evidence from solved crimes over the years. There is an early police motorcycle on display as well as uniforms worn at different times by Akron police. It is a small but interesting museum, located in the Justice Center.

▲ **Akron Police Department Historical Museum**   ☎ 330-375-2390
Harold K. Stubbs Justice Center, Room 201, 217 S. High St. · Akron

PRO BASEBALL UP CLOSE

If you would like to see some future members of the Cleveland Indians, visit one of their farm clubs, the Akron Aeros, in their very own state-of-the-art baseball stadium in downtown Akron.

You can see pro baseball close up at Akron Aeros's Canal Park Stadium

You can get a behind-the-scenes look at how a minor league team operates and a close-up look at the facilities on a tour of the place. The best tour time is on an off-game day, when you can also visit the locker rooms and the dugouts.

There's another attraction here, too.

Do you remember names like Don Novello, Virgil Dominic, and Martin Savidge? They, and a host of other celebrities who once appeared on radio and television in Ohio, are enshrined in the Radio and Television Broadcasters Hall of Fame, which is located inside the public area of the Aeros Stadium. Call the stadium for hours of operation.

▲ **Akron Aeros** ☎ 800-972-3767
Canal Park Stadium, 300 S. Main St. · Akron

A DELICIOUS AKRON RITUAL

It's not officially spring until Strickland's ice cream stand opens. The homemade custard, made fresh each day, has been prepared from the same recipe for generations. Strickland's is right across the street from the old Akron Airport, and their parking lot is a good place to see the air dock while enjoying an ice-cream cone. Open seasonally, closed in winter.

▲ **The Original Strickland's Frozen Custard** ☎ (no phone)
1809 Triplett Blvd. · Akron

STAN HYWET HALL AND GARDENS

The magnificent mansion owned by the Seiberling family, who owned Goodyear, is now open to the public. Its 60-some rooms range from the great hall to a wonderful music room where Paderewski once played. There is an indoor swimming pool, game room, and formal gardens,

Stan Hywet Hall has more than 60 rooms

which are a favorite with newlyweds for picture backgrounds. During the holidays, the mansion is decorated as it was during the time the Seiberling family lived there. (Hywet, by the way, is pronounced Hee-wit.)

⛰ **Stan Hywet Hall and Gardens**   ☎ 330-836-5533
714 N. Portage Path · Akron

THE HE-MAN BREAKFAST

There is a restaurant in Akron that gives new meaning to the words "hearty breakfast." The Lamp Post Restaurant is open 24 hours a day, but since they consider breakfast "the most important meal of the day," they serve it any time. Their special is "The He-Man Breakfast," a true heart-clogger made for those with stomachs of steel and bowels of brass: three eggs (any way you like 'em), two servings of meat (patties, links, or bacon), pancakes or French toast, two massive servings of hash browns, two slices of toast (white or wheat), and the required biscuits and sausage gravy, all served on a gigantic pizza platter. It looks more like a breakfast for five instead of one. The price is $9.99. I asked the young lady behind the counter what you get if you can eat the whole thing. She replied, "A pat on the back and maybe a belly-ache later."

It's a friendly kind of place where the servers call the customers "honey," and in at least one instance, when a regular brought in a couple of fish he had just caught in Lake Erie, the accommodating staff offered to cook them for him.

⛰ **The Lamp Post**   ☎ 330-733-5308
2081 E. Market St. · Akron

Crowne Plaza Quaker Square Hotel, made from grain silos

SLEEP IN A ROUND ROOM

You can literally spend the night in a round room at the Quaker Square Inn in Akron. The hotel was created out of the concrete silos that stored oats for the Quaker Oats Company. The silos have been transformed: Windows were cut through the concrete, and modern plumbing and air conditioning were added to make one very unusual hotel. Talk about a soundproof room: The walls are six inches thick. The hotel has gone through a lot of name changes in the last several years, and most of the stores in an attached mall in the old Quaker Oats factory have closed except for the General Store, which still sells the trademark fresh-baked oatmeal cookies.

▲ **Quaker Square Inn at the University of Akron**   ☎ 330-253-5970
135 S. Broadway · Akron

A BIT OF LAS VEGAS IN AKRON

With its Middle Eastern façade, the Tangier has been an entertainment landmark in the Rubber City for a half-century. In its heyday in the 1950s and '60s, all kinds of major show business names would play Tangier or at least visit when they passed through the Buckeye State. TV talk-show host Phil Donahue and his wife, Marlo Thomas (daughter of comedian Danny Thomas), held their wedding reception here.

It is still an upscale dining great spot and a cabaret where you can see some up-and-coming acts as well as some nationally-known entertainers, like the comedian Gallagher, with his watermelon smashing act, or the Scintas from Las Vegas.

▲ **The Tangier**   ☎ 330-376-7171
532 West Market St. · Akron

The Original Hamburger

Alliance, Hartville, North Canton, Uniontown

THE ORIGINAL HAMBURGER

I once provoked a firestorm of protest (all right, six letters and a few phone calls) from people who wanted to take issue with a story I wrote about how the hamburger originated. It seems there are at least four areas of the country that claim to be the birthplace of the ground-meat sandwich.

First a little history. Hamburger, the ground-up remains of parts of the cow usually deemed not worthy of a separate cut of meat, or the trimmings from the better parts, has been around a long, long time. Historians have traced its history all the way back to the Mongolian and Turkish tribes known as Tartars, who first cut up pieces of tough beef into small chunks to make it more tender. The practice spread through the Balkans and into Germany before the fourteenth century. Here, it is thought, the meat product gained its name when it allegedly became the meat of choice of the poorer classes in Hamburg, Germany, becoming known, derisively, as "Hamburger."

Historians also believe that it made the leap to the United States in the late 19th century with the heavy wave of German immigration to this country. However, there are reports that a dish called "Hamburg steak" was featured on the menu at a New York restaurant as early as 1834.

But for our purposes, the real question seems to be: Who was the first to take this piece of meat called "hamburger" and place it between two pieces of bread? That brings us back full circle to my original story about the Menches brothers of Akron. In 1885, while working their sausage concession at the Hamburg, New York, fair, they ran out of sausage on a hot day and found that the local butcher also had none available. So they took some beef, ground it up, added a few ingredients—like coffee and brown sugar—grilled it over their gasoline-powered stove, slapped it between some bread, and a new taste sensation was born.

But wait a minute. Out in Athens, Texas, they have a plaque on the side of a building proclaiming that this was the site of Fletch Davis's Cafe. It is said that in the 1880s, Davis, a laid-off pottery worker, started a cafe and was selling a sandwich he invented consisting of ground beef between two pieces of bread.

Still another claim comes from New Haven, Connecticut. Danish immigrant Louis Lassen leased a lunch wagon in 1895. At first he specialized in a sandwich made of thin slices of steak grilled and placed on toast. At night he would take the trimmings from the meat home and grind them up to make meat patties to fry and serve to his family. It was only a matter of time before he started serving the leftovers, which became the best seller in his lunch wagon.

And then there is the story of Charlie Nagreen out in Seymour, Wisconsin, who was selling meatballs at the Seymour fair in 1885. He decided to flatten the meatball, put it between two pieces of bread, and call it a "hamburger." By the way, local folks here take the story very seriously. They even hold an annual Hamburger Festival, where they once cooked the world's largest hamburger (over 5,000 pounds), which they served at the festival. Seymour is also home to the Hamburger Hall of Fame.

So who was first? The problem is that, until this century and the advent of the hamburger chains, the hamburger was just another sandwich, and there was little concern about its origin. Most of the information about how the hamburger started came in interviews supplied by the people claiming to have invented it, long after the event—sometimes as much as 50 or 60 years later. Memories tend to dim with time, and facts get fuzzy. Local pride can also get in the way as a legend begins to grow. Also historians have not spent a great deal of time or energy researching this topic.

Most, however, agree that the hamburger as we know it today was first served at the St. Louis World's Fair in 1904. And—surprise—attending that fair and serving their specialty were both Fletcher Davis of Athens, Texas, and Charles and Frank Menches from Ohio.

In fact, the Menches brothers seem to have the best claim to having originated the burger, since the dates they offer agree with the dates of the fair in Hamburg, New York. It's intriguing that they were also at the St. Louis World's Fair. As for the other folks, their claims were made much later and don't correlate with the time period when most historians say the hamburger was already being served. In the case of the Texas claim, Fletcher Davis was always vague about when he invented the hamburger, claiming it was sometime in the "late 1800s," which would imply the end of that century. The Menches claim is more specific: 1885. I'm going to stick with the Menches brothers as the developers of the hamburger. They also lay claim to having created the ice-cream cone, but here they seem to be on rather shaky historic ground. We'll have more about this controversy in another chapter.

By the way, if you would like to taste the original hamburger recipe, descendants of the Menches brothers operate a restaurant between Akron and Canton where they sell hamburgers made the same way their great-grandfathers made them—with a little coffee and brown sugar and other "secret" ingredients. At the entrance to the restaurant the a display of some of the equipment the brothers used for making their historic burgers.

▲ **Menches Brothers Original Hamburgers**   ☎ 330-896-2288
3700 Massillon Rd., Ste. 130 · Uniontown

LIBRARY IN A MALL

If you like to shop but have family members who don't, take them along to the Carnation Mall in Alliance, where you'll find one of the only public libraries located in a shopping mall. Nonshoppers can browse and relax in the reading room while the rest of the family hits the mall.

▲ **Rodman Public Library**   ☎ 330-821-1313
Carnation Mall, 2500 W. State St. · Alliance

SHOP 'TIL YOU DROP—ASLEEP

You can spend the night in the shopping mall, too. The Comfort Inn anchors one end of the Carnation Shopping Mall. The hotel offers many amenities: whirlpool baths in some rooms, an indoor swimming pool, an exercise room, and packages that include tickets to the movie theaters just off the lobby.

▲ **Comfort Inn**   ☎ 877-424-6423 reservations; 330-821-5555 local
Carnation Mall, 2500 W. State St. · Alliance

AN OLD-FASHIONED BANANA SPLIT

This candy store, soda fountain, and sandwich shop has been a Stark County institution for generations. Heggy's Candies are famous in many parts of the state, but local folks also head for Heggy's for fountain treats like old-fashioned banana splits made with vanilla, chocolate, and strawberry ice cream and mounds of whipped cream and cherries. It's the kind of place where you think about putting off that diet you were going to start today until tomorrow.

▲ **Heggy's Candies**   ☎ 330-821-2051
1306 W. State St. · Alliance

MY HART BELONGS TO CHOCOLATE

This small factory makes some fine candy and sells candymaking equipment, supplies, and molds. They specialize in personalized chocolates, such as you might use at a wedding. They also carry a good supply of sugar-free candies. Their candy maker once made candy for world-
Godiva Chocolates.

colate Factory   ☎ 330-877-1999
t Ave. · Hartville

iocolate Factory II   ☎ 330-587-0068
St. · Hartville

A HAMBURGER CHALLENGE

For more than half a century, folks in Alliance have been treated to a real-life *Happy Days* diner. Doug's Classic '57 Diner offers a lot more than good food and nostalgia. He also has some healthy offerings, like burgers made from buffalo and ostrich meat. (Both are considered low in fat but very tasty.) The restaurant started out in the 1950s as a Stewart's Root Beer stand. It's still one of the few places that has Stewart's on tap. But the real fun is when customers take the "King Kong Challenge." That means that they try to eat three of the giant-sized King Kong Burgers in a set amount of time. If they do it, they're free, and the customer gets his name on the Challenge Board in the restaurant. If they fail, they have to pay.

▲ **Doug's Classic '57 Diner**   ☎ 330-821-2887
2031 S. Rockhill Ave. · Alliance

A JUMBO FLEA MARKET

If you want to go to one of the classiest flea markets in the state of Ohio, head for Hartville.

The Hartville Marketplace and Flea Market is one of the biggest attractions in northeast Ohio. It started in the 1930s as a livestock auction, the idea of Sol Miller. As Hartville grew and farmland diminished, the livestock auction evolved into an egg auction, with a flea market on auction days. The flea market continued to grow until it became a business in the mid-1970s. By then it was a hodgepodge sprawl of buildings and gravel parking lots that on Mondays and Thursdays attracted upward of a thousand vendors on warm sunny days.

Marion Cobleentz, the third generation of Sol Miller's family to run the enterprise, moved the operation across the street and into modern quarters in 2002. Today the marketplace building houses more than 110 permanent businesses ranging from antique dealers to food-based operations to sports memorabilia and much more. The permanent booths are open on Monday, Thursday, Friday and Saturday, while outside in covered aisles are the temporary flea market vendors, who change from week to week. The parking lot covers 25 acres, and it is all paved. Inside the marketplace building are the offices, modern public restrooms, and restaurants.

▲ **The Hartville Marketplace and Flea Market**   ☎ 330-877-9860
1289 Edison St. NW · Hartville

THE MOST ORNATE AMISH-STYLE RESTAURANT

The Hartville Kitchen Restaurant has come a long way from its humble beginnings as a snack bar near an auction barn to a multimillion-dollar palace with sweeping stairways, huge chandeliers, artwork, and a series of shops. Oh, yes, there is a restaurant in there, too.

Most people expect an enormous restaurant when they see the building—the building and parking lots take up nearly 45 acres along Edison Street in Hartville. But inside, the center is taken up by a candy store and bakery, and on the other end are a huge gift shop and a coin store. The restaurant, for all of the building's size, only seats about 400, with banquet facilities in the back for another 500. The Hartville Kitchen has been famous for years for its homemade salad dressings, which can be purchased in most northern Ohio grocery stores. You can sample the various dressings on your salads in the dining room here and stop at the bakery to buy it by the bottle, or even the case, to take home. Not surprisingly, there are lines at lunch and dinnertime, but they usually move quickly. The biggest lines are on Mondays and Thursdays, when the Hartville Flea Market is held across the street. They offer the usual Amish-style restaurant fare—fried chicken, ham, and beef, as well as some daily specials. Be sure to try their noodle dishes, and save room for the Hartville Kitchen homemade pies.

▲ **The Hartville Kitchen Restaurant**   ☎ 330-877-9353
  1015 Edison St. · Hartville

OHIO'S BIGGEST CANDY FACTORY

This 80,000-square-foot candy factory and store sits just off I-77 next to the Akron-Canton Airport. You can see it from the highway. They offer my kind of factory tour: Someone offers you a piece of candy as soon as you walk through the door. The free samples just keep on coming as you see a short movie about candy making and then start trooping the corridors to watch through windows and see how the candy is actually made.

They make over 500 varieties of chocolate and gourmet candies, including the official candy version of the Ohio State symbol—the Buckeye (peanut butter with chocolate wrapped around it). There is a small charge for the tour, but you will probably get that back in the number of free samples they give you. Tours are Monday through Saturday from 10 A.M. until 3 P.M. April through June. Call for reservations and other tour dates. Their attractive store is also open, and you can buy just about any product they make.

▲ **Harry London Quality Chocolates**   ☎ 800-321-0444
  5353 Lauby Road · North Canton

THE LARGEST MILITARY MUSEUM IN OHIO

The Akron-Canton Airport has a secret. The second largest military museum in Ohio is located here. The Military Air Preservation Society (MAPS) has a hangar full of old war birds on the west side of the airport. This is where you can find everything from the gondola from a Goodyear blimp to a beautifully restored F4 Phantom to a Polish-

Historic aircraft are restored and displayed at the Military Air Preservation Society

built MIG17. The bright hangar lets them display the restored planes, with room to spare. There are other exhibits besides the planes, some of which are aircraft now undergoing restoration, link trainers, anti-aircraft guns, uniforms, model airplanes, and more. What they have accomplished here, with much of the work being done by volunteers, is incredible. This is one attraction you won't want to miss if you have any affection at all for airplanes.

⚠ **Military Air Preservation Society** ☎ 330-896-6332
Akron-Canton Airport, 2660 International Pkwy. · North Canton

A VACUUM CLEANER MUSEUM

The folks who make the Hoover vacuum cleaner turned their founder's boyhood home in North Canton into a museum for their machine. Included in the displays are cleaning devices that go back hundreds of years, as well as early Hoover models. A good stop for a rainy day.

⚠ **Hoover Historical Center** ☎ 330-499-0287
1875 E. Maple St. · North Canton

First Ladies and Football

Canton, Massillon

CLASSIC CARS ON DISPLAY

Where's your car? That's the question I get asked most often by viewers of my long-running "One Tank Trips" TV reports in Cleveland. The two best-known cars—a tiny yellow 1957 BMW Isetta that I used on the show for 15 years and the red and white 1959 Nash Metropolitan that was a symbol of "One Tank Trips" for more than a decade—are both on display at the Canton Classic Car Museum. The museum is well worth the visit. In addition to my cars, they have an outstanding collection of famous cars from America's history, including the Queen Mother's 1939 Lincoln and an armored police car used by the Canton police in the 1930s that may be the longest serving police car in history. You'll also see muscle cars from the 1950s and even a little car that could be driven on the highways and was also able to swim!

▲ **Canton Classic Car Museum**   ☎ 330-455-3603
104 6th St. SW · Canton

THE FOOTBALL HALL OF FAME

Canton is the birthplace of professional football and the home of the Pro Football Hall of Fame. Busts of football heroes and artifacts from past years of gridiron glory are on display; you can also match wits with football experts via interactive exhibits. The hall adds new members each August, and the ceremonies are held on the lawn in front of the football shrine. There is also a gift shop.

▲ **Pro Football Hall of Fame**   ☎ 330-456-8207
2121 George Halas Dr. · Canton

FUMBLEBALL

There really is such a game as fumbleball, and its hall of fame is right here in Canton. Fumbleball is like softball and is usually played by persons over the age of 35. There are only two leagues in the country, and one is in Canton, where a hall of fame has been established to honor its members.

▲ **Fumbleball Hall of Fame**   ☎ 330-453-1552
Greater Canton Amateur Sports Hall of Fame
1414 Market Ave. N · Canton

National First Ladies' Library / The Ida Saxton McKinley Home

THE WOMEN BEHIND THE PRESIDENTS

Just about every president of the United States has a library or museum somewhere named for him. But what about the power behind all these famous men—the first ladies of America? These women, with the exception of Eleanor Roosevelt and Jackie Kennedy, have remained in the shadow of their famous husbands and have been footnotes to history.

That changed with the opening of the National First Ladies' Library in the Canton home of the wife of the twenty-fifth president. Ida Saxton McKinley lived in this South Market Street home before and after she married William McKinley. Today, the historic home has been turned into a beautiful tribute to all first ladies.

The museum displays pictures and personal possessions of many of the women. The library contains an eclectic assortment of books about first ladies, many of them out of print.

Tours of the Saxton-McKinley home are available Tuesday through Saturday by reservation only.

▲ **National First Ladies' Library / The Ida Saxton McKinley Home** ☎ 330-452-0876
331 S. Market Ave. · Canton

A PARK FOR ALL PEOPLE

The Stark County Park District has attempted to make Sippo Lake a park that everyone—old, young, middle-aged, and the physically challenged—can enjoy. For openers, there is the fishing pier, once claimed to be the largest inland fishing pier in Ohio. The Exploration Gateway, which includes three community rooms, the park's educational staff, and an exhibit hall that features the natural and cultural history of the

Ohio and Erie Canalway. And, in an unusual partnership between the park system and the county library, there is a branch of the Stark County Library in the Gateway Center. In the marina you'll find one of the largest fishing tackle collections in the state. You can also rent a rowboat for $3 to $5 dollars an hour, and small motorboats are equally inexpensive.

For the youngsters there is a nature center, where abandoned and injured animals are cared for and nursed back to health, as well as an outstanding display of stuffed animals from around the world.

⛰ **Sippo Lake Park**   ☎ 330-477-3552
Stark County Park District , 5300 Tyner Ave. NW · Canton

A PRESIDENT AND A DINOSAUR

William McKinley was our twenty-fifth president. He was born in Niles and spent most of his adult life in Canton. He was a major in the Civil War, served as a congressman from Ohio, and served three terms as governor of Ohio. McKinley had been elected to his second term as president when he was assassinated while speaking in Buffalo, New York, in 1901. He was brought back to Canton, and today his tomb dominates the city skyline. At the time of his death he was the third U.S. president in 36 years to be assassinated. The others were Abraham Lincoln in 1865 and James A. Garfield in 1881.

The tomb sits on a bluff overlooking a park and the building that houses the William McKinley Presidential Library and Museum. This is a wonderful museum that offers a glimpse not only into the life of William McKinley but also into the industries and national firms that were either founded or have grown in Canton and affected our way of life. Also in the museum is a discovery section for children that includes a life-size animated dinosaur, an electrical display that will really

The William McKinley Presidential Library and Museum also features a life-sized dinosaur

stand your hair on end, and a host of other interesting things for kids to see and do. One final bit of ironic trivia: the discovery museum was designed by the firm operated by New York environmental designer Edwin Schlossberg. His wife is Caroline Kennedy Schlossberg, the daughter of President John F. Kennedy, who also was assassinated in office in 1963.

▲ **William McKinley Presidential Library and Museum**
☎ 330-455-7043
800 McKinley Monument Dr. NW · Canton

A REAL OLD FASHIONED ICE CREAM PARLOR

During the Football Hall of Fame festivities each year, you can usually find some football greats dropping into this Canton landmark, which has stood in the same spot since 1926. You might even find initials from the 1930s carved in some of the tables.

What they serve here is real homemade ice cream, made the same way for nearly seven decades. The big seller is a dish made with three-quarters of a pound of vanilla ice cream, homemade chocolate syrup, and fresh-roasted pecans, all blended together and topped with a mound of whipped cream. It's called a "Bittner." No one seems quite sure how the name originated. It's believed that it was named for an early employee who developed the treat, which is served in a soda glass with a spoon.

▲ **Taggart's Ice Cream**   ☎ 330-452-6844
1401 Fulton Rd. NW · Canton

STAY THE NIGHT AT A COUNTRY CLUB

When was the last time you slept in a country club? This is one of Ohio's most beautiful, and it's open to the public. Glenmoor started out as a seminary, built in the 1930s, and was later sold and converted to a private golf club. Today there are 74 nicely furnished rooms inside a building that resembles a Scottish castle. There is also a European spa and fitness center, as well as a Jack Nicklaus–inspired golf course just outside the front door. This is also the site of one of Ohio's top classic car shows.

▲ **Glenmoor Country Club**   ☎ 330-966-3600
4191 Glenmoor Rd. NW · Canton

THE HISTORY OF MASSILLON

The Massillon Museum is not just another small-town eclectic collection of local folks' memorabilia. This is a well-done, professional, modern museum—a tribute to the community that respected their historical past enough to do it right. From a lifelike miniature circus carved by Massillon doctor Robert Immel that covers 100 square feet to a 5,000-piece costume collection covering the period of the 1840s to

modern times, each gallery is a delight. And with the constantly changing temporary exhibits, there is always something new to see.

▲ **Massillon Museum**   ☎ 330-833-4061
121 Lincoln Way E · Massillon

SEE A MOVIE IN A REAL THEATER

The Massillon Lions Club is keeping alive one of the fine old movie
theaters that used to be the focal point of nearly every large town in
Ohio. The Lions Lincoln Theatre was declared "Finest Theater in Ohio"
when it opened in 1915. Now, nearly a century later, the local Lions have
purchased the building and are renovating it while keeping it alive,
showing classic movies every weekend at cut-rate prices. You can see
a major motion picture for as little as $3! The movies are shown every
Friday, Saturday, and Sunday.

▲ **Lions Lincoln Theatre**   ☎ 330-833-2413
156 Lincoln Way E · Massillon

OHIO MILITARY HISTORY MUSEUM

This small-town museum honors not only local veterans, but also
Congressional Medal of Honor recipients throughout the state. There is
a good collection of uniforms and weapons from various wars in which
Ohio soldiers have fought and a library of more than 2,000 reference
books about the services.

▲ **Ohio Military History Museum**   ☎ 330-832-5553
316 Lincoln Way E · Massillon

The Northeast Corner

Andover, Austinburg, Hartsgrove, Jefferson, Rome

This bridge in Harpersfield is one of 17 covered bridges in Ashtabula County

A FESTIVAL COVERING COVERED BRIDGES

Ashtabula County is the covered bridge capital of Ohio, with 17 bridges. Not only do they preserve their old bridges here, they're still building new ones! Probably the most photographed bridge is at Harpersfield, where a 228-foot-long structure spans the Grand River. The newest, completed in 2008, is the Smolen-Gulf Bridge across the Ashtabula River on State Road outside of Ashtabula. It's the longest covered bridge in the United States. The county throws a Covered Bridge Festival each October at the fairgrounds in Jefferson. A map of the bridges and other details about the event are available at the festival headquarters, open year-round, or from their Web site: www.coveredbridgefestival.org.

▲ **The Ashtabula County Covered Bridge Festival**　☎ 440-576-3769
25 W. Jefferson St. · Jefferson

A WORKING RAILROAD

There is still a working railroad in Ashtabula County. The Ashtabula, Carson & Jefferson Railroad, or AC&J for short, is a six-mile short-line railroad that serves industrial customers and on weekends hauls tourists on a 12-mile round trip over the last remaining portion of the old New York Central Ashtabula-to-Pittsburgh passenger mainline.

The passenger train runs only in the summer and autumn; call for the schedule. *[SEASONAL]*

▲ **Ashtabula, Carson & Jefferson Railroad** ☎ 440-576-6346
122 E. Walnut St. · Jefferson

A BABY CARRIAGE MUSEUM

With more than 200 antique baby carriages on display, twin sisters Judith Kaminski and Janet Pallo can safely claim that they have the world's largest-known collection of early wicker baby and doll carriages. What started out as a hobby has grown into a full-blown museum for the sisters. In fact, the collection grew so large that it took over their home. There is more than baby carriages; you will also discover sleighs, dolls, early tricycles, buckboard wagons, and other toys.

▲ **The Victorian Perambulator Museum** ☎ 440-576-9588
26 E. Cedar St. · Jefferson

CUT YOUR OWN CHRISTMAS TREES

Ashtabula County offers some of the larger Christmas tree plantations in the state. Two of them provide an uncommon way to get your annual treat: ride a horse-drawn wagon back into the fields, cut your own tree, throw it on the wagon, and haul it back to the office. It makes a great family holiday tradition. Usually open from late November/ early December until Christmas. *[SEASONAL]*

▲ **Manners Pine Tree Lodge** ☎ 440-294-2444
780 Dodgeville Rd. · Jefferson

▲ **Henson's Hideaway Tree Farm and Nursery** ☎ 440-294-2292
1155 Brockway Rd. · Rome

PYMATUNING STATE PARK

Pymatuning Lake is a 1,500-acre body of water sprawling across the state line into Pennsylvania. The state park on the Ohio side of the lake offers a host of activities and places to spend the night, from modern cabins, some equipped with fireplaces and hot tubs, to campsites where you can even rent a replica of a Mongolian yurt (a structure made of canvas and wood traditionally used by sheepherders). Pymatuning Lake is renowned for its fine walleye and muskellunge fishing and is also the place where ducks walk on the fish (on the Pennsylvania side, at the Linesville Spillway). There are boat rentals and swimming beaches.

▲ **Pymatuning State Park** ☎ 440-293-6030
6260 Pymatuning Lake Rd. · Andover

A QUAINT PLACE TO EAT

This quaint restaurant right on the square in Andover is just a stone's throw from Pymatuning State Park. It is decorated in antiques and offers some healthy "heart smart" recipes and specializes in soups. The day I visited, they even let me help make one of the daily specials, Italian wedding soup. It was delicious. A lot of local folks eat here.

▲ **Cranberry Station Restaurant**   ☎ 440-293-6651
    68 Public Square · Andover

A BISON FARM

This large American bison (buffalo) farm is open to the public. They offer wagon rides through the pastures where the buffalo roam for kids for a close personal look at the giant creatures. There is also a petting farm with goats, calves, and small domestic animals. The farm also includes a store where frozen buffalo meat is sold, as well as buffalo leather goods, wool clothing, artwork, and stoneware. Open on a seasonal basis May to September. *[SEASONAL]*

▲ **Buck Farm Bison**   ☎ 440-275-1415
    2500 Forman Rd. · Austinburg

GO PROSPECTING

You can actually pan for diamonds and other precious stones here in Ashtabula County. The NOEMA Gemstone Mine lets you take a bucket and sift through "tailings" purchased from mines around the world. Any precious or semiprecious stones are yours to keep. A jewelry business on site can mount any stone you find. While you may not find the Hope diamond, they claim that most people do find some kind of semiprecious stone that can be turned into a necklace or bracelet.

▲ **NOEMA Gemstone Mine**   ☎ 440-275-3211
    1788 Mill St. · Austinburg

THE EIGHT MISSING PRESIDENTS

In the small community of Williamsfield in Ashtabula County stands the "Real" Presidential Museum that, among other things, honors our first President, John Hanson.

George Washington was our first President, you say? Not according to museum owner Nick Pahys. Nine years before Washington was elected President, John Hanson was named to preside over America under the Articles of Confederation that we used until we had a U.S. Constitution. Obviously many historians do not agree with Pahys's reasoning, but he believes he has the straight story and built a museum to demonstrate his contention that Barack Obama is actually the 52nd U.S. President, not the 44th. (There were eight other people elected President between Hanson and George Washington.) If you love Presidential trivia, this place is for you.

▲ **One and Only Presidential Museum**   ☎ 440-344-0523
    6585 Howard Rd. · Williamsfield

Where Ashtabula Meets Lake Erie

Ashtabula, Conneaut, North Kingsville

ASHTABULA COUNTY

Historic Ashtabula County, tucked away in the northeast corner of the state, is not only the largest county in land size, it also stands out for some unusual attractions, like the 50-foot-tall statue of Our Lady of Guadalupe in Windsor and the unusual U.S. Presidential Museum in Hartsgrove. This is also home to a perambulator museum, lighthouses, beaches, and a historic harbor district.

UNDERGROUND RAILROAD HISTORY

Ashtabula played a big role in the Underground Railroad and was one of the stops for escaping slaves from the South as they tried to make their way to safety and freedom in Canada in the years prior to the Civil War. William and Catherine Hubbard made their home on the lakefront available as a haven, giving shelter, food, and comfort to the escaping slaves. Today the Hubbard home is a museum. Exhibits showing life in the early Western Reserve of Ohio are on the first floor. The second floor is dedicated to the home's being part of the Underground Railroad. A collection of early American and Civil War memorabilia is in the basement.

 ▲ **Hubbard House Underground Railroad Museum**
 ☎ 440-964-8168
 1603 Walnut Blvd. · Ashtabula

ASHTABULA HARBOR DISTRICT

The whole area of West 5th Street in Ashtabula from the 1200 block to the river has been placed on the National Register of Historic Places. That's 25 buildings sprawled over 45 acres. A great place to get a bird's-eye view of the harbor is from an overlook at the end of Walnut Boulevard, just across from the Great Lakes Marine and Coast Guard Memorial Museum.

The little hillside park offers great views of the harbor, as well as a chance for an up-close look at the leg of one of the giant Hulett ore unloaders that once quickly emptied ore ships at the dock below. The unloaders were so large that they could take 17 tons of ore off the boats

Great Lakes Marine and Coast Guard Memorial Museum also has a great view of the harbor

with just one bite. Inside the museum, you can see the only working model left of the Huletts. The museum also offers lots of Coast Guard memorabilia, including ship models, guns, and even the pilot house from an old ore boat. There is also a working model of early radar used by the Coast Guard, on which you can see the Canadian shore. The harbor district is a great place to start a visit to Ashtabula.

▲ **Great Lakes Marine and Coast Guard Memorial Museum**
☎ 440-964-6847
1071 Walnut St. · Ashtabula

A HARBOR VIEW

The Gilded Swan Bed and Breakfasts lives up to its name. The stately restored Victorian home has been updated and modernized inside but still keeps its charm. There are whirlpool baths and fireplaces in some of the bedrooms, and you can keep watch on the busy traffic below in Ashtabula harbor.

▲ **The Gilded Swan**   ☎ 888-345-7926
5024 West Ave. · Ashtabula

EAT IN A BANK VAULT

What do you do with a former bank building with its giant vault? In Ashtabula they turned one into a restaurant.

Casa Capelli decided to keep the look of the former bank, which has Tiffany-style arched glass ceilings. The vault has been turned into a separate private dining room. (Imagine a dining room with a door that weighs 14,000 pounds. Talk about privacy.) The specialties here are a blend of Italian and Mexican foods, which seem to complement each other. One of my favorites is the appetizer ravioli Español. It's Italian cheese ravioli filled with jalapeños, deep-fried, and served with a fresh marinara sauce.

▲ **Casa Capelli Restaurant** ☎ 440-992-3700
4641 Main Ave. · Ashtabula

RAILROAD MEMORABILIA

Railroads played a big part in the history of Ashtabula County. You can learn about days of the "iron horse" at the Conneaut Historical Railroad Museum. Located in the former New York Central depot built more than 100 years ago, there are relics of the terrible train wreck that occurred when a railroad bridge in Ashtabula collapsed in 1876, sending many of the passengers to their deaths. An actual steam locomotive and caboose are on display, and the kids can climb aboard and look around. The station building houses other railroad memorabilia.

▲ **Conneaut Railroad Museum** ☎ 440-599-7878
363 Depot St. · Conneaut

A HEALTHY SANDWICH STOP

One of my favorite places to stop for a sandwich in northeast Ohio is just before you leave Ohio and head into Pennsylvania. The White Turkey Drive-In Restaurant in Conneaut is like a frozen piece of history. The old root beer stand still has shutters that fold into the roof to create a curbside counter. The specialty here is not hamburgers but a much healthier cooked turkey breast ground into a patty and served on a bun. They still serve everything they served in the 1950s; only the prices have changed. *[SEASONAL]*

▲ **White Turkey Drive-In** ☎ 440-593-2209
388 E. Main Rd. · Conneaut

PIZZA UNDER COVER

If you want to mix a little history with your pizza, there is a perfect place to do it in Ashtabula County. A pizza restaurant there is built inside half of an old covered bridge that once spanned a stream in Ashtabula County. When it was determined the bridge could no long carry traffic, the county put it up for sale. The pizza shop owner bought it and cut it in two halves. One of them is now a pizzeria in North Kingsville. The other half was also made into a restaurant, in Andover, Ohio, which is also in Ashtabula County. People who like to tour covered bridges will love this place because he has kept the interior of the bridge as it was, graffiti and all. Instead of cars, there are tables and chairs on the bridge today. You can eat a pizza and contemplate all the history that this old bridge has seen.

▲ **Covered Bridge Pizza Parlor** ☎ 440-224-2252
6541 S. Main St. · North Kingsville

Winery Capital of Ohio

Conneaut, Geneva, Madison

With a dozen wineries within the county and more located nearby, Ashtabula can rightly be called the Winery Capital of Ohio. The best time to visit is late summer and early fall, when the grapes are heavy on the vines and the air is perfumed with their smell. Many of the wineries have tasting rooms and retail stores where you can sample and take home some of the best wines to be had in the Buckeye State or the entire country. No matter what time of the year it is, most of the wineries are open, and you can not only enjoy the vineyards but also the many other attractions in this county known as the cornerstone of Ohio.

A YOUNG WINERY

Tarsitano Winery is just up the road from a covered bridge. The wine cellar is in the basement of the 1850 farmhouse, and a nearby cedar barn doubles as a wine store, café, and tasting room. While the winery still offers only a few varieties of wine, they have already won some prestigious awards. The owners are local residents and can give you good tips on other sights to see in the county.

▲ **Tarsitano Winery** ☎ 440-224-2444
4871 Hatches Corners Rd. · Conneaut

SLEEP AT A WINERY

Buccia Vineyards is a small winery tucked away on the Ohio-Pennsylvania border. What makes it unusual is that you can sleep in the winery. Buccia's offers a bed and breakfast that is open year-round, right inside the winemaking building. Each of the rooms offers a six-person hot tub, as well as a private bath. Their tasting room is open year-round, and they say they are "children and pet friendly" with prior consent.

▲ **Buccia Winery Bed and Breakfast** ☎ 440-593-5976
518 Gore Rd. · Conneaut

WINERY IN A CHURCH

One of the more unusual wineries in Ashtabula County is located on its namesake, South River Road. The South River Vineyard not only makes great wine, it is located in a former church that dates back to 1892. Today, it has been restored to much or its original charm and doubles not only as a winery but as a wedding chapel. The church building was originally located in Portage County, where it was abandoned for nearly 30 years. Heather and Gene Siegel bought it and moved it board by board to its new location is in the midst of acres of grapes on a hill overlooking Lake Erie.

▲ **South River Vineyard**   ☎ 440-466-6676
6062 S. River Rd. · Geneva

ROMANTIC DINING

How about a romantic lunch or dinner in the middle of a vineyard? You can do it at Ferrante's in Geneva. The Ferrante family offers fine Italian cuisine as well as some of their fine wines to go with your meal. One of my favorites is the pepe carciofo, an appetizer made of Romano, mozzarella, and cheddar cheeses mixed with roasted red peppers, artichoke hearts, black olives, and fresh herbs. It's baked and served with bread for dipping, and it is almost a meal in itself. For a main course, I like their pollo pasta Rockefeller. It's chicken breast sautéed with fresh spinach, bacon, tomatoes, and Swiss cheese, tossed with white wine and served on a bed of linguine.

By the way, they also have a wine tasting room and store in the restaurant where you can sample and purchase bottles of wine to take home. Tours of the winery are available.

▲ **Ferrante Winery and Ristorante**   ☎ 440-466-8466
5585 State Rte. 307 · Geneva

A LUXURY STAY AMONG THE VINES

When you first arrive at the Polly Harper Inn, you would swear the building has been standing in the middle of a field of grape vines for centuries, but you would be wrong.

The Polly Harper Inn, although designed to look like it has been part of the Western Reserve for a couple of hundred years, is, in fact, a modern home with many nice amenities. It was built as a bed and breakfast. The bedrooms come with queen-sized four-poster beds. There are gas fireplaces in each room, and for a luxurious touch each of the rooms has a whirlpool bath for two people, as well as private bathrooms. It's located in the middle of wine country and sits right in the middle of a vineyard, yet it is close to many restaurants, covered bridges, and other activities.

▲ **Polly Harper Inn**   ☎ 440-466-6183
6308 S. River Rd. · Geneva

ICE WINE (AND MORE)

The last time Tony Debevec invited me out to watch his crew pick grapes, I should have noticed something a bit unusual. It was January, the temperature was near zero, there was a foot of snow on the ground, and the wind was blowing more snow all over. But sure enough, out in the vineyards atop a windy hill were a dozen frozen grape-pickers bundled against the near-blinding blizzard, all of them picking frozen grapes off net-covered vines. Later, in the warmth of the winery, clutching a cup of hot spiced wine, Tony explained that this is how they make a special wine called ice wine, just one of the many wonderful wines produced at Ohio's largest estate winery. During the summer months, they offer both food and entertainment, too.

▲ **Chalet Debonne Vineyards**   ☎ 440-466-3485
7743 Doty Rd. · Madison

Our Great-Grandparents Vacationed Here

Geneva, Geneva-on-the-Lake, Unionville

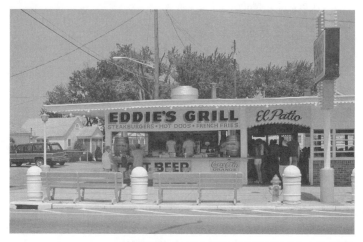

Eddie's Grill looks much like it did during its heydey in the 1950s

OHIO'S FIRST SUMMER RESORT

Geneva-on-the-Lake can trace its beginnings all the way back to 1869, four years after the end of the Civil War. That makes it Ohio's first summer resort.

Today it looks much as it did during its glory days in the 1950s. The main street is surrounded by restaurants and resort businesses, everything from game rooms to tee-shirt shops. You can still sit at a sidewalk counter at Eddie's for one of his trademark foot-long hotdogs or walk across the street to Madsen Donuts, which has been around since the 1930s, for a hot cruller. You can still ride the go-carts and merry-go-round at Adventure Zone, or enjoy the view of Lake Erie from the Ferris wheel at the Old Firehouse Winery. Wineries, miniature golf, water slides, and wonderful Lake Erie fishing can be found at your doorstep. *[SEASONAL]*

▲ **Geneva-on-the-Lake** ☎ 800-862-9948
   Geneva-on-the-Lake Chamber of Commerce
   5536 Lake Rd. · Geneva-on-the-Lake

A SUMMER HOT DOG

There are those who swear the greatest hot dogs are those that can only be obtained in the summer at Ohio's first resort, Geneva-on-the-Lake. They are referring to the hot dogs at Eddie's Grill and Dairy Queen. A part of the strip for half a century, Eddie's has been making foot-long hot dogs the same way since first opened back in 1949.

He deep-fries the dog and puts it on a toasted bun. Summer residents of the resort say they have never had a hot dog that tastes as good.

I think part of the mystique about Eddie's is its location. The counter, where you can sit, is actually the front of the building. When they are ready to open for the day, they just raise a large shutter, and you sit down partly on the busy strip of downtown Geneva-on-the-Lake. This way you can eat and people-watch at the same time.

There is no air conditioning, just gentle breezes from Lake Erie, mixed with the smell of hot grease, onions, and suntan lotion. It fairly screams "summer" at you. I thought the hot dogs were good, and the ambiance of Eddie's made them taste even better. *[SEASONAL]*

▲ **Eddie's Grill and Dairy Queen**   ☎ 440-466-8720
   5377 Lake Rd. · Geneva-on-the-Lake

A LAKE ERIE VIEW

This B&B on the edge of Lake Erie was built in the 1960s as the home of a local doctor. The bedrooms are all air conditioned and have private baths. There is a hot tub on a screened porch overlooking Lake Erie. A gazebo on the lawn is a great place to sit and read or just watch boats go by.

▲ **Charlma Bed and Breakfast**   ☎ 440-466-3646
   6739 Lake Rd. W · Geneva-on-the-Lake

A FIRST-RATE PLACE TO STAY

I discovered the Lakehouse Inn and Winery on a cold January day. We sat in the glassed-in porch of the winery in front of a fire and watched swirls of snow dance over frozen Lake Erie as we sampled some of the nearly one dozen types of wine they produce here. Summer or winter, the wine and the accommodations at this lakefront property are first rate. Some of the rooms offer whirlpool baths as well as fireplaces. The great room has an incredible view of the lake that you can enjoy with your breakfast. The Lakehouse Inn and Winery is located between Geneva State Park and the strip in downtown Geneva-on-the-Lake. In other words, it's convenient to everything.

▲ **Lakehouse Inn and Winery**   ☎ 440-466-8668
   5653 Lake Rd. E · Geneva-on-the-Lake

Old Firehouse Winery and Restaurant

EAT AT THE FIREHOUSE

This really was the firehouse that served the lakefront resort community of Geneva-on-the-Lake for many years. Today it has been converted into a restaurant and winery on the banks of Lake Erie. The dining room patio offers spectacular views of passing boats and the famous Lake Erie sunsets. The winery also offers wines that incorporate the flavors of peaches, raspberries, and apples, as well as the traditional grape wines of the region.

▲ **Old Firehouse Winery and Restaurant**   ☎ 440-466-9300
5499 Lake Rd. E · Geneva-on-the-Lake

A PLACE FOR FUN IN THE SUN

Old and new mix at the edge of the village where Adventure Zone now stands. The merry-go-round that was part of Erieview Park for many years has found a new home here, along with new go-kart tracks, bumper boats, batting cages, and a climbing wall. Adventure Zone has pretty much taken the place of old Erieview Park. It is walking distance from the downtown strip and also not far from the new Geneva State Park Lodge. This is a town that loves miniature golf and you will find one of the newer courses here at Adventure Zone. There is plenty here to keep the kids busy on a hot summer day.

▲ **Adventure Zone**   ☎ 440-466-3555
5600 Lake Road E · Geneva-on-the-Lake

LAKE ERIE SUNSETS

Geneva State Park is on the very edge of Lake Erie. With 109 rooms, a dramatic four-story lobby, and octagonal rooms that overlook the lake and house the swimming pool, the park's Lodge and Conference Center

Geneva State Park

is a mighty popular place, both summer and winter. The lodge is only a stone's throw from the state park and marina. Fishing, swimming, biking, and a multitude of other attractions are available without leaving the property. Reservations here are a must, especially in the summer season. There's a terrific view of those incredible Lake Erie sunsets.

▲ **Lodge and Conference Center at Geneva State Park**
☎ 800-801-9982
4888 N. Broadway · Geneva-on-the-Lake

GENEVA STATE PARK

You can often find charter-fishing captains at the concession stand at the marina. Marina officials can usually supply you with names and phone numbers of fishing guides. Besides one of the best marinas on the eastern end of Lake Erie, the park also has campgrounds and cabins available for rent, some with lakefront views. The cabins are equipped with just about everything you need; just bring your food and clothing. Reservations for the cabins are a must.

▲ **Geneva State Park**   ☎ 440-466-8400
4499 Padanarum Rd. · Geneva

Lake County Highlights

Fairport Harbor, Grand River, Kirtland, Mentor, Painesville, Willoughby

Headlands Beach and Fairport Lighthouse

A LIGHTHOUSE MUSEUM

The old lighthouse at Fairport Harbor is home to the Fairport Marine Museum and Lighthouse. The lighthouse was built in 1825 and was 30 feet high. In 1871 it was rebuilt, and the new light was raised to 60 feet high with a house for the lighthouse keeper at the base. Today the house is the museum, which was founded in 1945. Visitors can climb the 69 steps to the observation platform at the top of the lighthouse. It's a great view of Lake Erie and Fairport Harbor. You can also enter the pilot house from the Lake Carrier *Frontenac* and stand at the wheel imagining what it must have been like to sail the Great Lakes and depend on lighthouses like the one here in Fairport Harbor.

▲ **Fairport Marine Museum and Lighthouse**
☎ 440-354-4825
129 2nd St. · Fairport Harbor

OHIO'S BIGGEST BEACH

It stretches for a mile along the south side of Lake Erie. Headlands Beach State Park near Mentor is the longest beach in the Buckeye state. Its popularity in the summer sometimes sees it covered with people for the entire mile. Besides the natural sand beach, there are picnic shelters and picnic tables and a children's playground. There are some hiking trails in a nearby marsh area. The big beach and shallow waters near shore make it an ideal place for swimming or just relaxing.

🔺 **Headlands Beach State Park**   ☎ 216-881-8141
9601 Headlands Rd. · Mentor

HAVE A MENTOR ADVENTURE

The city of Mentor owns a U.S. Navy launch, the BB64, once used on the battleship the U.S.S. *Wisconsin.* They use the launch, which can carry up to 13 people, to offer a 45-minute cruise of the Mentor Lagoons. The lakefront canal area was created in the 1920s when a developer planned a community to be built on the lagoons. The development was never realized, but the lagoons have become both a popular docking area for boaters as well as a nature preserve bordering the famed Mentor Marsh. On a typical cruise you will see deer, all kinds of waterfowl, as well as lots of beautiful boats. You even pass under "The Bridge to Nowhere," a bridge built by the original developer that was to have connected to the main highway and streets in the lagoon community. It, too, was never finished, and today is a curiosity for boaters.

🔺 **Mentor Lagoons Nature Preserve and Marina**   ☎440-205-3625
8365 Harbor Dr. · Mentor

A RESTAURANT WITH PANACHE

According to my dictionary, the word "panache" means "something with flair." That certainly applies to Pickle Bill's Restaurant in Grand River.

I first met the restaurant's founder, Jerry Powell, back in 1967, when he opened a restaurant with the same name in the Cleveland Flats. It wasn't the three-dollar pitchers of beer or the steak for under five dollars that attracted me to the place. It was the personality of the owner, who had this great affection for movie actor W. C. Fields. Powell would show his comedies over and over at his riverfront restaurant. The food was good, the entertainment was cheap and while the restaurant wasn't much to look at, Powell was a great host.

Why was it called "Pickle Bill's"? W. C. Fields first name was William, and there was a legend that his large nose was partly caused by his love of booze. It looked like his nose was "pickled."

In 1982 Powell moved his eclectic restaurant to River Street in Grand River, where it has stood ever since. Surviving floods and even a fire that burned the place to the ground in 1998, Powell rebuilt—actually, he built an entirely new building, this one even bigger and better than before. And while the five-dollar steaks are a thing of the past, the food is still good, and as always, the focus is on seafood.

There aren't too many restaurants along Lake Erie that still offer "all you can eat" items on their menu. Jerry does. You can eat your fill of fresh Lake Erie walleye, prime rib, or barbecue ribs until they roll you out the door. I usually find it pretty hard to visit Grand River without stopping in for dinner at Pickle Bill's.

▲ **Pickle Bill's Restaurant**   ☎ 800-352-6343
  101 River St. · Grand River

HOLDEN ARBORETUM

Lake County has one of the largest arboretums in the United States. With over 3,400 acres of land, Holden Arboretum contains woods, meadows, and ponds. It is a great place for bird watchers. You'll find well-marked trails with signs identifying the various trees, wildflowers, and grasses. Especially beautiful in the spring and fall, Holden is a four-seasons destintation.

▲ **Holden Arboretum**   ☎ 440-946-4400
  9500 Sperry Rd. · Kirtland

FARMS AND RAILROADS

At Lake Farmpark you can wander around a barn, help milk a cow, crawl through a maze made of straw, or even take a horse-drawn hay-ride through the park. There are gift shops and even restaurants here.

The park's holiday lights display is one of the most popular holiday attractions in northern Ohio, selling out almost as soon as it opens each holiday season. If you are lucky enough to buy a ticket, you and your little ones get a horse-drawn wagon ride through the Farmpark's holi-day light display. Thousands and thousands of lights spread over acres and acres light the winter night. When the wagon ride is over, the kids get to climb into Santa's sleigh to tell the jolly old elf their Christmas wishes. From there they are escorted into Santa's workshop, where elves help kids build a wooden toy that they then can take home.

The number of guests are limited for maximum enjoyment. Tickets sell out each Christmas season; get yours early so you won't be disap-pointed.

▲ **Lake Farmpark**   ☎ 800-366-3276
  8800 Chardon Rd. · Kirtland

AN INN FOR ROMANCE

For a romantic place to get away to for a weekend or just overnight, try Rider's Inn in Painesville. The tavern has been around since the early 1800s. Today, while still maintaining a historic look, it offers modern-ized bedrooms with private baths and beautiful furnishings.

If you want to surprise someone special, give the inn a call and they can arrange for someone to go shopping and perhaps buy a slinky negligée or robe in the right color and size that will be waiting on the bed when you arrive. Also, you can schedule a romantic dinner at the inn and, when you are finished eating, the hostess will offer to give you a tour of the premises. Upon reaching your room (which is the last stop on the tour), she hands you a key and gently closes the door leaving the two of you alone.

▲ **Rider's Inn** ☏ 440-354-8200
792 Mentor Ave. · Painesville

OHIO'S PRESIDENTIAL TRAIL: JAMES A. GARFIELD

The 20th president of the United States made his home here in Mentor. Lawnfield is the house Garfield purchased in 1876 and summered in until he was elected president in 1880, when he went to Washington and was assassinated just months after taking office.

▲ **Lawnfield, James A. Garfield National Historic Site**
☏ 440-255-8722
8095 Mentor Ave. · Mentor

AN OLD-FASHIONED SODA FOUNTAIN

You can find phosphates, ice-cream sodas, and some big ice-cream cones at this old-fashioned soda fountain in downtown Willoughby. It looks like it's been there forever, but it was opened in the 1990s. The present owners have done a good job of capturing the atmosphere of the soda fountains of a half-century ago.

▲ **Scooter's Soda Fountain** ☏ 440-946-7632
4127 Vine St. · Willoughby

SEGWAY ADVENTURE IN THE METROPARKS

If you and the family have been wanting to experience what it is like to ride the futuristic Segway two-wheeled transporter device but can't pony up the thousands of dollars it takes to purchase one, I have a solution. A Cleveland-area company that sells the vehicles also offers a scenic tour of the Cleveland Metroparks North Chagrin Reservation using rental vehicles. The tour takes you on paved and gravel paths past a waterfall, under and over bridges, and past ponds and woods. It is an easy way to see much of the park in a very short time.

The tours, which cost about $40 and last at least 90 minutes, include a short instruction period on operating the stand-up transporter, which just about anyone can drive as long as they are at least 14 years old.

The tours run by reservation only year-round, weather permitting.

▲ **Tomorrow's Transport Segway Sales and Tours** ☏ 440-725-3353
3037 SOM Center Rd. · Willoughby Hills

The Amishland of Northeast Ohio

Burton, Chardon, Garrettsville, Mesopotamia, Middlefield

NATURE'S CANDY

For something natural and sweet, stop at the log cabin on the square in Burton. The rustic building houses the Burton Chamber of Commerce's community maple syrup operation. In early spring when the sap is running, maple sap is collected here and turned into maple syrup and maple sugar. You can enjoy the big fireplace in the salesroom and, watch them make the candy, and buy some fresh syrup.

🔺 **Burton Log Cabin and Maple Sugar Camp** ☎ 800-526-5630
Burton Village Park, State Rte. 87 · Burton
At the intersection of State Rte. 87 and State Rte. 6

A SMALL HISTORIC VILLAGE

The Burton Historical Society runs a small village, just off the historic square district in downtown Burton, that takes visitors back a hundred years or more. Century Village consists of a one-room schoolhouse, a general store, early wooden churches, and other buildings around a village square. All were originally located within the Western Reserve. The

Century Village

Society offers a series of living history programs from April to December each year. Contact the Society for a calendar of events.

▲ **Century Village**   ☎ 440-834-1492
Geauga County Historical Society, 14653 E. Park St. · Burton

AN AUTHENTIC COUNTY FAIR

One of the last really authentic Ohio county fairs is the Great Geauga County Fair in Burton, held each summer on Labor Day weekend. The fair has changed little in the last hundred years. Farmers bring their crops and livestock to be judged. There are exhibits of farm equipment and 4-H and Future Farmer exhibits. They even have chicken-flying contests, and, once in a while, a cow race. It's a little bit of yesterday still existing today. *[SEASONAL]*

▲ **Great Geauga County Fair**   ☎ 440-834-1846
14373 N. Cheshire St. · Burton

A MILLION DOLLAR VIEW

If there is such a thing as a million dollar view, the Red Maple Inn has it. It's located on top of a hill on the edge of the village, and on a clear day you can see for a dozen miles or more over the Amish farmlands spread out below. While the architecture resembles the New England style of two centuries ago, the building is modern, with amenities you would expect in a fine inn. There are 17 bedrooms, several with fireplaces. A dining room on the first floor has a magnificent view of the countryside, and you are only steps away from downtown Burton.

▲ **Red Maple Inn**   ☎ 440-834-8334
14707 S. Cheshire St. · Burton

MA AND PA'S GIFT SHACK

If your idea of a romantic afternoon or evening is being tucked into an antique sleigh pulled by a spirited horse and feeling the snow hit your cheeks as you trot through a wooded snow-covered winter paradise, I have just the place for you: "Ma and Pa's Horse Drawn Sleigh Rides," a family-operated business east of Cleveland in Troy Township in Geauga County. The sleigh rides operate from the first heavy snow in November through the end of February—weather permitting—and since Troy is in northeast Ohio's snow belt, it's a good bet that conditions will be favorable. They operate every Friday, Saturday, and Sunday. A weekday ride for special occasions, like getting engaged or a wedding anniversary, might be arranged, but call first. By the way, all rides are by reservation only.

▲ **Ma and Pa's Gift Shack**   ☎ 440-548-5521
15161 Main Market Road (S.R. 422), Burton

Swine Creek Reservation

EVERYTHING MAPLE

Since 1910, this business has been making and selling maple products like syrup and candy—and even the equipment to make your own syrup. One of my favorite things is to stop by when they are making candy in the kitchen and get a sample of fresh maple cream right out of the pot. Richardson's has a store that has local maple syrup products year-round. They always have the syrup, maple spread, maple sugar candy, and gift boxes.

▲ **Richards Maple Products**　☎ 800-352-4052
545 Water St. · Chardon

PANCAKES, SYRUP, AND . . . SAUERKRAUT

In Chardon, during the annual Maple Festival, you can find pancakes served with fresh-made maple syrup and . . . sauerkraut! I know, I can hear you saying, "Yukk!" already. That was my reaction, too, before I tried it. But the taste—sweet and sour and reminiscent of a Chinese egg roll—was very good. The Maple Festival is held each year on the first weekend after Easter. *[SEASONAL]*

▲ **Geauga County Maple Festival**　☎ 440-286-3007
Chardon

UNSPOILED NATURE

The Geauga County Park District has a dozen parks with more than 6,000 acres spread across the county. One of my personal favorites is Swine Creek Reservation, just outside of Middlefield. I like it partly because of its homely name and mostly because there is much to do in this unspoiled park filled with woods and ravines, from the annual sugar-bush experience, where visitors can follow a horse-drawn wagon as it collects sap from the maple trees, to the sugarbush itself, where the sap is turned into maple syrup. In the spring they offer horse-drawn wagon rides in the park, and for hikers, this is a wonderful area, filled with a variety of terrain.

▲ **Swine Creek Reservation** ☎ 800-536-4006
Geauga County Park District, 9160 Robinson Rd. · Chardon

EXOTIC GAME ON THE MENU

The first time I ever tasted wild game was at the Bass Lake Taverne in Chardon. The tavern, part of the Bass Lake Inn, is a rustic but elegant place to eat, just south of downtown Chardon. There's a roaring fire in the fireplace in the dining room and a kitchen that offers many specialties, including some exotic game dishes. If you're looking for someplace romantic and restful for lunch or dinner, this is the place.

▲ **Bass Lake Taverne** ☎ 440-285-3100
426 South St. · Chardon

SKYDIVING

Have you ever had the inclination to jump out of a perfectly good airplane? I must confess that it has never been one of my life's ambitions, but if you have always had a fantasy about skydiving, here is the place to go. The Cleveland Sport Parachute Center offers skydiving lessons for beginners and more advanced students. They offer tandem jumps—beginners can jump while attached to a more-experienced skydiver, using a larger chute to handle the weight.

▲ **Cleveland Sport Parachute Center** ☎ 440-548-4511
15199 Grove Rd. · Garrettsville
2 miles south of Parkman

AN AMISH FARMERS CO-OP

We hear a lot about Amish cheese-makers in Ohio. This company in Middlefield that turns out cheese year-round really is almost entirely owned and operated by the Amish. This co-op is 98 percent Amish farmers who bring their milk to the factory in 10-gallon cans and then turn it into cheddar and other kinds of cheeses. There is a viewing window in the salesroom where you can watch the process. The salesroom also offers jams, jellies, and other Amish-made products.

▲ **Middlefield Original Cheese Co-op** ☎ 440-632-5567
16942 Kinsman Rd. · Middlefield

MIDDLEFIELD CHEESE-MAKERS OF FINE SWISS CHEESE

This business was for years the only cheese manufacturer in Geauga County. Then Amish farmers decided to start their own cooperative. Middlefield Cheese still accepts only grade-A milk (from a four-state area) to make sure each pound of their cheese is the highest quality. They make five kinds of Swiss cheese, which is their specialty: Baby Swiss, mild, sharp, baby eye Swiss, and no-salt Swiss. They also carry approximately 50 other types of cheese, some of it imported. At their retail store there is a small museum that explains the story of how cheese was and is made, and there is a short movie showing the cheese-making process. Closed on Sundays.

▲ **Middlefield Cheese Company**   ☎ 440-632-5228
   15815 Nauvoo Rd. · Middlefield

A COUNTRY MARKETPLACE

On Mondays and Saturdays you can find a lot of Amish folks and tourists gathered at the Middlefield Market Complex on Nauvoo Road. This is the site of the local flea market. There are permanent vendors inside the marketplace selling everything from shrubs to fresh bakery, and outside, weather permitting, you will usually find dozens of flea market vendors selling anything and everything.

▲ **Middlefield Market Complex**   ☎ 440-632-3196
   15848 Nauvoo Rd. · Middlefield

AMISH STYLE FOOD

While the owner isn't Amish, many Amish work here in the kitchen and in the restaurant. The food is Amish-style: lots of chicken, ham, and roast beef, mashed potatoes, and a huge salad bar with pickled eggs and just about anything else you can put on a salad. This is a big tourist stop, but they handle crowds quickly and efficiently. The gift shop also carries local Amish-made crafts.

End of the Commons General Store

▲ **Mary Yoder's Amish Kitchen, Bakery, and Gift Shop**
☎ 440-632-1939
14743 N. State St. · Middlefield

A REAL AMISH STORE

When you visit Mesopotamia, you are in part of Ohio's second-largest Amish settlement. Horses and buggies can be seen routinely on the main and side roads, and the crossroads of State Route 87 and Route 534 is a picture postcard of the early Western Reserve come to life, with its tree-lined streets and New England architecture of the churches and homes. At the top of the square is the End of the Commons General Store, where both Amish and English (the Amish name for the rest of us) do their shopping. Here you can find bulk foods, candy, and ice cream, as well as some Amish collectibles.

▲ **End of the Commons General Store**   ☎ 440-693-4295
8719 State Rte. 534 · Mesopotamia

Home of the Hotdog

Hubbard, Niles, Warren

A WARREN TRADITION

Just about anyone who has ever lived in Warren or even just stopped by for a visit has had at least one hotdog at this downtown Warren institution. Here they have a secret, closely guarded sauce that they use on the hotdogs, and they go through hundreds of them every day. Many fans buy the dogs by the bagful.

▲ **The Hot Dog Shoppe** ☎ 330-395-7057
740 W. Market St. · Warren

FIRST FLIGHT LUNAR MODULE

The first landing on the moon by humankind, and the role that Warren, Ohio, played in that history-making achievement, is commemorated next to a fast-food restaurant on the edge of town.

Once an airport that served Warren, it was also where, in the late 1930s, a young Neil Armstrong, living in Warren, was brought for his very first airplane ride.

A local businessman spearheaded a drive to create a scaled-down version of Armstrong's Lunar Landing Module and has created a small park where the Lunar Lander is on display. Armstrong, a real moonwalker, was here for the dedication.

▲ **First Flight Lunar Module** ☎ 330-898-3116
2487 Parkman Rd. · Warren

First Flight Lunar Module

National Packard Museum

ASK THE MAN WHO OWNS ONE

It's pretty hard these days to "Ask the man who owns one." That was once the proud motto of the Packard Automobile Company, but Packard automobiles have not been manufactured since the 1950s. You can still see many of these famous autos that once set the standard for excellence in motor cars at the National Packard Museum in Warren. Why Warren? Because this was the hometown of James and William Packard, who designed and built the first car bearing their name near the turn of the twentieth century. The museum entrance is built to resemble the famous Packard grill and hood ornament. Inside you will find various models of the famous car, from the earliest up to the final models. There is also a store that sells all kinds of things with a Packard logo.

▲ **National Packard Museum**   ☎ 330-394-1899
1899 Mahoning Ave. NW · Warren

WHERE CELEBRITIES STAY AND PLAY

The Avalon Inn attracts both local folks and the rich and famous who visit here. A fine restaurant, lovely rooms, and a championship golf course with beautiful grounds make this a great getaway for families. Some of the biggest names in golf have played this course.

▲ **The Avalon Inn**   ☎ 330-856-1900
9519 E. Market St. · Warren

THE GHOSTS OF THE PAST

Warren offers an unusual Halloween tradition. Each October, the Fine Arts Council gets actors to portray famous residents who once lived along "Millionaires' Row." In the evening, as you walk along the street, "ghosts" of these residents drift by to tell stories of the grief and scandal they faced. Tours leave from the First Presbyterian Church, located at 256 Mahoning Avenue, and include a visit to the Pioneer Cemetery.

Of course celebrating Halloween is not the only thing the Fine Arts Council does for the city. Call them for a current schedule of events. *[SEASONAL]*

▲ **Fine Arts Council of Trumbull County**   ☎ 330-399-1212
    Warren

WAKE UP AND GOLF

If you have a die-hard golfer in the family, plan an overnight visit to this part of Northeast Ohio and book a room at Julia's Bed and Breakfast in Hubbard, Ohio. It's located on the edge of the Pine Lakes Golf Club, which has just been totally renovated. The bed and breakfast was once the home of a former Ohio governor. It was built in 1875, but it is now modernized inside so that the suites have private baths, and some have fireplaces and whirlpool bathtubs. You can even set up a tee time when you make your reservation.

▲ **Julia's Bed and Breakfast**   ☎ 888-758-5427
    6219 W. Liberty · Hubbard

AN ORIGINAL

I love diners. I especially love Erika's Emerald Diner in Hubbard. This is one of those rare places where they mix comfort food, like meatloaf and garlic mashed potatoes, with things like fancy French-style cooking, homemade salad dressings, and checkerboard cakes. The diner is an original that was purchased from Connecticut and brought to Ohio, where it was refurbished and taken back in time to the 1950s in appearance. But it's the good food that makes this almost worth the trip to Northeast Ohio.

▲ **Erika's Emerald Diner**   ☎ 330-534-1441
    825 N. Main St. · Hubbard

EQUARIUM

You can go nose-to-nose with a real live shark right here in northeast Ohio and not even get your feet wet.

Eastwood Mall in Niles has opened what may be the first huge aquarium inside a shopping mall. They call it Equarium.

It consists of three monster tanks, one containing almost 5,000 gallons of seawater that is home to the aforementioned sharks. There are two other smaller tanks that have other sea creatures and fish. Best of all, the attraction is free.

▲ **Equarium**   ☎ 330-652-6980
    5555 Youngstown Warren Rd. · Niles

Bandits, Flea Markets, and Pottery

Columbiana, East Liverpool, Hanoverton, Rogers

PLAIN AND SIMPLE FOOD

Das Dutch Haus Restaurant and Bakery usually has lines of hungry people waiting every lunch hour. It serves Amish-style food, and there's a huge salad bar and lots of fresh homemade pies and other baked goods. Service is usually fast and efficient. The restaurant is located in a complex that also has an inn and several shops offering a variety of products ranging from books to pet supplies.

▲ **Das Dutch Haus Restaurant and Bakery** ☎ 330-482-2236
14895 South Ave. Extension · Columbiana

OHIO'S LEAST-KNOWN STATE PARK

This is one of Ohio's least-known state parks, and one of the loveliest. A small village has been re-created near a lock on the old Sandy Canal that once ran through here. You can climb to the top of one of the locks and do what lockkeepers did a hundred years ago: close the huge wooden locks by hand to allow water to run into the chamber, raising canal boats several feet to get them to the next level of the river. There is also an old gristmill and a one-room schoolhouse that looks as though the children left just moments before. There are wonderful walking trails throughout the park, and this is one of the few facilities in the state that allows camping with your horse. On the edge of the park you can see the historical marker where "Pretty Boy" Floyd was gunned down by lawmen on October 22, 1934. In another area of the park, you can find an abandoned village where it is said the ghost of a young woman still walks, searching for her betrothed who never returned from the Civil War.

▲ **Beaver Creek State Park** ☎ 330-385-3091
12021 Echo Dell Rd. · East Liverpool
On State Rte. 7, just north of East Liverpool

THE POTTERY CITY

East Liverpool still clings to its pottery heritage. Aside from the local ceramics museum, there are still several active companies making pottery here in the Ohio Valley. Hall China has been famous for their teapots since 1903. They are the largest manufacturer of specialty chinaware in the country.

When visiting East Liverpool, you can stop at the factory and visit the company retail shop, called the Hall Closet. They sell seconds and one-of-a-kind items from their foodservice product line. This is a good place to get some really durable chinaware at a reduced price.

  ▲ **Hall China Company** ☎ 800-445-4255
    1 Anna St. · East Liverpool

POTTERY AND ANTIQUES

More than 200 dealers are gathered in an abandoned department store in downtown East Liverpool. A specialty is local pottery. East Liverpool once was the pottery-making capital of Ohio. Several local potteries also have outlet stores inside this mall and offer discontinued series or seconds at discounted prices.

  ▲ **Pottery City Galleries, Antiques and Collectibles Mall**
    ☎ 330-385-6933
    409 Washington St. · East Liverpool

A BED AND BREAKFAST WITH A TOUCH OF HISTORY

When 1930s gangster Charles Arthur "Pretty Boy" Floyd was gunned down by lawmen outside East Liverpool, his body was taken to the local funeral home, where he was embalmed and then put on display for the local townspeople in the "viewing room." Today that funeral home is a beautifully furnished Victorian-style bed and breakfast, and the viewing room is now the breakfast room where guests eat each morning. However, if you ask, you can go into the basement and see the embalming room, complete with pictures, just as it was when they prepared Floyd for his last journey. Modern amenities include six rooms with private baths, air conditioning, phones, and TV.

  ▲ **Sturgis House Bed and Breakfast** ☎ 330-382-0194
    122 W. Fifth St. · East Liverpool

A HISTORIC HIDEAWAY

Built in 1837, the Spread Eagle Tavern was an important part of the early nineteenth century canal era. When the canal was the main form of transportation across Ohio, the three-story Federal-period brick tavern served as both a hotel and food stop for passengers on the canal boats. But when the canal period ended in the early 1900s, Hanoverton was pretty much bypassed and became just another small Ohio backwater town. It was probably saved by the fact that the first continental road, the Lincoln Highway (today, U.S. Route 30) was built through the community. A century and a half after the Spread Eagle Tavern was built, Peter and Jean Johnson spent more than two years and countless dollars in a total restoration of the historic building that today offers five luxurious guest rooms and a very impressive restaurant with gourmet cooking. One of my favorites is their walnut-encrusted salmon served on a bed of garlic mashed potatoes with a red onion-celery compote. The tavern is a great Ohio destination for a special occasion or a romantic getaway.

▲ **The Spread Eagle Tavern and Inn**   ☎ 330-223-1583
10150 Historic Plymouth St. · Hanoverton

BACK IN TIME

If you want to really experience what a diner in the 1950s was like, head to Lisbon, where you will find a grand old O'Mahoney diner that has been restored to the "Happy Days" of the 1950s.

They serve real mashed potatoes and hand-cut french fries. Fresh pies fresh every day. (Their oatmeal pie is so good that it has been written up in national diner magazines.) A jukebox plays songs of the '50s, and neon signs makes the place glow at night like a giant caterpillar.

It's diner food, pure and simple—breakfast, lunch, and dinner done right. The food is fresh, well prepared, and served hot. You can't ask for much more. They make their milkshakes with ice cream, so thick that the straw stands up in the middle.

Open 24 hours a day most of the time.

▲ **Steel Trolley Diner**   ☎ 330-424-3663
140 E. Lincoln Way · Lisbon

A BIG FLEA MARKET

This flea market and auction operates every Friday, year-round. Several buildings house more than 600 vendors and an auction; in warmer weather upwards of 1,000 more vendors set up outside, surrounding the buildings. This event attracts residents from all 50 states. Parking lots are often some distance from flea market. Get there early in the day for close-in parking during peak season.

▲ **Rogers Community Auction and Open Air Market**
☎ 330-227-3233
45625 State Rte. 154 · Rogers
½ west of Rte. 7 on State Rte. 154, halfway between Youngstown and East Liverpool.

Water, Ghosts, and Sandstone

Elyria, Lorain, Oberlin, South Amherst

WATER FROM WHISKEYVILLE

At the intersection of State Routes 113 and 58 in Amherst Township is an area called Whiskeyville. It got its name more than a century ago, when there were several taverns located near the four corners, as well as a stagecoach stop. There has always been local suspicion that there was some illegal whiskey-making in the area before the turn of the last century, which also may have contributed to the name. I've always believed this to be true because of the ready source of spring water in the area, a necessary ingredient in "moonshine."

The owners of one spring opted for the more mundane name of "Cherry Knoll Spring," probably because of the number of cherry trees on the site. A small brick building near the intersection houses spigots and coin machines where you can fill your own jugs with cold, clear spring water. Their water is also sold commercially throughout northern Ohio.

▲ **Cherry Knoll Spring Water**   ☎ 440-986-2197
8470 Leavitt Road (State Rte. 58) · Amherst

"ANNE'S FOUNTAIN"

Newton Baus was a Lorain County farmer in 1956 when he decided to build a new home near the corner of State Route 113 and West Ridge Road on the west side of Elyria. Water for a home in the country in those days meant digging a well. There were no city water lines outside of city limits. So Baus had a well dug on the lot where he was building his home, never realizing that that well was going to change not only his life, but the lives of his children and grandchildren. Baus hit water, but the source he hit was unlike those of most farm wells. He hit an artesian well, a source of large quantities of water under so much pressure that the water shoots up like a geyser when tapped.

Not only did he have a practically unlimited source of water for his home and farm, the water tested out as pure as water can be. It was a marvelous stroke of luck for Baus. He decided to share the water with others by building a quaint little sandstone house over the well. On the roof there was a small waterfall, and the inside of the building was equipped with drinking fountains and two faucets that accepted coins from people who wanted to take five or ten gallons home with them. He really didn't make much money off the water; it was just to help offset the cost of building the little sandstone structure and for its upkeep.

But when his son, Wayne, got out of the service in 1959, he had an idea. Why not bottle the water and sell it to places like offices and plants that wanted some really pure water? They bought a couple of trucks and built a small bottling building to the rear of the property, and the White House Artesian Springs water company was born.

Today they still sell the same water from the wells, which have never gone dry since they were first discovered back in 1956. The little stone house is still there, and a traveler can still stop to have a free drink of artesian spring water at the drinking fountain inside or bring a bottle and take home a few gallons.

Another feature is "Anne's Fountain," a memorial Wayne created for his wife, who lost a long battle with cancer and died in 1990. The fountain has 111 lights and 42 nozzles, which can be programmed to do dozens of different things to change the way the fountain sprays water. It becomes a magical scene at night as the lights come on and turn the water all the colors of the rainbow. The fountain is open to the public each summer.

▲ **White House Artesian Springs**   ☏ 440-322-1317
8100 W. Ridge Road · Elyria

A CITY PARK WITH GREAT SCENERY

Cascade Park is another of those little hidden treasures you find all over Ohio. This one is a city park tucked along the Black River that meanders through the town; twin waterfalls highlight the union of the east and west branches of the Black River. Geologists say that the waterfalls are probably older than Lake Erie, since they were sculpted when an ancient lake, before Erie, had its shore just north of where the park is today. The park offers lot of scenic views, and there is a nearby arboretum and a playground. In winter there is a sledding hill, and any time of year the view of the falls is worth the walk from the parking lot. It's a great place for a picnic lunch.

▲ **Cascade Park**   ☏ 440-326-1500
Cascade Park Dr. · Elyria

HOME OF AN INVENTOR

He helped make bicycle riding more comfortable with his invention of a padded bicycle seat. He also invented an automobile that bore his name. He was Arthur Garford of Elyria, and his massive home on Washington Avenue is now the home of the Lorain County Historical Society. Tours of the home are available, and if you have a Lorain County connection, this is the place to start your search for your family history.

▲ **The Hickories**   ☎ 440-322-3341
Lorain County Historical Society, 509 Washington Ave. · Elyria

AN ARTFULLY RESTORED THEATER

This jewel is one of a handful of beautifully restored theaters that refused to die. The Palace Theatre of Lorain covers more than a half acre of space and houses 1,400 seats; at one time it was considered the largest one-floor theater in the state of Ohio. From its great crystal chandelier to its concession stand, where you don't have to take a second mortgage to have a box of popcorn, it's a great place to watch a movie or a stage show. Speaking of movies, this theater has just one screen, and it's enormous! When was the last time you saw a movie the way it was supposed to be shown, larger than life on a screen that dwarfs the audience, not one of the multiplex screens that's only slightly larger than a bedsheet? Call for current offerings and admission prices.

▲ **Lorain Palace Theatre**   ☎ 800-889-4842
617 Broadway Ave. · Lorain

LAKEFRONT DINING YEAR-ROUND

This is one of my personal favorites, especially on beautiful late summer afternoons. Their lakefront location in Lorain and open-air deck add to a pleasant summer dining experience. In winter, they have a cozy fire blazing in the dining room fireplace. The specialty here is rotisserie-cooked prime rib. Sandwiches are accompanied by freshly made home-cooked potato chips. They have a full bar and are very close to the Spitzer Lakeside Marina, so you'll see lots of the boating crowd here. It's also a great place for late dinner after visiting the Palace Civic Center.

▲ **Jackalope Lakeside Restaurant**   ☎ 440-288-2051
301 Lakeside Ave. · Lorain

11,000 WORKS OF ART

The museum is one of the best-kept secrets in Lorain County. It has more than 11,000 acquisitions spanning the history of art, including seventeenth century Dutch and Flemish paintings, European art of the nineteenth and twentieth centuries, and, my favorite, contemporary American art. The best part is that admission is free.

The collection is now considered to be one of the finest university or college collections in the United States.

▲ **Allen Memorial Art Museum**   ☎ 440-775-8665
Oberlin College, 87 N. Main St. · Oberlin

Allen Memorial Art Museum

WATER CANNONS AND TUMBLE BUCKETS

This year-round aquatic center is run by Lorain County Metroparks. In the summer, there is a 6,000-square-foot outdoor pool to get wet in. There are two 24-foot-tall water slides and a host of other things, like water cannons and tumble buckets, to make sure you really get wet. In the winter, there is the inside pool, fitness room, and even a giant frog in the kiddie pool, where you slide down the frog's tongue into the water.

▲ **Splash Zone** ☎ 440-774-5059
95 W. Hamilton St. · Oberlin

HAUNTED OR NOT, A COZY PLACE TO STAY

Historic and haunted is the way some visitors have described the Shurtleff Cottage Historic Bed and Breakfast in Oberlin, Ohio. The Victorian-era home was built in 1892 by Oberlin hero General Giles Shurtleff. Shurtleff was the first leader of African-American troops from Ohio in the Civil War. The restored building, which for many years served as a college dormitory, now contains four bedrooms with private baths and all modern amenities. The new owners spent several years restoring the home and modernizing its facilities. The county gave the restored home an award for the "most beautiful renovation," and the bed and breakfast has been featured on cable-TV channel HDTV's *If Walls Could Talk*. Guests find themselves within walking distance of historic downtown Oberlin, the college campus, and the many activities going on there.

As for the report that the house is haunted, owner Marsha Marsh told me, "When General Shurtleff decided he wanted to build the house on a slight rise on Morgan Street, there was just one problem. It was the site of the town's first cemetery. So the general paid to have contractors come in and dig up and move the bodies to nearby Westwood Cemetery. The only problem: there are rumors that when the foundation for the basement of the house was excavated, workers discovered several bodies that the contractors had missed when they dug up the original graveyard."

I asked her if the ghost stories hurt business. She laughed and said, "No, as a matter of fact, I get some guests who come here just so they can say they spent the night in a house that was supposed to be haunted."

▲ **Shurtleff Cottage Historic Bed and Breakfast**   ☎ 440-774-8033
46 Morgan St. · Oberlin

SANDSTONE CENTER OF THE WORLD

In 1868 the first sandstone was quarried by workers in the farmlands of western Lorain County. Today the 1,000 acres in and around the small village of South Amherst contain more than 300 million cubic feet of sandstone and are believed to be the oldest and largest sandstone quarries in existence. Now known as the Sandstone Center of the World, you can get a look at the vastness of these quarry holes from Quarry Road, a public highway that runs among several of the larger quarry holes.

▲ **Cleveland Quarries**   ☎ (no phone)
Quarry Rd. · South Amherst
The quarries can be seen from Quarry Road. They are so massive they cannot be missed; there is no street address for the quarry holes.

JAMIE'S FLEA MARKET

This flea market has been a Lorain County landmark since the 1970s. Open Wednesdays and Saturdays year-round, it has permanent buildings, and during warm weather several hundred additional vendors set up on one side of the parking lot and around the front of the market property. There is usually a good mix, from folks selling from the trunks of their automobiles to established vendors who specialize in tools, antiques, or other specialty items. The parking lot is unpaved, and on busy days after a rain, it can get a bit muddy. Bring boots.

▲ **Jamie's Flea Market**   ☎ 440-986-4402
46388 Telegraph Rd. · South Amherst
Near I-90 and the Ohio Turnpike on State Rte. 113

Canoe Capital of Ohio

Loudonville, Lucas, Perrysville

LOUDONVILLE CANOE LIVERY

There are several places to rent canoes near Loudonville. All offer trips varying in length, from a couple of hours to adventures that go on for days. This one has canoes, rafts, and kayaks, as well as large inner-tubes for those who want to spend a hot day just floating down the river. One reminder: always bring along some extra clothing. It's a rare visitor who takes a canoe ride and doesn't end up getting wet. *[SEASONAL]*

🛶 **Loudonville Canoe Livery and River Room** ☎ 888-226-6356
424 W. Main St. · Loudonville

CANOES AND MORE

This longtime attraction rents canoes and kayaks and organizes float trips. They also have go-karts, mini-golf, and rental cabins. Located just a short distance from Mohican State Park.

🛶 **Mohican Adventures** ☎ 800-662-2663
3045 State Rte. 3 · Loudonville
1 mile south of Loudonville

OHIO'S OFFICIAL WAR MEMORIAL

Not many folks know that Ohio's official state memorial to nearly 20,000 sons and daughters who lost their lives in wars since the beginning of World War II is located in rural Ashland County. A small sandstone shrine, built from local materials and dedicated in 1947, stands in the corner of a field in the Mohican Memorial State Forest. Inside the shrine is a large book with names of all of the fallen Ohioans from World War II, Korea, Vietnam, and the Gulf Wars. In the surrounding park and state forest, more than 300,000 tress have been planted as a living memorial to the war dead. Open seven days a week.

🛶 **Memorial Forest Shrine** ☎
Mohican Memorial State Forest, State Rte. 97 · Loudonville
West of State Rte. 3

AN 1860s BED AND BREAKFAST

This is an excellent place to spend a night and also to learn more about Ohio's Amish lands. The red brick Italianate mansion was built in 1865, the year the Civil War ended. Today it is owned by journalist Sue

Landoll's Mohican Castle

Gorisek. You may recognize Sue's name from the many stories she has written for *Ohio Magazine*. The bed and breakfast has six guest rooms and two suites with double beds, all with a private bath and air conditioning. The furnishings reflect the Goriseks' love of antiques and range from colonial to Victorian. The beauty of this spot is that the home is located only a block or so from downtown Loudonville, so it's an easy walk to several attractions. Rates are moderate. There's no smoking in the residence, and children are allowed only by prior arrangement. Open year-round.

   ▲ **The Blackfork Inn** ☎ 419-994-3252
      303 N. Water St. · Loudonville

A FANTASY CASTLE

This fantasy inn will make you think you have just stepped into a movie set. Perched on a wooded hillside is a castle that looks like something designed by Disney. There are 11 luxurious suites and some beautifully furnished cabins. This is one place you have to see to believe.

   ▲ **Landoll's Mohican Castle** ☎ 800-291-5001
      561 Township Rd. 3352 · Loudonville

WHERE BOGIE AND BACALL WERE WED

This is where Humphrey Bogart and Lauren Bacall were married and where they spent their honeymoon. It's also where movie legend Jimmy Cagney manned a produce stand beside the road, selling fresh vegetables to surprised tourists. The former farm home of Pulitzer Prize-winning author Louis Bromfield, located in aptly named Pleasant Valley, near Mansfield, is today a state park.

Inside the big main house you can still see the stairway where Bo-

Malabar Farm State Park

gey and Bacall tied the knot and the wedding suite upstairs (with twin beds!). Bromfield, who also worked as a writer in Hollywood, had many movie star friends who came to the quiet farm to get away.

The farm buildings still house cattle, goats, horses, and chickens, and wagon tours are available of the farm fields during the summer. There is also a hiking trail, fishing, and, in the winter, sledding and ice skating.

Also, just down the road is a house with a great ghost story. Be sure to ask the rangers.

▲ **Malabar Farm State Park**   ☎ 419-892-2784
4050 Bromfield Rd. · Lucas

A MODERN LODGE

This beautiful state park offers a lodge tucked away far from highways and towns. Hollywood types like Alan Alda and Paul Newman have stayed here more than once. Besides a modern lodge, cabins, camping, and seclusion, the park offers lakes with fishing, some great wooded hiking trails, and Ohio's Veterans' Memorial Chapel.

▲ **Mohican Resort and Conference Center**   ☎ 419-938-5411
1098 County Rd. 3006 · Perrysville
Off McCurdy Rd., north of State Rte. 97

Home of the Big House

Lexington, Mansfield

The Ohio State Reformatory at Mansfield has been used as a location for several movies

THE MANSFIELD REFORMATORY

The first time I was in the Mansfield Reformatory, I was there to do a story on the inmates' formation of a behind-the-walls Rotary Club chapter. I had even received a written invitation to be their speaker. I accepted partly out of curiosity and, also, because it seemed like a good feature story. On the day of the visit, after the meeting, one of the guard captains gave me a quick tour of the prison. It is a gothic-style building that is instantly depressing, even from the outside.

Being on the inside was even worse. The captain took me to one of the cell blocks, which was six stories high. The prisoners were mostly at work, and the tiny cells were standing open. We had climbed the winding steel stairs to the sixth range and walked down the steel grid walkway, where I could look down all the way to the cement floor at ground level.

I asked if I could step into one of the cells and see what it was like to be inside. The captain motioned to me to help myself. I walked inside one about halfway down the long corridor. It seemed to grow even smaller as I entered; I could almost touch the walls on both sides. The only furnishings were a one-piece steel toilet, a wash basin, and two folding cots attached to the wall. Gray blankets covered both beds, and there were small piles of personal possessions—magazines, candy bars, paperback books—stacked on the floor near the bunks. The smell was what really hit me: a cross between stale food and body odor. Paint on the steel walls was flaking off because of the humidity.

As I was turning around to leave, the door suddenly slammed shut! The captain had activated the electronic locking device to show me what it was really like to be locked in a cell. My heart was pounding, my chest was tight, and I felt claustrophobia building; I almost wanted to scream out as I grabbed the bars and looked through. I must confess that I was very happy to hear the captain say "Stand clear!" and see the door slide open again. I quickly left the cell and the range and really had no desire to ever visit a prison again. That is, until the summer of 1996.

By then, the Mansfield Reformatory had finally closed and had been taken over by a historic preservation group that was raising money by giving guided tours. I decided to visit once more.

The 25-foot stone wall that surrounded the prison was gone, leaving the gothic buildings, battered by several years of neglect, exposed. Windows were broken, and the interior seemed even more ragged because of the peeling water-based paints used by Castle Rock when filming the movie *The Shawshank Redemption.*

As we approached the cell blocks, they seemed even more threatening and desolate than they did all those years ago. Missing were the sounds of life. Now all that could be heard was the chirp of birds that had flown in through broken windows. It was a fascinating tour as the guide, a former guard, told tales of criminals who once were imprisoned here—including one prisoner, a baseball player on the prison team, who was so good that scouts from the Detroit Tigers showed up to watch him play. When he was released, they gave him a job. But when we climbed to the sixth range of the cell block, I again felt the claustrophobic feeling I had had years ago and opted to skip that part of the tour, instead going for a look at the solitary cells in the basement and wandering through the prison gift shop, Convictions, where souvenirs are now sold to tourists.

The Preservation Society hopes that the tours will produce enough money to help restore the old prison and preserve it as a reminder of what criminal justice in this country once was. Tours are from early June through early September, Sundays 1 P.M. to 4 P.M. and Tuesday-Friday at 2 P.M. There is an admission charge.

At last report, there was still no heat in the building, so on cool days wear a sweater. Because of the thickness of the stone walls, it will seem much cooler inside. *[SEASONAL]*

🔺 **The Ohio State Reformatory**   ☎ 419-522-2644
   100 Reformatory Rd. · Mansfield
   On the north side of U.S. Rte. 30

SHAWSHANK REDEMPTION TOUR

If you are a true movie buff, you will want to take the *Shawshank Redemption* Trail tour in the Mansfield area.

The local convention and visitors bureau has created a list of nearby places used in the making of the award-winning movie back in 1994.

Of course, most of the filming was done at the old Ohio State Reformatory building in Mansfield. Here you can see the warden's office, the "hole" where Tim Robbins as Andy Dufresne was imprisoned, as well as the historic old building that figures so prominently in the film.

You can download a map from their Web site that will lead you to other sites used as a background in the film, such as Malabar Farm State Park, seen in the final scenes of the movie where Red uncovers Andy's note that leads him to Mexico. In nearby Upper Sandusky you can see the county courthouse that was used for the filming of the trial in the opening scenes of the movie.

All in all it makes for a great road trip for a fan of the movie. Just remember that many of the locations are on private property and not open to the public, so you can only photograph them from the street. Fortunately, the Convention and Visitors Bureau's map clearly marks the places that are not available for tours.

▲ **Mansfield and Richland County Convention and Visitors Bureau** ☎ 800-642-8282
124 North Main St. · Mansfield

A CONEY ISLAND DOG

It's like walking into a time warp, except for the prices. The Coney Island Diner in downtown Mansfield looks, and probably smells, much as it did when it opened its doors in 1936.

Jim and Cathy Smith, the third owners of the business, were responsible for taking the longtime restaurant back to the way it looked in the 1930s. Of course, back then hot dogs came in one long tube and had to be cut every six inches. They cost a nickel apiece in 1936! The "secret" sauce, to which Jim and Cathy attribute the restaurant's longevity, has been handed down from owner to owner. The neon sign over the diner has remained the same, and so have many of the customers, who are quick to tell you they came here for hot dogs as children and now bring their grandchildren.

While hot dogs are what it's all about here, they do offer some other items for those who don't eat hot dogs.

Located right across the street from Richland Carousel Park.

▲ **The Coney Island Diner** ☎ 419-526-2669
98 North Main St. · Mansfield

The hand-carved carousel at Richland Carousel Park

WHERE WOOD COMES TO LIFE

If you have a fascination for merry-go-rounds and would like to see how they make a pile of ordinary wooden boards come to life as a carousel horse, head for this magic place. It's a carousel factory, and they offer guided tours of the plant where you can watch master carvers at work creating horses and other kinds of animals from wood. The tours are Tuesday through Saturday from April through December. The factory is located in downtown Mansfield very near Richland Carousel Park, which is open for rides year-round.

▲ **Carousel Magic** ☎ 419-526-4009
44 W. 4th St. · Mansfield

A HAND-CARVED CAROUSEL

Mansfield is home to the first hand-carved carousel built in Ohio, and perhaps America, since the 1920s. There are 52 carousel animals, all made of wood, and two chariots for those who don't like to go up and down while going 'round and 'round. Another feature that makes this carousel unusual: it is handicapped accessible. There is a special ramp and chariot where a wheelchair can be taken on board and secured for the ride. Open year-round.

▲ **Richland Carousel Park** ☎ 419-522-4223
75 N. Main St. · Mansfield

THE GARDEN CENTER OF MANSFIELD

One of the most beautiful sights in the city of Mansfield is Kingwood Center. The garden center began life as the estate of Mr. and Mrs.

Charles Kelley King. The mansion, known as Kingwood, and 47 acres were given to the city of Mansfield by the Kings in 1953.

The mansion today houses the offices and a horticultural library for the foundation that operates the garden center for the city. The gardens outside sprawl down a hillside from the mansion, and you can find something in bloom at almost any season of the year. In a greenhouse on the property there is a cactus garden with rare plants that stretch almost 10 feet high.

My favorite spot at Kingwood is at the end of the lawn, near a small fountain and pool that in the spring are surrounded by tulips. From a stone bench by the pool you have a clear view of the hillside and the mansion that overlooks the estate. Many wedding pictures have been taken at this spot. The gardens are open seven days a week; admission is free.

▲ **Kingwood Center**   ☎ 419-522-0211
900 Park Ave. W · Mansfield

A BIBLICAL WAX MUSEUM

One of the more unusual attractions in Mansfield is this one dedicated to the Bible. Sixty-two life-sized dioramas, with special effects and sound, tell the story of the life of Jesus Christ and the miracles of the Old Testament. This is the state's only wax museum, and it also houses a collection of rare Bibles, woodcarvings, and American votive folk art.

▲ **Living Bible Museum and Bible Walk**   ☎ 419-524-0139
500 Tingley Ave. · Mansfield

A HISTORIC VETERANS' HALL

The oldest continuously used veterans' hall in Ohio is the Mansfield Memorial Building. Originally founded by veterans of the Civil War, it's been used ever since. It has also at one time housed Mansfield's first zoo and the city's first library. It might even have a resident ghost, of its very first curator. Be sure to ask about the strange things that have happened in this historic building.

▲ **Mansfield Memorial Museum**   ☎ 419-525-2491
34 Park Ave. W · Mansfield

SEARCHING FOR ROOTS

The Ohio Genealogical Society has its library in Mansfield, and what a wonderful treasure this is for persons wanting to research their family history. With more than 25,000 volumes of census records, Bible records, cemetery listings, newspapers, and a host of other research materials, it's a perfect place to begin your search. While the library is mainly for the use of society members, visitors are allowed to use the facility for a small fee on a daily basis. Helpful staff members are always on hand to answer questions and to point you in the right direction. Who knows what you might discover in your family tree?

▲ **Ohio Genealogical Society**   ☎ 419-756-7294
713 Main St. · Mansfield

OHIO'S OLDEST SKI RESORT

Dick Goddard, the dean of Ohio TV weathermen, often mentions Possum Run Road near Mansfield. Because of its unusual topography— a valley in the highest elevation in the state—they often have record low temperatures. It's a perfect spot for Ohio's oldest ski resort, which has been operating here since the 1950s. Because of the colder temperatures, they are sometimes able to make snow when other Ohio ski areas can't. *[SEASONAL]*

▲ **Snow Trails**   ☎ 419-774-9818
3100 Possum Run Rd. · Mansfield

AN INN FOR SKIERS

If you want to stay close to the skiing area, you won't do much better than Spruce Hill Inn and Cottages literally right next door to the top of the ski hill. In fact, you can probably ski right off your porch at some of the cottages. There are 28 cottages with whirlpool bathtubs, and if you have a big family, you might want to consider the Victorian Manor House that sleeps eight people in luxury.

▲ **Spruce Hill Inn and Cottages**   ☎ 419-756-2200
3230 Possum Run Rd. · Mansfield

VROOM, VROOM!

Does the sound of a race car get your blood pumping? Does your foot start to twitch when you hear the roar of high-speed autos careening around a race track? If so then the Mid-Ohio School in Lexington may be just the ticket for you. This famous race track, where movie star Paul Newman used to race, now also offers a driving school that's not just for professional drivers but for anyone who would like to learn to drive high-performance automobiles. I sat in on one of the schools and in the class with me were ambulance drivers; a family of husband, wife, and two sons; and a host of other folks who just wanted to experience the thrill of tooling around a race course in a car capable of speeds over 100 MPH.

It's by reservation only and only at certain times of the year, so call for information and reservations. *[SEASONAL]*

▲ **The Mid-Ohio School**   ☎ 877-793-8667
7721 Steam Corners Rd. · Lexington

Another Taste of Amish Country

Brewster, Canal Fulton Fredericksburg, Kidron, Orrville, Shreve, Wilmot

A POTATO CHIP FACTORY

This well-known local potato chip company has some real bargains in its company store. They usually have clear plastic bags filled with three pounds of chips that didn't make it through the inspection line. The best part is that the chips are very fresh. They are considered "seconds" only because their color might be a bit dark (due to the sugar in the chip, not because it is burned) or because the chips are broken when they leave the production line. Other products are made here (such as caramel corn) that are not sold to distributors; they are only available locally. Pretzel "seconds" are also sold at bargain prices—nothing wrong with them, they're just broken. No tours of the potato chip plant are offered, but while in the outlet store, just look to the rear and you'll see fresh, hot chips coming off the conveyor belt into containers.

 ▲ **Shearer Potato Chips**   ☎ 330-767-3426
   692 Wabash Ave. · Brewster
   State Rte. 93 N, south of Canton

OHIO'S PAST AFLOAT

You can get a glimpse of what life was like in early Ohio by riding an authentic canal boat down a restored part of the old Ohio and Erie Canal. The *St. Helena III* sails every day from June to August from the Canal Fulton Community Park. The ride, usually pulled by a pair of work horses, glides silently down a mile or so of the old canal. It's so quiet that the only sound is the steady clop of the horses' hooves and the songs of birds or the croaking of frogs. At the far end of the ride, the crew turns the boat around at the Lock Four Turning Basin and then brings you back to the starting point at the park. On the ride I took, a crew member told us the history of the canal and anecdotes about what life was like along the canal. Canal Fulton was a community that was created by the coming of the big ditch, as the canal was then called. *[SEASONAL]*

 ▲ *St. Helena III* **Canal Boat**   ☎ 800-435-3623
   103 Tuscarawas St. W · Canal Fulton

Lehman's—like a general store from the old days, only bigger

STAY ON A QUIET COUNTRY ROAD

This bed and breakfast is located halfway between Berlin and Wooster on a quiet country road with Amish neighbors all around. Although originally built as a home for their family, the owners later added a wing when they decided to go into the bed-and-breakfast business. Bedrooms have 12-foot-high ceilings, large French doors that lead onto a deck that surrounds the building, gas fireplaces, giant whirlpool tubs, and a full private bath. All rooms appear to have been professionally decorated. The house sits in the middle of five acres of lawn, and the bedrooms overlook a large lake. Visitors are encouraged to go boating and fishing on the lake. All rooms have a private entrance. Children are allowed, but no pets. They do accept credit cards.

▲ **Gilead's Balm Manor Bed and Breakfast**   ☎ 330-695-3881
  8690 County Rd. 201 · Fredericksburg
  Ask for directions when making reservations.

A NON-ELECTRIC HARDWARE STORE

This store has always carried the things the Amish use in their simple, non-electric lifestyle. You can still buy a wood-burning cook stove here, brand new. You can also find things like lanterns, wringers, hand-operated washing machines—even a kerosene-powered freezer. It's like wandering through a general store from your grandmother's time.

How does such a store survive in the twenty-first century? Very well, thank you. Jay Lehman, the founder, told me that he started his unusual store in 1955 to supply the local Amish families and others who do not have electricity readily available, like missionaries and people who spend lots of time far away from civilization. Apparently, there were a lot of people who still liked wood-burning cook stoves, kerosene lamps, and old fashioned non-electric appliances. The store has continued to grow over the years, and is now considered the world's largest purveyor of historical technology. It has also become a major tourist attraction in northeast Ohio. Here you can find everything from Amish cookie cutters to a hand-operated non-electric kitchen blender. They sell many kinds of wood-burning stoves and even refrigerators and freezers that run on natural gas or kerosene. The products are also mailed to people all over the world. Visiting Lehman's is like taking a trip into the past.

▲ **Lehman's**   ☎ 877-438-5346
1 Lehman Circle · Kidron

A COLLECTION THAT JUST GREW

An Orrville man who had always wanted to be a truck driver started collecting toy trucks. The collection grew and grew and is still growing. When his collection grew so big it required a separate building, he decided to share it with the world. The Toy and Hobby Museum of Orrville is the result. More than 4,000 toy trucks line the walls. But it doesn't stop there. He also has many of his friends' collections of other things, like salt and pepper shakers and Indian arrowheads on exhibit. The main featured item is an exact replica, in miniature, of a local farm, complete with the tractors and vehicles that work each of the fields. Since it is a private collection hours are rather spotty. Call for an appointment to see the collection.

▲ **Toy and Hobby Museum**   ☎ 330-683-8697
531 Smithville Rd. · Orrville

WITH A NAME LIKE SMUCKERS . . .

When J. M. Smucker started his cider mill in 1897 and began selling apple butter from the back of a wagon in the town of Orrville, he probably never dreamed that he was beginning a business that would one day be known across America.

More than a century later, the J. M. Smucker Company (Smucker's, to you and me) is still based in Orrville. And at the company's barn-like company store, just south of Orrville, you can find all kinds of Smucker's jams and jellies and also hundreds of other items the company now produces or markets. The store building also contains a museum telling the company history and a café where hungry shoppers can taste some of the latest additions to the Smucker line as well as fresh baked items hot from the oven.

The store has become a major tourist attraction in Wayne County.

J. M. Smucker Company Store and Café   ☎ 330-864-1500
333 Wadsworth Road, Orrville

The Smucker Company Store also contains a museum and a café

HAVE LUNCH IN A BUGGY

This is a little out of the way of the usual Amish restaurants, but there are plenty of Mennonite and Amish folks who live in and around Shreve to give it authenticity. There is an Amish buggy in the restaurant set up as a table so you can say you had lunch in a buggy. There is also a large bakery where diners can see the Amish women baking pies, and a large fireplace where, in the winter, you often find ladies working on a large quilt. The name of the restaurant means "the Dutch eating house." The menu is pretty typical of Amish-style restaurants. Chicken, beef, and ham headline, with mashed potatoes, salad bar, homemade bread, rolls, and pies.

▲ **Des Dutch Essenhaus** ☏ 330-567-2212
176 N. Market St. · Shreve

AN AMISH WEDDING SPREAD

The Amish areas of Ohio feature a wonderful snack concoction known as an "Amish Wedding Spread." There are several different recipes. The one I like best is a combination of peanut butter, marshmallow, and maple syrup blended and served on fresh, homemade Amish bread. It is difficult to write about without salivating. You can find it, among other places, at the Amish Door Restaurant. Part of a large tourist stop here in Tuscarawas County on the edge of Amish country, this place started out as a restaurant in a replica of a small barn that just grew and grew. Today the complex consists of a huge new restaurant that resembles an old farmhouse and a new inn that from the lobby makes you think you are on board a riverboat. The barn that once housed the restaurant as well as an adjacent house are now occupied by shops. A nearby farmhouse serves as a bed and breakfast. The banquet center offers family entertainment in the form of dinner theaters and gospel concerts, both held monthly.

The restaurant, like so many of the places in this part of the state, reflects the craftsmanship of local Amish talent. Lots of polished oak, winding stairways, and large chandeliers—everything modern and well appointed. They have the obligatory salad bar with what I already described as the best coleslaw in Ohio. The menu regularly offers family-style meals. A bakery not only supplies the restaurant but offers its surplus for sale to diners and visitors. This is another of those huge Amish-style restaurants that can handle several busloads of tourists quickly and efficiently. The line may be long, but the wait isn't.

▲ **The Amish Door Restaurant**   ☎ 330-359-5464
  1210 Winesburg St. · Wilmot

A LUXURIOUS PLACE TO SPEND THE NIGHT

This 52-room Victorian-style hotel is part of the Amish Door restaurant, a longtime fixture in this area. The rooms all feature queen- or king-size beds, and there is even an indoor swimming pool and hot tub to help relax the kinks at the end of a long day of exploring. Some of the suites even have whirlpool bathtubs and fireplaces.

▲ **The Inn at the Amish Door**   ☎ 888-264-7436
  1210 Winesburg St. · Wilmot

NORTHWEST
OHIO

Gateway to the Islands

Lakeside, Marblehead, Port Clinton, Sandusky Bay

Marblehead Lighthouse

THE GUARDIAN OF SANDUSKY BAY

Marblehead Lighthouse has been the guardian of Sandusky Bay on Lake Erie for nearly 200 years. In fact the light, built in 1822, is the oldest lighthouse in continuous operation on the entire Great Lakes. Tours of the historic lighthouse are available on weekdays and on the second Saturday of each month through October. There is a fee for the tours. The nine acres around the lighthouse are now a state park and offer some great views of the Lake Erie islands and the boat traffic in and out of Sandusky Bay. One of my favorite uses is to have a winter picnic on the grounds when the lake is frozen over and you have the lighthouse and the lake all to yourself.

▲ **Marblehead Lighthouse**   ☎ 419-798-9600
110 Lighthouse Dr. · Marblehead

A VIEW OF THE LIGHTHOUSE

While you can't sleep in a lighthouse here, you can spend the night just a stone's throw away from the rocky shore and the historic light. The Lighthouse Resort offers suites for larger families or groups that need more than one bedroom. They also offer some smaller single rooms. Some of the suites are spectacular, with a great lake view and a balcony off the great room. They have whirlpool bathtubs and giant TV sets here, and you are in walking distance of the Marblehead Lighthouse State Park.

Ritski's Bar & Grill, located inside the hotel, serves lunch and dinner with homemade soups, desserts, and more.

▲ **Lighthouse Resort**   ☎ 419-624-1119
  614 E. Main St. · Marblehead

ART OF MARBLEHEAD

Marblehead is home to an incredibly talented man, Ben Richmond. Ben is an artist, a sculptor, and an author. His paintings of nautical scenes from Lake Erie and the islands grace homes all over the world. If you drive in Ohio, you have probably seen his work—the license plate that depicts the Marblehead Lighthouse is his. His gallery in downtown Marblehead is loaded with prints of most of his paintings and other works. It's a fun place just to browse, and you will probably find something that you will want to take home as a souvenir.

▲ **Richmond Galleries**   ☎ 800-441-5631
  417 W. Main St. · Marblehead

ELECTRIC TRAINS

In Marblehead, there is a summer exhibit of electric trains that will warm the heart of any model railroader. A huge room is filled with hundreds of trains in just about every gauge, from the tiny N-gauge to the large German style G-gauge. The exhibit is open daily, all year.

▲ **Train-O-Rama**   ☎ 419-734-5856
  6732 E. Harbor Rd. · Marblehead

A WALK BACK IN TIME

If you have a kid who just loves dinosaurs, or who enjoys optical illusions, I have just the place for you. It's been around since the 1950s.

Chances are, your parents or grandparents may have visited this manmade attraction. There's Mystery Hill, a place where water runs uphill, a room that makes you feel like you are falling as you try to walk from one door to another, a place where chairs placed high on the wall refuse to fall to the floor. The last time I visited, I leaned against the wall and felt like I was glued to the surface. You will probably hear a lot of mumbo-jumbo from the guides about magnetism in the earth, but it's just an optical illusion. It's also a lot of fun.

The other attraction here is Pre-Historic Forest. You walk along a path through a wooded area, and around every corner you meet nearly

The drive-through portion of African Safari Wildlife Park

life-size prehistoric animals, like dinosaurs Triceratops and Tyranno-saurus Rex. Some just stand there, and others are automated. There is a waterfall that you walk behind in a fiberglass volcano. Some basic cabins are available for rent, so you can even spend the night at the Pre-Historic Forest. *[SEASONAL]*

▲ **Pre-Historic Forest & Mystery Hill**   ☎ 419-798-5230
8232 E. Harbor Rd. · Marblehead

AUTOMOBILE SAFARI

If you'd enjoy being slobbered on by a llama or a camel, this is the place for you. As you drive your car through this compound, be pre-pared to be very popular if the animals spot you with one of the little white feed buckets. Your windshield will probably be licked clean by an eland or a zebra. Also, if you have the window down far enough, a deer with halitosis may give you a big, wet kiss while trying to steal the entire bucket of food.

Besides the drive-through portion of the park, you can also visit a walk-through petting zoo, see some baby animals, and get a pony or camel ride. *[SEASONAL]*

▲ **African Safari Wildlife Park**   ☎ 800-521-2660
267 Lightner Rd. · Port Clinton

SPEND THE NIGHT AT A HISTORIC MILITARY BASE

Historic Camp Perry, just east of Port Clinton, has been many things over the years. Most notably, it has been and continues to be the home of the National Matches, sometimes called the World Series of Shooting. During World War II, it served as both an induction post for new soldiers who were being sent off to war and, later, as a prison camp for Italian and German prisoners of war. Recently, it has been a staging area twice for reservists and national guardsmen called to active duty. What many people don't realize is that the base is usually open to the public, and it has one of the better fishing piers on the south shore of Lake Erie. There is also a nice sandy beach and a clubhouse that caters parties and events on the lakefront, as well as cabins and motels available to civilians who would like to spend the night at the base. Reservations are on a first-come, first-served basis, and during the National Matches each summer the camp is usually booked. For a really different and historic place to spend a night, give it a try.

▲ **Camp Perry Military Reservation** ☎ 888-889-7010
100 Lawrence Rd., Building 600 · Port Clinton

NEW WAVE SNORKEL AND SCUBA CENTER

Now, you may not think of Lake Erie as a place for diving or snorkeling, but all that has changed in the past few years, thanks, in part, to that pest, the zebra mussel. In many spots, the mussels have cleared the lake, and you can actually see the bottom on a clear, still day. This business near Port Clinton not only offers to teach you to dive and snorkel, it will also lead you on dives to some of the many shipwrecks that dot the bottom of Lake Erie. We were taken to one in about 40 feet of water just off the Lake Erie Islands. The sunken vessel could easily be seen in the water. In fact, using an underwater video camera, we shot pictures of fish and of the hulk on the bottom of the lake.

▲ **New Wave Snorkel and Scuba Center** ☎ 419-734-2240
1425 W. Lakeshore Dr. · Port Clinton

CHARTER FISHING

Some of the best charter boat fishing on Lake Erie can be found in the Port Clinton area. The downtown dock has a host of charter boats available. The favorite catches here are walleye and Lake Erie perch. There are also "headboats"—boats where you can walk on board with your fishing gear and, for a nominal sum, spend the morning or afternoon fishing with many others in one of the lake's best fishing spots. A charter service we used was:

▲ **Shore-Nuf Charters** ☎ 419-734-9999
Drawbridge Marina, 247 Lakeshore Dr. · Port Clinton

A FAST WAY TO THE ISLANDS

A 3,500-horsepower hydrojet catamaran is the fastest ferryboat working Lake Erie. The craft can carry nearly 400 people at a time, and

The Jet Express, the fastest ferry working Lake Erie

it makes the run from downtown Port Clinton to Put-in-Bay on South Bass Island in just about 20 minutes. It's a refreshing way to get there, but a word of caution: there are no public bathrooms on board.

⚓ **The Jet Express**   ☎ 800-245-1538
3 N. Monroe St. · Port Clinton

TAKE YOUR CAR TO THE ISLANDS

When you visit the Lake Erie islands, you can take your car along on your visits to South Bass and Middle Bass. Miller Boat Line has hauled just about anything you can imagine, from a house (in sections) to hearses carrying bodies. Tourists share the boat with trucks loaded with supplied for the islands. The ferryboat line is based on South Bass Island, but docks at Catawba Island and Middle Bass. It usually runs throughout the year as long as lake conditions allow.

⚓ **Miller Boat Line**   ☎ 800-500-2421
239 Bay View Ave. · Port Clinton

A STAY JUST MINUTES FROM THE FERRY

Take a retired Air Force pilot, mix in his great-grandmother's home on Catawba Island, and you end up with a massive, surprisingly comfortable, 28-room bed and breakfast. John Davenport made use of a decade-long search of attics and basements, then turned the finds into unusual and useful furniture to fill his unusual bed and breakfast. For example, an old ladder is now a pot rack in the kitchen. You can see Lake Erie from the tower in the home. The location puts you only minutes from Port Clinton, Marblehead, or the ferryboats to the Lake Erie islands. For rainy days, there is a large fireplace to curl up in front of with a good book. If you want to explore a bit, John is an expert on the

Sandusky Bay area, and can offer good suggestions and directions. Like many of the bed and breakfasts in this popular vacation area, they offer many packages for special weekends.

   ▲ **Sunnyside Tower Bed and Breakfast**   ☎ 888-831-1263
      3612 N.W. Catawba Rd. · Port Clinton

FRESH LAKE ERIE PERCH AND WALLEYE

If you are visiting anywhere along the edge of Lake Erie, you have to try the fresh Lake Erie perch or walleye. Many restaurants feature the famous Lake Erie fish, but a few do it better than most.

The Garden at the Lighthouse Restaurant in Port Clinton is actually the original site of Port Clinton's first lighthouse. It was built in 1832, a lovely Victorian home later replaced with a lighthouse that was moved closer to the lake. The restaurant is a favorite of local residents and also many tourists who have discovered it over the years. It offers both perch and walleye on the menu every day. However, for something really special, try poulet d'elegance. It's a lobster tail and Swiss cheese stuffed into a breast of chicken, then baked inside puff pastry. Not only is it elegant, it's delicious!

   ▲ **Garden at the Lighthouse Restaurant**   ☎ 419-732-2151
      226 E. Perry St. · Port Clinton

OHIO'S CHATAUQUA

The Lakeside Resort on the Marblehead Peninsula has been Ohio's Chatauqua for over a century and a quarter. Everyone from presidents of the United States to some of the world's top entertainers have passed through the gates of this Victorian lakefront community. Founded in the 1800s by the Methodist Church, it evolved into a combination religious and cultural center. Famous evangelists to world-famous entertainers like Ray Charles have spoken and performed in the 3,000-seat Hoover Auditorium. The lobby of the hotel looks much as it did when President Ulysses S. Grant visited here for a reunion of Civil War soldiers.

On the day we visited, a sailing school was just getting started for youngsters in the park on the beach in front of the hotel. A shuffleboard tournament was going on, and kids were riding bicycles up and down tree-shaded streets heading for the lake to go swimming. The Lakeside Symphony Orchestra was holding a rehearsal for an evening concert, and a host of other activities and meetings were going on. Once you have paid the admission fee to enter the complex, there are many places to stay, from the historic hotel to quaint bed and breakfasts and inns, and many of the century-old cottages are rented by the week each summer.

There are restaurants and stores inside the park, but you are only minutes away from Sandusky and Port Clinton, as well as the Lake Erie

Confederate Cemetery, Johnson's Island

islands. Lakeside is the kind of vacation place where you can be as busy as you want to be. It's also a very quiet place if you just want to kick back and relax in an atmosphere of yesteryear.

▲ **Lakeside**   ☎ 866-952-5374
236 Walnut Ave. · Lakeside

HISTORIC JOHNSON'S ISLAND

During the Civil War, Confederate officers were imprisoned on Johnson's Island in Sandusky Bay. Some escaped, while others died or were killed here. Today, a Confederate cemetery and a statue of a Confederate soldier are all that remain of this tragic chapter in Sandusky Bay's history. The cemetery is open to visitors (there is a toll gate fee) and can be reached by boat or by causeway from the mainland. The rest of the island is strictly private.

▲ **Confederate Cemetery**   ☎ no telephone
Johnson's Island · Sandusky Bay

Lake Erie's Big Island

Kelleys Island

THE FERRY TO KELLEYS ISLAND

The Kelleys Island Ferry Boat, which some locals refer to as the "BOB" (for Big Orange Boat), is the lifeline between Kelleys Island and the mainland. It runs throughout the year as long as the weather permits. The boat is big enough to carry people and several cars or trucks. The ride takes about 20 minutes from Marblehead to the dock on Kelleys Island. If you want to take a car or RV to the island, it's a good idea to call first for space availability. In the summer, at the peak of tourist season, there is usually a boat coming or going about every 30 minutes. The number of boats drops when cold weather arrives, and when the ice gets solid they stop altogether. (Then the only way to the island is by airplane.) *[SEASONAL]*

▲ **Kelleys Island Ferry** ☎ 419-798-9763
510 W. Main St. · Marblehead
Boats leave from downtown Marblehead across from the Marblehead Police/Fire Department.

THE MARKS OF TIME

We'll never know just how huge and impressive the glacial grooves on the north side of Kelleys Island in Lake Erie once were. Much of them were destroyed a century or more ago when the island's limestone quarry carved many of them into stones that were shipped off the island. What remains is still very impressive, though. Believed to be the largest such grooves in the entire world, these include a trough 400 feet long, 35 feet wide, and over 10 feet deep that shows the immense power of the great glacier ice that covered this part of North America 18,000 years ago. The ice was nearly a mile thick, and on the bottom were hard granite boulders frozen to the ice that were pushed and dragged by the melting and freezing action of the ice. As the boulders moved, they scoured great grooves in the softer limestone that made up the land mass. Today you can visit the Glacial Grooves Memorial next to the state park on the north side of Kelleys Island. Open daily; no admission fee.

▲ **Glacial Grooves** ☎ 419-746-2360
4049 E. Moores Dock Rd. · Kelleys Island

Glacial Grooves, a remnant of the last ice age

KELLEYS ISLAND WINE COMPANY

Winery owner Kirt Zettler's father was a retired diplomat when he decided to start a winery on the grounds of his favorite summer vacation spot on Kelleys Island. The wines have become very successful, some even winning national awards for excellence. Today, Kirt and his wife, Robby, not only offer wine tastings, they also operate a delicatessen at the winery, offering imported cheeses and meats from around the world. They also welcome children by providing them with a play area off the dining deck outside the winery.

▲ **Kelleys Island Wine Company**   ☎ 419-746-2678
418 Woodford Rd. · Kelleys Island

OUT ON THE ISLANDS

This is one of the first places you spot when you step off a boat at the docks on Kelleys Island. It's been around since 1854, and over the years has housed the post office, an undertaker, a doctor's office, and a candy store. After Prohibition, it became a bar and evolved into the restaurant-tavern that it is today. I have always enjoyed stopping here because of their house specialty, fresh Lake Erie perch dinners. Like many island businesses, it is seasonal, March through December. *[SEASONAL]*

▲ **The Village Pump**   ☎ 419-746-2281
103 W. Lakeshore Dr. · Kelleys Island

GUESTROOMS ON THE LAKEFRONT

This is one of those beautiful lakefront homes that also doubles as a popular bed and breakfast. They have this enormous screened-in front porch overlooking Lake Erie, where, weather permitting, they serve breakfast to their overnight guests. The home, built in 1905, offers a downstairs suite with a king-sized bed and private bath, while upstairs are two other suites that share a bathroom. The bed and breakfast is located close to what passes for Kelleys Island's downtown, so you are within walking distance of the docks, the restaurants, and the other business places. This is a seasonal bed and breakfast, open from April to November. *[SEASONAL]*

   ▲ **Cricket Lodge Bed and Breakfast** ☎ 419-746-2263
     111 E. Lakeshore Dr. · Kelleys Island

A TOUCH OF ISLAND LUXURY

This Victorian mansion looks like it has stood on the island for a century or more, but it was built in the 1990s. It combines the beauty of the Victorian look with lots of modern conveniences, like hot tubs and a whirlpool. A few of the air-conditioned rooms have fireplaces. Gourmet breakfasts are included, and they also offer packages that can include a sunset sail in the owner's sailboat.

   ▲ **Water's Edge Retreat** ☎ 419-746-2455
     827 E. Lakeshore Dr. · Kelleys Island

Water's Edge Retreat

Caves, Wineries, and Island Adventure

Put-in-Bay

HOME OF THE WANDERING STATUE

Few people who see this statue of Commodore Oliver Hazard Perry, hero of the Battle of Lake Erie, realize how much it has traveled.

It all started back in 1860, when veterans of the War of 1812 honored Perry with a statue placed in the center of Cleveland's Public Square. It stayed there a while, but, wouldn't you know, along came progress: the city fathers decided to cut the square into quadrangles. After much debate, Perry's statue was moved to the new southeast quadrant, where it was expected to remain forever. Wrong.

In the 1890s, veterans of the Civil War wanting to commemorate their service cast their eyes on Commodore Perry's corner of Public Square. By that time most of the vets of the War of 1812 were gone, and the veterans of the latest war got their way. The Perry Monument was carefully taken down to make room for the new Soldiers and Sailors Monument. But what to do with Commodore Perry?

A home was eventually found in Gordon Park, overlooking Lake Erie. But the monument was showing years of wear, and it was decided that a new statue should be cast before the good Commodore was placed. Now the question was, what about the old statue?

A group of patriotic citizens in the small town of Perrysburg had followed the debate over the Commodore's statue and contacted Cleveland officials. Since their town was actually named after the Commodore, why not give them the old statue? Although there is some debate over whether the statue was actually given to the town or whether they had to pay for it, the old monument indeed ended up in Perrysburg.

But just when the statue seemed to have a permanent home, it moved again. In 2002, the National Park Service opened a new visitor center on South Bass Island at the foot of the Perry Peace Memorial. The Park Service approached the folks in Perrysburg, who decided to give the monument to the Park Service and now it has yet another new home—this time indoors.

The Perry Peace Monument on South Bass Island, 352 feet high, dominates the skyline. From the observation platform at its top, on a clear day, you can see the Canadian shoreline. It's a great spot from

Perry Victory and International Peace Memorial

which to view all the islands. Park rangers will point out where Commodore Oliver Hazard Perry defeated the British fleet during the War of 1812. The monument also serves as a grave marker for British seamen whose bodies washed ashore after the battle.

▲ **Perry Victory and International Peace Memorial**　☎ 419-285-2184
Bayview Ave. · Put-in-Bay

A MUSEUM ALL ABOUT CHOCOLATE

This is one of the most fun museums in all of Ohio if you love chocolate. The exhibits not only explain the history of the cocoa bean and how it came to be developed into the wonderful concoction we call chocolate, but you can also sample some exotic chocolate drinks here in a small café in the museum. *[SEASONAL]*

▲ **Chocolate Cafe and Museum**　☎ 419-285-2268
820 Catawba St. · Put-in-Bay

THE WATER TAXI

If you stay on the island late into the night, you might find the ferryboats have stopped running for the day. What do you do if this happens, or if you have an emergency on the island and must get to the mainland right away? Not to worry. Ladd's Water Taxi has been carrying forgetful tourists back to their cars for years. They use speedy cabin cruisers and are on call 24 hours a day. This is a good number to tuck into your pocket before heading out for a day of fun on the islands. *[SEASONAL]*

▲ **Ladd's Water Taxi**　☎ 419-366-1147
Ladd's Marina, 229 Bayview · Put-in-Bay
Call their office on Put-in-Bay; they'll come to you.

PERRY'S CAVE

Legend has it that this cave was discovered when Commodore Oliver Hazard Perry made South Bass Island his headquarters during the Battle of Lake Erie in 1813. The cave is large enough that it contains an underground lake of fresh water that has been used over the years as a water source by some island establishments. Today it is a tourist attraction. There is a classic automobile museum on the property, a faux gem mine, where you can pan for semi-precious stones, and a butterfly garden in the summertime. *[SEASONAL]*

▲ **Perry's Cave & Gemstone Mining** ☎ 419-285-2405
979 Catawba Ave. · Put-in-Bay

WINERY AND CAVE

Heineman Winery, right across the street from the Perry Cave, has its own cave as a tourist attraction. The difference is that Crystal Cave has the world's largest celestite crystals. It is unlike any cave you have ever been in. Upstairs, in the winery and garden, you can sample some of the famous island wines. *[SEASONAL]*

▲ **Heineman Winery and Vineyards** ☎ 419-285-2811
978 Catawba Ave. · Put-in-Bay

SLEEP ON THE ISLAND

The beautiful Bayshore Hotel sits on the water's edge, and all rooms have a lake view. There is even a 30-person whirlpool tub and a swim-up bar in the swimming-pool area. Needless to say, you want to get your reservations in early here if you want to spend a weekend on the island. *[SEASONAL]*

▲ **Bayshore Resort Hotel** ☎ 866-422-9746
328 Toledo Ave. · Put-in-Bay

Cedar Point and Sandusky Bay

Sandusky

Cedar Point, home of the thrill rides—and more

THE WORLD'S TOP COASTER PARK

At my last count Cedar Point Amusement park had 16 roller coasters. They claim that's more than any other amusement park in the world. If you like to be thrilled, hurled, twisted, tossed, bounced, and scared, this is the place to go.

The historic park has been entertaining families for generations. (It was here that football legend Knute Rockne developed the forward pass while working as a lifeguard.) Some of the original buildings are still here from nearly a century ago when it opened as a beer garden on the edge of Sandusky Bay. The old dance hall where the big bands in the 1930s and 1940s played is still here, the famous Hotel Breakers on the water's edge has grown and has been modernized, but still offers one of the best views of Lake Erie.

There is so much to do at Cedar Point that you will need several days to do it all—and then there is the rest of the Sandusky Bay area with many other things to see and do. *[SEASONAL]*

▲ **Cedar Point** ☎ 419-627-2350
1 Cedar Point Dr. · Sandusky
On a peninsula in Sandusky Bay off State Rte. 2

CEDAR POINT SWIMMING YEAR-ROUND

Cedar Point's water park, Castaway Bay, is a year-round attraction that certainly will make you think you're in Florida or the Caribbean. The resort is located near the entrance to Cedar Point and covers almost a quarter million square feet. What they did was take the original Radisson Harbor Inn and spent $22 million to convert it into an indoor water park with luxury guest rooms and restaurants.

The actual water park contains a 35-foot-tall, 520-foot-long water roller coaster that uses jets of water to propel riders uphill. Of course, they have waterslides—12 of them—and a couple are more than 30 feet tall. Even if you don't like to swim, you can really get wet here. Castaway Bay offers a giant water-filled bucket that dumps 1,000 gallons of water on the folks below every two minutes. You can even go body surfing inside at Castaway Bay. There is a 100,000-gallon wave-action pool.

In the swimming pool area are lots of fun activities that include basketball hoops, floating sea creatures to make pool crossings with, and a floating treasure chest that tests skills and agility.

The only drawback to the resort is that you can't just drop in to use the water park for an afternoon; you must be an overnight guest.

▲ **Castaway Bay** ☎ 419-627-2106
2001 Cleveland Rd. · Sandusky

PARASAIL OVER LAKE ERIE

Here is your chance to soar under a huge parachute towed behind a speedboat. It's relatively easy. You ride out into the bay on a speedboat equipped with a platform at its rear. You strap on a harness hooked to a huge parachute that trails out behind the boat. As the boat speeds up, a cable connecting the chute and the boat unwinds. The chute gently lifts you off the boat, and in seconds you are flying several hundred feet in the air behind the boat as it cuts through the water. On a clear day you can see the Canadian shoreline. As the ride ends and you are being winched back onto the boat, the crew will take a picture of you flying behind them so you can prove to your friends that you really did it. *[SEASONAL]*

▲ **North Coast Parasail** ☎ 419-627-2279
Oceana Midway Beach, Cedar Point · Sandusky
Off public beach at Cedar Point Amusement Park

WHERE LIFE GOES ROUND AND ROUND

If two places ever were meant for each other, they're the old post office building in Sandusky and the Merry-Go-Round Museum. After the U.S. Postal Service moved out, the beautiful art deco building with the rotunda on the front was a perfect match for a museum dedicated to merry-go-rounds. There are dozens of posters and carousel art on

The Merry-Go-Round Museum includes memorabilia from hundreds of amusement parks

the walls, and you can also see authentic hand-carved carousel antique horses and other animals.

In the center of the big room is the restored Allen Herschell carousel with its band organ. Every visitor gets a chance to ride. The animals on the carousel are antiques that have been restored. You can find memorabilia from hundreds of amusement parks that once called Ohio home, like Crystal Beach in Vermilion. You can see and hear about the legend of the haunted Cedar Point carousel. There is also a display of tools and carvings from the Dentzel Carving shops in 1867, and there are also demonstrations by a carver who makes and repairs the horses. A gift shop is also on the premises. Open year-round.

▲ **Merry-Go-Round Museum**   ☎ 419-626-6111
301 Jackson St. · Sandusky

FLYING OVER THE BAY

Griffing Flying Service has been providing a year-round lifeline to the folks on the Lake Erie islands since the 1950s. The airline offers both island flights and sightseeing flights over the entire Sandusky Bay area. In the summer, you can either fly or float to the island, but when winter comes, the airplane becomes the islanders' only link with the mainland for travel, emergencies, and food, as there is air service to the islands year-round.

▲ **Griffing Flying Service**   ☎ 419-626-5161
3115 Cleveland Rd. · Sandusky

MORE YEAR-ROUND SWIMMING

Great Wolf Lodge in Sandusky was the first of the commercial indoor water park resorts to be built in Ohio, and it is still going strong. Besides the obligatory giant pail that dumps tons of water on guests below, at-

Great Wolf Lodge

tractions include dueling water slides—even one that goes to the top of the four-story activity center. There is also a soft-play aquatic tree house for the little kids. Use of the water park here is restricted to overnight guests. The lodge has 271 suites, several restaurants, and game rooms in addition to the indoor water park.

▲ **Great Wolf Lodge**   ☎ 888-779-2327
4600 Milan Rd. · Sandusky

CRUISE TO THE ISLANDS

A wonderful way to see Sandusky Bay and the Lake Erie islands is to take one of the many cruise boats that offer day-long cruises through the bay and around the islands, stopping at several before heading back to Sandusky that evening. *[SEASONAL]*

▲ *Goodtime I* **Cruises**   ☎ 419-625-9692
Jackson St. Pier · Sandusky

FISH DINNERS

The Lake Erie perch and walleye are always fresh, never frozen. Now, this is not your white-tablecloth-and-crystal-stemware kind of restaurant. The tableware is strictly plastic, with little packets of lemon juice and salt and pepper. There is no table service. You walk up to the counter and order what you want, or drive up to the window at the side of the building and pick up a carry-out order. But what you get is worth it. They sell fresh-cooked perch, either deep fried or broiled, by the pound. Be sure to have a bowl of their homemade turtle soup with your lunch. This is the kind of place where you'll find a lot of local residents who really know their fish stopping by for lunch and dinner. The service is quick and the food is good. What else do you need?

▲ **DeMore's Fish Den**   ☎ 419-626-8861
302 W. Perkins Ave. · Sandusky

BEST MILK SHAKE

One of the best milk shakes I've had in recent years can be found in a most unusual place: the snack bar here at Griffing Flying Service's Sandusky Airport. They make it with several dips of ice cream, and they test it by standing a straw up straight. If the straw leans, they put in more ice cream.

▲ **Snack Bar, Griffing Flying Service**   ☎ 419-626-5161
3115 Cleveland Rd. · Sandusky

A BIG ICE-CREAM CONE

Toft's Dairy of Sandusky is an institution. Generations of Sanduski-ans have made a pilgrimage to this dairy store on a summer's day for a single, double, or triple ice-cream cone. Newcomers get a real surprise. Their "single" is really two large dips of ice cream; there are three dips for a "double"; and a triple—well, you have to have a milk-shake cup to keep all the dips upright on the ice-cream cone. It's a true ice cream lover's kind of place.

▲ **Toft's Dairy and Ice Cream**   ☎ 800-521-4606
3717 Venice Rd. · Sandusky

SLEEP INN

This motel is located near the Sandusky Mall, just a short distance from the Cedar Point entrance and close to all the attractions of San-dusky Bay. It offers some rooms that have gas fireplaces, king-sized beds, and whirlpool baths, all for a price lower than you might pay for a bed and breakfast in this area. They also throw in a free continental breakfast in their dining room, which has a fireplace. Add to this an indoor swimming pool and fitness room, and you get a fine place for a couples escape that's not far from home.

▲ **Sleep Inn**   ☎ 419-625-6989
5509 Milan Rd. · Sandusky
Near the intersection of State Rte. 2 and U.S. Rte. 250.

Sea Stories and Worm Races

Birmingham, Vermilion

Caterpillar races at the Woollybear Festival

A HUGE PARADE OF CATERPILLARS

You can usually tell if a person lives in northern Ohio by whether they know that a woollybear is a caterpillar, not a four-legged bear with a heavy coat.

My TV colleague Dick Goddard, the dean of Ohio weather forecasters, has raised the lowly woollybear caterpillar to near-legendary status. How many worms do you know that have a festival named after them?

It started in my living room back in the 1970s. The local elementary school Parent-Teachers Association officers were holding a meeting there one evening as I arrived home from work.

"Does anyone have any idea how we can raise some money?" one of the ladies asked.

"Start a festival named after that woollybear caterpillar that Goddard is always talking about," I suggested, as I passed through the room.

They did, and Dick agreed to participate. He not only made a personal appearance; he has been spearheading the festival for more than a quarter of a century. It is now the largest single-day festival in Ohio, attracting upward of 150,000 people to watch a two-hour parade through the streets of Vermilion, where the festival is now held. There are also races, games, and woollybear look-alike contests for kids and pets. My personal favorite is the woollybear races. This is where anyone who has a woollybear caterpillar can enter him in a race. It's so exciting. Almost as much fun as watching, say, paint dry, or grass grow.

In all seriousness, the festival has remained true to Dick's original concept. All of the proceeds go to charity. None of the TV or radio personalities, including Dick, makes any money from the festival, which has raised thousands of dollars through the years for local organizations and provided northern Ohio families with a wonderful way to spend an autumn afternoon. The festival is held each year at the end of September or beginning of October, depending on the Cleveland Browns' schedule. (Dick is the statistician for the team, so he has to schedule the festival when the Browns aren't playing.) *[SEASONAL]*

▲ **The Woollybear Festival**   ☏ 440-967-4477
Vermilion Chamber of Commerce, 5495 Liberty St. · Vermilion

A RIDE ON THE VERMILION RIVER

A great way to see were the Vermilion River empties into Lake Erie is right in downtown Vermilion, aboard the good ship *Mystic Belle*. It may be small, but the floatboat, disguised as a paddlewheel riverboat, can carry up to 21 people, and Captain Don Parsons gives an excellent narrated tour that lasts nearly an hour and provides glimpses of the big yachts anchored here, the exclusive Vermilion Lagoon riverfront homes, and even a peek out into Lake Erie, weather permitting. The *Mystic Belle* sails May through September. Call for reservations. *[SEASONAL]*

▲ ***Mystic Belle* Boat Ride**   ☏ 440-967-7910
636 Sandusky St. · Vermilion

SOME HOMEMADE CHOCOLATES

Bob Brummer is the third generation of his family to make chocolates. His family's candy is well known in New Jersey. Bob married a lady from Vermilion and decided to bring his expertise to Ohio. They offer dozens of flavors of chocolates, all made fresh in the candy kitchen at their store. They will even custom-pack a gift box of your favorite chocolates if you give them some advance notice. They also offer more than 18 varieties of sugar-free candy.

▲ **Brummer's Homemade Chocolates**   ☏ 440-967-2329
672 Main St. · Vermilion

GREAT LAKES LORE

One of the attractions in Vermilion year-round is the Great Lakes Historical Society Museum. Here you can find parts of Commodore Oliver Hazard Perry's flagship, which was sunk in the War of 1812. There

Inland Seas Maritime Museum

is an actual lake freighter wheelhouse, where you can stand and see the lake through the windows. The museum also has an extensive display of artifacts from famous ships that sailed Lake Erie and the other Great Lakes.

▲ **Inland Seas Maritime Museum**   ☎ 440-967-3467
  Great Lakes Historical Society, 480 Main St. · Vermilion

CAPTAIN LARRY'S AND ADMIRAL DEBBIE'S

One of my favorite stops during the Woollybear Festival is Captain Larry's Restaurant and Admiral Debbie's Desserts.

It has been a downtown Vermilion institution for years. You can get everything from a Lake Erie perch dinner to a veggie burger. But my personal favorites are the desserts. They offer an old-fashioned soda fountain with chocolate sodas the way they used to be made. If you really are hungry, they make from scratch a homemade cheesecake that will melt in your mouth. The menu also offers beer and wine.

The walls of the restaurant are lined with memorabilia and photos from the long-gone Crystal Beach Amusement Park that once attracted fun-seekers to the town.

▲ **Captain Larry's Restaurant and**
  Admiral Debbie's Desserts ☎ 440-967-1003
  5561 Liberty Ave. · Vermilion

A CAPTAIN'S GUEST HOUSE

This Victorian guest house in Vermilion is just one block from the lake and two blocks from historic Harbourtown. It has four guest rooms, all with private baths and all air-conditioned. For breakfast they offer an assortment of things, including cake, pastries, cereals, and hard-boiled eggs. The guest house offers a large wraparound porch—a favorite of guests during the summer.

▲ **Captain Gilchrist Guest House Bed and Breakfast**
☎ 440-967-1237
5662 Huron St. · Vermilion

FORMAL GARDENS AND NATURAL WOODLANDS

Just a few miles south of Vermilion is the crossroads of Birmingham. Here you will find another example of the great things that surprise us in the many Metropark districts scattered all over the state. Schoepfle Garden consists of 70 acres of botanical gardens and natural woodlands that run right to the edge of the Vermilion River. In the formal gardens you'll find topiaries, trees, collections of many kinds of roses, rhododendrons, canna, hostas, and various shade plants. It's a wonderful, relaxing place to spend an afternoon. Be sure to bring along a camera. While beautiful any time of the year, my favorite time to visit is late summer, when most everything is in bloom.

▲ **Schoepfle Garden**   ☎ 440-965-7237
Market St. · Birmingham
Off State Rte. 113

Children's garden at Schoepfle Garden

Railroads and Caves

Bellevue, Huron, Milan

WORKING ON THE RAILROAD

If someone in your family loves railroading, you don't want to miss a visit to this railroad museum in Bellevue. The Mad River Railroad was one of the earliest lines to pass through this part of Ohio. Today rail fans have gathered an impressive amount of rolling stock here next to the old railroad tracks and depot. The locomotives are open to allow kids, both big and little, to climb in and out and pretend to be engineers. Cabooses are open for exploring, as are both the diesel and steam engines. It's a chance to get up close and personal with some historic railroad equipment.

▲ **Mad River and NKP Railroad Museum**   ☎ 419-483-2222
233 York St. · Bellevue

THE "CAVIEST CAVE"

The "Caviest Cave in the United States": That's what some cave fanciers have tagged Seneca Caverns, near Bellevue. That's because although the caves have been a tourist attraction for a half century or more, they have been left much as they were found or first excavated. In other words, there are no smooth, measured steps down to each level, just a path and sometimes narrow passageways and uneven rocks to climb on. There are several levels to the caverns, and more than half of the caverns are still unexplored. If you like your caves to look like caves, this is the one for you. But it's not for everyone, especially if you have trouble walking and climbing or you don't like tight passageways.

The Seneca Caverns complex was discovered in 1872 by two boys who fell into part of it while searching for their dog. It has seven levels and runs to 110 feet deep; the largest room is 250 feet long. A crystal-clear stream is located on the lowest level. Bring a sweater or coat—the temperature inside the caverns is always 54 degrees. This cave is unusual because it was formed from a crack in the earth. Owner Dick Bell says his father commercialized the caverns and first opened them to tourists in the early 1930s, during the Depression. (His father was an attorney and sometimes would let clients work off their bills by helping clean clay out of the upper cavern passages.) When we have an especially wet spring or summer, the lower levels of the caverns are often

filled with water. Today the caverns are a Registered Natural Landmark.
[SEASONAL]

> ▲ **Seneca Caverns**   ☎ 419-483-6711
> 15248 E. Thompson Rd. · Bellevue
> Township Rd. 178, near the small town of Flat Rock, south of Bellevue.

CEDAR POINT FRIES

If you visited Cedar Point in the 1970s or before, you might remember the famous french fries stands in the park. The fries were served with lots of malt vinegar and salt and had a very distinctive taste. The Berardi family, who operated the french fry stands, went through tons of potatoes every week to keep up with the demand. Times changed and Cedar Point decided to take over the food service in their park; the Berardis were out. Those fries live on, though. Berardi's operates several restaurants in the area, and they still serve the original fries with malt vinegar. They also make some great homemade pies and have some wonderful lunch specials. I've stopped several times at the restaurant in Huron.

> ▲ **Berardi's Restaurant**   ☎ 419-433-5984
> 218 Cleveland Rd. E · Huron

PARTY IN A BOXCAR

If you are looking for a spot to hold a family reunion or an interesting place to take a scout group for an overnight trip, this might be just right. One of the smaller metroparks in Erie County, the Coupling Reserve consists of just a train caboose, a boxcar, and a turn-of-the-century train station that has been converted into a party room, complete with a living room with gas fireplace, a kitchen, and modern bathrooms. The park system will rent the cabooses and boxcars to groups for overnight stays. The train cars now have heat and electric light, but no bathrooms. Bathrooms as well as a place to cook your dinner and breakfast can be found in the station house. By reservations only; call ahead.

> ▲ **The Coupling Reserve**   ☎ 419-625-7783
> Erie Metroparks, 3910 Perkins Ave. · Huron
> Between Huron and Milan

YOUNG TOM EDISON

Thomas Edison was born a Buckeye. He started life in a tiny house in Milan in 1847. The house still stands, and today it is a museum where you can see a collection of some of Edison's inventions, as well as manuscripts and family photographs. Legend has it that Edison visited the home in the 1920s and was embarrassed to discover that the house had no electricity installed. It was soon electrified. Although Edison only spent seven years of his life in Milan, his family continued to own prop-

erty in town for many years, and his descendants still have an association with the village.

▲ **Thomas Edison Birthplace**   ☎ 419-499-2135
9 Edison Dr. · Milan

THE OTHER MUSEUM

Milan has more museums than most small towns its size do. Beside
the Thomas Edison connection, the Milan Historical Museum is actually a block-long collection of historical buildings and homes that
house an eclectic assortment of collections, from the Galpin House,
named for an early doctor in the community who built the house in
1846, and that now houses the Robert Mowry Glass Collection with
more than 1,500 pieces on display, to the Doll and Toy House, another
old home that includes more than 350 antique dolls and other early
playthings. There is also a general store, a blacksmith shop, and myriad
other antique attractions here open year-round.

▲ **Milan Historical Museum**   ☎ 419-499-2968
10 N. Edison Dr. · Milan

The General Store at the Milan Historical Museum

Toledo Area

Bowling Green, Grand Rapids, Oregon, Perrysburg, Sylvania, Toledo, Waterville, Whitehouse

HUNTING FOSSILS IN OHIO

The Olander Park System in Sylvania, near Toledo, is home to Fossil Park. You can dig for real fossils left behind by a long-ago sea that covered our state and take home your findings. Now, understand we are not talking about the bones of a T-Rex or a Variraptor. What you will find here are tiny Devonian-era brachiopods, echinoderms, corals, and trilobites. Experts say there are only two places in the world where you may find major concentrations of these fossils: Devon, England, where they first were found, and Sylvania, Ohio.

Fossil Park is located on the bottom of an abandoned shale quarry west of Toledo. The gritty shale material that contains the fossils is trucked in from another quarry about a mile away. That quarry, owned by the Hanson Quarry Company, is a major repository of the fossils, but their business is mining limestone, not fossils, so they worked out a partnership with the Olander Park System to create Fossil Park. They bring in the shale they remove to reach the limestone and deposit it in Fossil Park several times a month. Visitors to the park can then search through the shale and keep any fossils they find.

No tools are allowed in the quarry. The shale is soft, and if you don't mind getting your hands dirty, by using a little ingenuity you can break the shale and ancient mud apart and hopefully discover one of the small seashell-like fossils. The park does keep a large water tank on the quarry floor so you can wash away dirt and debris and more easily identify your find. There is usually one of about a dozen park employees who have been trained to spot the fossils on hand to help visitors identify what they have just discovered. There are also posters nearby with large pictures of each of the fossils to help in identifying them.

▲ **Fossil Park** ☎ 419-882-8313
5705 Centennial Rd. · Sylvania

A REPLICA CANAL BOAT

The *Sandpiper* cruise boat in Toledo looks just like the boats used a hundred years ago to make this a center of commerce on the edge of the Great Lakes. The *Sandpiper* is a modern-day replica of a long-ago canal boat that carried freight and passengers across Ohio and Indiana. Today the boat just carries passengers on the Maumee River.

The 65 foot-long steel boat can carry 100 passengers. And, unlike the original canal boats that were pulled by horses or mules, this boat has its own diesel power and does not need assistance from the shore. Cruises usually include a tour upriver, where you can see beautiful riverside homes and yacht clubs, as well as some great scenes of the Toledo skyline. The sailing season runs May through October. *[SEASONAL]*

> ▲ *Sandpiper* **Canal Boat**　☎ 419-537-1212
> Promenade Park, Jefferson Ave. · Toledo

A MUSEUM SHIP

A 600-foot-long lake freighter has become a permanent part of the downtown skyline in Toledo. The ship, which once hauled ore and steel through the Great Lakes, has been retired and turned into a floating museum. Be aware that a lot of walking and climbing are required to see this exhibit.

> ▲ **S.S.** *Willis B. Boyer* **Museum Ship**　☎ 419-936-3070
> International Park, 26 Main St. · Toledo

THE TOLEDO FIREFIGHTERS MUSEUM

A former fire station in the city of Toledo has been put to excellent use. It has become a museum where much of the Toledo Fire Department's old equipment is now on display and real, active-duty firefighters are assigned to teach fire safety and to recall a proud history to visitors.

Tour guides point out such things as an early lantern from the days when firemen still pulled their pumper to the fire by hand. The youngest member of the department would take the lantern and run ahead of the sweating firemen hauling their pumper down the street, screaming at the top of his voice, "FIREMEN COMING! FIREMEN COMING!" He was a sort of predecessor of the siren and red light used today to clear the way for fire trucks.

The museum also offers a look at how firemen lived a hundred years ago. There are the shiny brass poles down which they would slide when answering a fire alarm.

> ▲ **Toledo Firefighters Museum**　☎ 419-478-3473
> 918 Sylvania Ave. · Toledo

A FARMER'S MARKET, PLUS

Downtown Toledo's old civic center has been converted into a marketplace. This Toledo attraction has a nice assortment of vendors selling everything from antiques to crafts. Outside is a farmers' market with fresh produce in season, and the building has a Libbey Glass Compa-

At the Toledo Museum of Art you can also buy art to take home

ny outlet store. The market is open Wednesday through Sunday; the antique mall, Tuesday through Sunday; and the Libbey outlet store is open seven days a week.

▲ **The Erie Street Market** ☎ 419-936-3743; Superior Antique Mall:
419-243-1800; Libbey Glass Outlet: 888-794-8469
219 S. Erie St. · Toledo

A MUSEUM WHERE YOU CAN TAKE HOME THE PAINTINGS

Wouldn't this be nice: You go to an art museum, see a painting you like, and buy it to take it home and enjoy the very next day. Sounds like fiction, you say? Not really. The famous Toledo Museum of Art has been doing just that since the 1970s.

Now, I don't mean that if you see a Rodin or a Van Gogh in the museum you can just take it off the wall and head to the cash register. It doesn't quite work that way. While they have some of the world's most famous art on display, those aren't for sale. But a department in the museum called Collector's Corner does display actual paintings, glass, textiles, and artworks in other media that are for sale. These aren't by old masters, but they are, for the most part, by artists who are recognized professionals. For a few dollars—or several thousand dollars—you can take home one of their juried works of art.

At one time, many museums offered area artists a chance to show and sell their works. Today, the Toledo Museum of Art is exceptional for its strong commitment to helping aspiring artists not only display, but sell their work.

Admission to the Toledo Museum of Art is free.

▲ **Toledo Museum of Art** ☎ 419-255-8000
2445 Monroe St. · Toledo

Tony Packo's Café, where they keep their buns on the wall

A GLASS OUTLET STORE

Toledo is the world headquarters of the Libbey Glass Company, and local folks know that a good spot for bargain glassware is the Libbey Company Outlet Store at the factory. You can buy their discontinued stock, as well as seconds (cosmetically flawed glassware that can't be sold in stores) at a good savings.

 ▲ **Libbey Glass Factory Outlet Store**   ☎ 419-254-5000
    205 S. Erie St. · Toledo

A MEXICAN-GERMAN KIND OF PLACE

The operators of two Toledo restaurants, one of German ancestry and the other of Latino heritage, decided to merge their eateries into one establishment. The result: a delightful mix of ethnic cultures and food. Where else can you get a platter of sauerkraut and tacos? Seriously, the combination seems to work. The kitchen turns out specialties of each culture; customers can order straight German, straight Mexican, or mix them as they desire. The restaurant has become very popular; reservations are a must, especially on weekends.

 ▲ **Fritz and Alfredo's Restaurant**   ☎ 419-729-9775
    3025 N. Summit St. · Toledo

CORPORAL KLINGER'S FAVORITE RESTAURANT

Jamie Farr, who portrayed the character Corporal Max Klinger on the popular TV show *M*A*S*H*, really did grow up in Toledo. The Tony Packo's Restaurant that his character used to recall with fondness on the TV show really does exist. In fact, Tony Packo's is a Toledo institution. The walls are covered with—believe it or not—autographed hot dog buns, some of them bearing the names of customers like former

B&B Railroad Depot Bed and Breakfast is surrounded by a miniature railroad

president Jimmy Carter and Burt Reynolds! As for the food, spicy Hungarian hot dogs and chili sundaes are a couple of the specialties. The tavern is a very popular spot for lunch and dinner, so be prepared to wait for a seat.

▲ **Tony Packo's Café**   ☎ 419-691-6054
1902 Front St. · Toledo

A LIVING HISTORY CAR MUSEUM

The owners of this small car museum call it a "living museum" because each of the autos—from the 1930s to the 1960s—has been lovingly restored to perfect working condition. They're often driven in parades and at other times. Bill and Jeff Snook have constructed a replica of a 1940s-era Texaco gasoline station as their museum and showroom. They also do repairs and restoration on other folks' classic automobiles.

▲ **Snook's Dream Cars**   ☎ 419-353-8338
13920 County Home Rd. · Bowling Green

ANOTHER OF OHIO'S BEST-KEPT SECRETS

Ohio's many metroparks are one of our greatest, but least known attractions. Take, for example, the Isaac Ludwig Mill in Providence Metropark, which is part of the Metroparks Toledo Area. Not only is this restored mill a living museum where you can see water power used to saw logs and grind grain, it is a link to the Miami and Erie Canal, a section of which is also part of the park. During the summer months, costumed guides will take you on an authentic mule-drawn canal boat for a trip down part of the canal. The canal was important to the settlement of Ohio. At one time, it stretched 249 miles between Toledo and Cincinnati, carrying goods and people between those destinations.

This is an area rich with history. It was not far from the park where "Mad" Anthony Wayne was victorious in the Battle of Fallen Timbers, which drove the British out of Ohio for the last time. (See "Two Graves For Anthony Wayne" in my book, *Strange Tales From Ohio*.)

Isaac Ludwig Mill and the canal ride are open from May to October. *[SEASONAL]*

▲ **Isaac Ludwig Mill**   ☎ 419-407-9741
   Providence Metropark, 13827 U.S. Rte. 24 · Grand Rapids
   At State Rte. 578

A B&B SURROUNDED BY TRAINS

The B&B Railroad Depot Bed and Breakfast is what happens when spouses mix their different avocations. Nate Brinkman had always wanted to operate a miniature railroad. His wife, Linda, had always wanted to operate a bed and breakfast. When Nate bought his first steam locomotive, Linda, a remodeling contractor, decided to redo their small home and increase its size. The result is this beautiful bed and breakfast surrounded by miniature railroad tracks, where guests can always catch a ride on the train. It's a fun place to spend the night, and it's just minutes from downtown Toledo or the Lake Erie Islands.

▲ **B&B Railroad Depot Bed and Breakfast**   ☎ 888-690-7137
   5331 Cedar Point Rd. · Oregon

A LAKE FRONT LODGE

Maumee Bay State Park offers great access to Lake Erie. The property is located just east of Toledo and includes not only a modern lodge with indoor and outdoor swimming pools and an exercise room but also tennis courts and a state-of-the-art golf course. Modern, furnished

Maumee Bay Resort and Conference Center

cabins are also available, scattered along the edge of the golf course on the north side of the park. The park is located only minutes from downtown Toledo and is also very close to the Port Clinton-Sandusky Bay area.

▲ **Maumee Bay Resort**
☎ 800-282-7275 reservations; 419-836-1466 local
1750 Maumee Bay Park Rd. #2 · Oregon

THE LARGEST RECONSTRUCTED FORT IN AMERICA

Fort Meigs, which dates back to the War of 1812, is the largest reconstructed fort in America. It covers several acres overlooking the Maumee River. The fort was built to defend against the British in the War of 1812 and was abandoned after the war. Today, during the summer, staff members at the fort wear the uniforms of the 1812 period and demonstrate weapons used at the fort. *[SEASONAL]*

▲ **Fort Meigs State Memorial**   ☎ 419-874-4121
29100 W. River Rd. · Perrysburg

A TOUR TRAIN

The *Bluebird* has been operating between Waterville and Grand Rapids, Ohio, since 1980. The trip covers a six-mile stretch along the Maumee River. Operating times change with the seasons; call for hours.

▲ *Bluebird* **Passenger Train**   ☎ 419-878-2177
The Toledo, Lake Erie and Western Railroad, 49 N. Sixth St. • Waterville

CARVINGS OF WHIMSY

The carvings are whimsical, and they are the work of sculptor George Carruth, whose stone carvings have become highly sought collectibles. He has his studio in Waterville, south of Toledo. Some of his work has been commissioned by the National Cathedral in Washington, D.C., and he has been asked to create a decoration for the White House Christmas tree. His outlet store is near his studio, where you can purchase seconds and discontinued items. The store, run by his wife, Deb, is called Garden Smiles.

▲ **Garden Smiles Shop**   ☎ 419-878-5412
211 Mechanic St. · Waterville

BUTTERFLIES ARE FREE—ALMOST

If you are looking for a gentle, quiet way to spend a warm summer afternoon, try this place. In the enclosed garden setting, you will find hundreds of species of butterflies, many from South America and Asia. As you wander or sit in the garden, butterflies flit and dart around you, sometimes landing on your arm or head. It may be that "butterflies are

Historical Construction Equipment Museum

free," but here you will pay an admission charge to commune with the colorful insects. One of the most popular events is a butterfly release program held each August.

▲ **Butterfly House** ☎ 419-877-2733
11455 Obee Rd. · Whitehouse

HISTORICAL CONSTRUCTION EQUIPMENT MUSEUM

The Historical Construction Equipment Association has a museum of antique heavy equipment located just outside of Bowling Green on Liberty Hi Road.

Here you will find everything from a horse-drawn grader used to smooth roads in the early years of the twentieth century to a working restored model of a giant Marion 21 electric shovel manufactured back in 1926.

There are more than 60 exhibits inside and out, and many that have been restored to like-new working condition by volunteers. Every three years or so the museum hosts a show where collectors and fans of big equipment gather. You can see many different pieces of equipment, from graders to giant shovels, doing their thing. Other times the museum is open weekdays from 9 A.M. to 5 P.M. Please call ahead of your visit.

▲ **Historical Construction Equipment Museum** ☎ 419-352-5616
16623 Liberty Hi Road Rd. · Bowling Green

Where History Lives

Archbold, Bryan, Defiance

Living history at Sauder Village

ERIE SAUDER'S DREAM

Perhaps the only museum in Ohio that spells out the history of the bathroom is located in Archbold at this historic village and farm. This is a collection of old buildings from northwestern Ohio. At the rear of the village, in a large building, is an eclectic museum chock full of equipment and paraphernalia used on early farms. In one corner an exhibit traces the history of the bathroom, complete with toilets of every description, bathtubs, and sinks.

The village contains living history exhibits featuring volunteers dressed in costumes of a century ago and demonstrating crafts such as broom making, blacksmithing, yarn spinning, and herb gardening. There are real farm animals, buggy rides, and barns to wander through. Nearby is a restaurant where fresh country foods are served.

If you would like to stay here, check out the Sauder Heritage Inn. It is a beautiful, rustic, barn-like inn with large, attractive rooms, each with private bath. Breakfast is included in the price of a night's lodging.

▲ **Sauder Village and Heritage Inn**   ☎ 800-590-9755
    22611 State Route 2 · Archbold

SOME BARGAINS ON FURNITURE

Erie Sauder, who founded the historic Sauder Village, made his fortune from inexpensive furniture. Many years ago, he founded Sauder Furniture, which today is sold across the country in Kmart, Wal-Mart, and many other department stores. The furniture is mostly office and home items, such as desks, entertainment centers, bookcases, and beds, much of it made from particle board and sold unassembled. The main plant is in Archbold, and they have a factory outlet here where they dispose of discontinued models, overruns, and some factory seconds, pieces that may have cosmetic blemishes but are perfect in every other way. You often can find these types of items at a savings here.

▲ **Sauder Store and Outlet** ☎ 419-446-2711
22611 State Rte. 2 · Archbold

BELLYSTICKERS

In the tiny northwest Ohio town of Archbold they make a concoction known as bellystickers. These are not for the diet conscious. They're sort of like sinful Parker House rolls. In fact, they start out as fresh-baked Parker House rolls, then fresh cream and sugar are poured on top and are allowed to seep through overnight. The next morning, the pan is inverted on a plate, and the bellystickers are served. If you don't care about calories, it's a wonderful way to start the day.

▲ **The Barn Restaurant and Doughbox Bakery** ☎ 800-590-9755
22611 State Rte. 2 · Archbold

A VILLAGE FROM THE PAST

As historic villages go, this one's pretty modern. AuGlaize Village, a restoration project of the Defiance County Historical Society, was founded in the 1960s. A local woman donated funds to create a community that would show future generations what life was like when this part of Ohio was first settled. Located just outside of Defiance, it consists of dozens of buildings, some replicas and some, like an unusual two-story log cabin, that have been moved here and restored to look as they did a century or more ago.

In the historic red barn you will find a street of shops that includes a dentist's office from a century ago, a cobbler, weaving shop, broom factory, and an unusual exhibit of household appliances down through the years.

One of my favorite special attractions here is the Old West Shoot-out that is offered on the third Sunday of each month from April through October. The AuGlaize Rough Riders, modern-day Old West gunslingers, walk the streets of Henry Hooker's town (a separate part of the museum) and battle desperados on five different stages. It's called Cowboy

Action Shooting, and instead of people the cowboys and cowgirls shoot at targets using authentic weapons, from pistols to shotguns.

Open on weekends and for special events.

▲ **AuGlaize Village** ☎ 419-784-0107
Krouse Rd. · Defiance

AS SEEN ON TV

Remember the title character in the TV series *Alice* and "Mel's Diner" where she worked? Well, it has been said that Lester's Diner, a fixture since the 1960s in Bryan, Ohio, was the model that the producers of the TV show used. They actually filmed the diner and superimposed "Mel's" on the sign.

The show is just TV history, but the diner is doing just fine. Two things have not changed through the years: the size of their coffee cup—a staggering 14-ounces, a caffeine lover's dream—and their "stacked-to-the-ceiling" club sandwiches. Both are signature items. But there is more: baked chicken and Swiss steak.

They use locally produced syrups on their pancakes and even make the coleslaw fresh each day. Very few things here come in tubs and cans. You can usually tell how good a place is by the crowd at lunchtime, and people are usually standing in line for a seat here. It could be because the prices are reasonable, but the food is fresh and good, too.

▲ **Lester's Diner** ☎ 419-636-1818
233 S. Main St. · Bryan

The President Slept Here

Bettsville, Bucyrus, Findlay, Fremont, Marion, Tiro,
Upper Sandusky, Waldo

Rutherford B. Hayes Presidential Center

OHIO'S PRESIDENTIAL TRAIL: FREMONT

After the state of Virginia, Ohio has the highest number of native sons who became president of the United States. They came from just about every corner of the Buckeye State, starting with a transplanted Virginian, William Henry Harrison, of North Bend near the Ohio–Indiana border, and ending with Warren G. Harding of Marion. In between there was Civil War hero Ulysses S. Grant, born in Point Pleasant at the bottom of the state, and James Garfield of Mentor in the northeast corner. There was also William Howard Taft of Cincinnati, and William McKinley of Niles and Canton. Benjamin Harrison was the grandson of William Henry Harrison, and was born at his grandfather's farm in North Bend. The president who is possibly the least known, but who left perhaps the biggest legacy to the state of Ohio, is Rutherford B. Hayes.

Hayes, known as "Ruddy" to his friends, had a distinguished record as congressman, governor of Ohio, and Civil War general. He was elected to the presidency in a disputed election that saw the outcome decided by an electoral commission. Hayes pledged not to run for re-election. In his inaugural address, he summed up his feelings with these words: "He serves his party best, who serves his country best."

Hayes was credited with helping bind up the wounds of the Civil War by ending the rule of carpetbaggers in the South. He also rooted out corruption in government and helped establish the civil service system.

When he was done with his one term, he came back to Ohio to Spiegel Grove, his estate in Fremont. Here he lived out the rest of his life. His son, Medal of Honor winner Col. Webb Hayes, encouraged the state to build a library dedicated to his father's memory on the estate grounds he donated. It was the first presidential library in American history.

Today the Hayes Presidential Center in Fremont honors not only President Hayes but also all the men who have served as the nation's chief executive. In the museum there are exhibits honoring each of the presidents.

The beautiful Victorian mansion where Hayes lived is also kept almost as it was in his day and is open to the public.

President and Mrs. Hayes were buried on the estate. His grave is covered with a simple stone that has only his name. There is no mention that he once was a general, governor, and president of the United States.

Don't overlook the bargains to be had at the Hayes Presidential Center. Surplus books from the library are often on sale, as well as limited-edition Christmas ornaments and several one-of-a-kind items for history buffs. No admission charge to enter museum store.

▲ **Rutherford B. Hayes Presidential Center**   ☎ 800-998-7737
Spiegel Grove · Fremont
Hayes and Buckland Avenues

OTHER THINGS TO DO IN FREMONT

Scuba diving in a quarry is one of the things you can do in the Sandusky County Park District in and around Fremont. At White Star Park there is a bathing beach and an abandoned quarry filled by clear spring water, which, according to divers, makes this one of the better places in northern Ohio for practicing dives.

Wolf Creek Park offers camping along a winding river not far from Fremont.

▲ **Sandusky County Park District**   ☎ 419-334-4495
1970 Countryside Dr. · Fremont

NEIGHBORS TO A PRESIDENT

When U.S. President Rutherford B. Hayes came home to Fremont after his term as the nation's chief executive was over, lots of movers and shakers in Fremont wanted to live close to a former president. They built large homes on the city's west side near Spiegel Grove, the presidential estate. One Romanesque mansion located very near the Hayes Presidential Center is now a bed and breakfast. Blessings Bed and Breakfast offers a wide, shady porch to relax on. The rooms inside still have much of the original woodwork from the nineteenth century, as well as antique furnishings. Yet the three bedrooms have been modernized and have private baths. You get a full breakfast with a night's stay.

▲ **Blessings Bed and Breakfast** ☎ 419-333-7829
903 Birchard Ave. · Fremont

A QUILTING BARN

If you have someone in the family who is into quilting, then you want to visit this barn not far from Fremont in Bettsville. The Door Mouse has quilting fabric, quilting supplies, and even holds classes to teach you how to make quilts. Located in a large beige barn, the rafters are filled with thousands of bolts of cloth. If you can imagine a pattern, they probably have it. It's a popular stop for bus tours and shop hops by quilting groups. Even if you are not a quilter, it's a fascinating place to visit.

▲ **The Door Mouse** ☎ 419-986-5667
5047 W. State Rte. 12 · Bettsville

A TINY WORKING STEAM RAILROAD

The Northwest Ohio Railroad Preservation Society has rescued a historic steam locomotive, restored it, and now are offering rides on the little train. It is quarter-scale, built for the House of David Amusement Park in Benton Harbor, Michigan, in the 1940s. Originally used to shuttle customers from the parking lot to the park, the little locomotive and its passenger cars is an exact replica of a full-sized train. Now located in Findlay, Ohio, the train runs on a half mile of 15-inch-wide track at the preservation society grounds, located at the intersection of I-75 and County Road 99. They also have a small railroad museum with some full-sized cars on the grounds. *[SEASONAL]*

▲ **Northwest Ohio Railroad Preservation Society** ☎ 419-423-2995
11600 County Rd. 99 · Findlay

YET ANOTHER LARGEST ANTIQUE MALL

This is owned by the same people who operate the Springfield Antique Mall. With 300-plus dealers all under one roof, it was once known as the "Largest Antique Mall in Northwest Ohio". It sells all types of antiques. Many of the dealers specialize in one thing, like silver or glassware. Restrooms are available. Open seven days a week.

▲ **Jeffrey's Antique Gallery** ☎ 419-423-7500
11326 Township Rd. 99 · Findlay
Near Findlay, exit 161 on I-75

A POPCORN MUSEUM

How many towns can claim a museum dedicated to popcorn? Marion can. The Wyandot Popcorn Company is located here, and their collection of popcorn machines and popcorn wagons has finally found a permanent home at the city's Heritage Hall. The museum also includes a huge stuffed Percheron horse reputed to have been from the stable of Napoleon III of France, exhibits reflecting other industries that once called Marion home, and a room dedicated to the memory of the town's most famous son, former U.S. president Warren G. Harding.

▲ **Heritage Hall / Wyandot Popcorn Museum**　☎ 740-387-4255
   169 E. Church St.　·　Marion

PRESIDENT WARREN G. HARDING

Although some might say there is a definite correlation between bologna and politics, I choose to think it is just coincidence that a few miles north of Waldo is Marion, the home and burial place of the last U.S. president to come from Ohio, Warren G. Harding.

The Harding home is just as he and Mrs. Harding left it in 1920 to go to Washington. President Harding died in office and was brought back to Marion to be buried in a magnificent tomb just a mile or so from his home.

Though Harding's administration was wracked with scandal and many of his appointees went to prison, Harding himself was never charged with wrongdoing. Some historians paint him as a man who relied too much on the advice of political cronies, while others are quick to point out that the good things he accomplished in office have been largely forgotten. One bit of interesting Harding trivia is the following phrase from a speech he gave in 1923: "We must have a citizenship less concerned about what the government can do for it, and more anxious about what it can do for the nation." Some believe it was that half-forgotten speech that inspired President John F. Kennedy's more famous line 40 years later.

The home and a small museum at the rear of the home are open for tours. Admission charged.

▲ **President Harding Home**　☎ 740-387-9630
   380 Mount Vernon Ave.　·　Marion

TIRO TESTICLE FESTIVAL

Tiro, Ohio is probably one of the more unlikely places to have an annual festival. It's really just a wide spot in the road with three or four businesses, but each April thousands of people travel from several states to take part in this home-grown event. What they celebrate is the part of a bull that makes a bull a bull. Yep, some people call them "mountain oysters" or "prairie oysters," but these oysters have never seen the sea.

It started simply back in the 1990s, when the owner of the Tiro Tavern was given a box of the delicacies. He fried them up and handed them out to his patrons. Since then it's become a tradition one weekend in April each year, and they now cook upwards of a half-ton of the gonads to satisfy the growing crowds. There is no parade, no queen selected, no rides—so what is there to do at this festival? As one woman told me last year: "We drink beer and eat testicles." And that is precisely what they do at the Tiro Testicle Festival.

▲ **Tiro Tavern**   ☎ 419-347-6922
102 S. Main St. · Tiro

A MEMORIAL TO THE WYANDOTS

The Wyandots were the last American Indian tribe to call Ohio home. Like other tribes, they were forced off their lands as the European settlers pushed westward. The reason that the Wyandots lasted longer was because they had fought on the side of the U.S. in the War of 1812 against the British. In fact, that is why the mill was built in 1820 along the Sandusky River near the Wyandot Village. It was a reward from a grateful U.S. government for loyalty during the war.

The Wyandots had sided with the U.S. in the war in hope of stopping the flood of pioneers onto their lands. They felt certain that the gratitude of the government would protect them in their little corner of Ohio. But that gratitude only lasted about 20 years. Then the big push was on again to take over Indian lands, and the Wyandots were forced to sell their property and leave Ohio.

In 1842, as the last group prepared to leave the state for the new home the government had picked for them in the western states, their chief, Squire Grey-Eyes spoke to them: "Here our dead are buried. We have placed fresh leaves and flowers upon their graves for the last time. Soon they shall be forgotten, for the onward march of the strong white man will not turn aside for the Indian graves."

He was right.

Today the rebuilt mill stands as a memorial to the Wyandots. Inside you can see exhibits that spell out the history of milling from prehistoric times to the present.

▲ **Indian Mill State Memorial**   ☎ 800-600-7147
Upper Sandusky Area Chamber of Commerce
108 E. Wyandot Ave. · Upper Sandusky
Three miles northeast of Upper Sandusky on County Rd. 47 at the Sandusky River

A REAL BARN BED AND BREAKFAST

This has the makings for a great practical joke. Tell your favorite person that you're taking them to a "really rustic" place to spend the

The Barn at Walnut Glen Bed and Breakfast: all barn outside, luxury apartment inside

weekend. Imagine their surprise when you pull up in front of a very weathered old barn out in the countryside. You lead them through the partly open 14-foot-tall barn door, and all you see at first is a tractor and some open-beam barn ceilings. By this time, they may suspect they are going to spend the night sleeping in a hayloft, but then you lead them through another door into a luxurious, modern apartment within the barn, complete with pool table, modern bath, and a kitchen.

▲ **The Barn at Walnut Glen Bed and Breakfast** ☎ 740-726-1000
4505 St. James Rd. · Waldo

FRIED BOLOGNA SANDWICHES

Does the mention of a fried bologna sandwich stir memories? Do you find yourself back in kindergarten? Well, there is a restaurant in central Ohio that has made fried bologna sandwiches an art form. The G & R Tavern in the small town of Waldo, south of Marion, offers a distinctive sandwich. It is made of a half-inch-thick slab of homemade bologna that is grilled to a crusty dark brown, covered with a slice of Monterey jack cheese, topped with large slices of sweet onion and sweet pickle, then flipped onto a fresh kaiser roll. To some, it is possibly the closest thing to true ambrosia.

It started back in the 1960s when the original owners, two men named George and Roy, decided to put a fried bologna sandwich on the menu. It wasn't anything unusual. Waldo is farm country, and many a young farmer carried fried bologna sandwiches to school each day, especially in the 1930s, '40s, and '50s. Well, George and Roy's new dish must have touched off memories, because their fried bologna sandwich became an instant hit. Their fame spread far from the only downtown street in Waldo. The news reached Columbus, and local newspaper food writers drove up Route 23 to see what all the fuss was about. Soon, food mavens from around the state were stopping in for a fried bologna sandwich. Television personalities from all over also started to get a nostalgic craving for the kindergarten soul food. More publicity followed.

Today a sign on the side of the building proclaims, "Best fried bologna sandwich in America." If you challenge that statement, the staff of the G&R will probably whip out a guest book that has comments from across the country by many who claim to have driven long distances just to taste their fried bologna sandwich. They can tell you that each week the little country tavern goes through over a half-ton of the specially made bologna. The ingredients are a closely guarded secret that will only be revealed to whoever buys the tavern—if it is ever sold.

If you visit the G & R, chances are you might find a nun sitting on a bar stool next to a truck driver, both enjoying fried bologna sandwiches. Also, it is not unusual to see people carrying large grocery bags filled with the sandwiches when they leave.

▲ **G & R Tavern**   ☎ 740-726-9685
103 N. Marion Rd. · Waldo

Caverns and Castles

Bellefontaine, Lakeview, West Liberty

THE BIGGEST CAVERNS IN OHIO

It was an observant farm hand in the late 1800s who noticed that rain water quickly disappeared on a stretch of rolling farmland near West Liberty. His curiosity led him to examine the hillside more closely, and he discovered a hole in the ground that was the opening to a subterranean series of passages. He had discovered the Ohio Caverns.

Today they are considered Ohio's largest and most beautiful caverns. (A note about caves and caverns: the words are usually interchangeable, but many folks consider caves to be above ground, while caverns are subterranean.) When these were first discovered, they were filled with mud and limestone, and it took years for workers, stooped and lying on their stomachs, to scrape and carry the goop and debris out of the underground formation, to make the caverns easily accessible to tourists.

The original part of the caves that was opened to the public in 1897 stretched for over a mile and half underground and offered visitors the largest collection of stalactites (the pointy things growing down from the ceiling) and stalagmites (the pointy ones growing up from the floor) in Ohio. The icicle-like formations are created by crystallization of minerals created by the slow, but steady, drip of groundwater down through the rock. It can take from 500 to 1,000 years for the stalactites to grow just one inch! To put this in perspective, some of the formations are four to five feet long and have grown only one inch since Columbus discovered America. So these caves have been around a long, long time.

As far as caverns go, these may be the easiest for able-bodied folks to visit. There is a short flight of stairs down to the first chamber, then a fairly level walkway that covers about a mile that meanders through the various chambers and rock formations, but when you get to the end of the tour there is a fairly long and steep set of steps back to the surface. They are wide enough to let others pass if you need to stop for a minute to catch your breath. One other note: the temperature, year-round inside the caverns is always in the fifties, so despite the heat outside, you might want to bring along a sweater or jacket.

▲ **Ohio Caverns**   ☎ 937-465-4017
2210 State Rte. 245 E · West Liberty

Piatt Castles: Mac-a-cheek and Mac-o-chee

TOUR THE CASTLES OF CENTRAL OHIO

Mac-a-cheek and Mac-o-chee Castles are the famous homes of the Piatt brothers in Logan County and one of Ohio's oldest tourist attractions. The castles, actually large stone homes, have been attracting tourists since the early 1990s. Abram Piatt, who built Mac-a-cheek, was a farmer and a Union general in the Civil War. His brother, Donn Piatt, who built Mac-o-chee, was a journalist and a poet. The homes were built on the enormous Piatt estate, which consisted then of hundreds of acres of land. Today the two castles are located less than a mile apart. Self-guided tours of the buildings are available. The castles are open seasonally; call for hours. *[SEASONAL]*

▲ **Piatt Castles** ☎ 937-465-2821
10051 Township Rd. 47 · West Liberty

WORLD FAMOUS MACARONI SALAD

This diner is famous for its macaroni salad. Some writers for *Gourmet* magazine happened to stop in for lunch and were so enthralled by the diner's macaroni salad that it ended up as the subject of an article they were doing for the magazine. The diner attracts a lot of local folks. You can stop in and see for yourself if the food is "stupendously good," as quoted in the magazine article.

▲ **Liberty Gathering Place Restaurant** ☎ 937-465-3081
111 N. Detroit St. · West Liberty

SLEEP IN A REAL AMERICAN INDIAN CAMPGROUND

Southwind Park, near Bellefontaine, is perhaps the only campground in Ohio owned and operated by American Indians. The Shawnee Nation, United Remnant Band of Ohio, the only state-recognized tribe in Ohio, has purchased more than 300 acres of land where their ancestors once roamed, including Zane Caverns and Southwind Park. The caverns, which are open to the public, contain many interesting geological formations and stretch for more than a third of a mile underground.

Nearby is a museum dedicated to the Shawnee and Ancient American Indian Culture that was once in Ohio.

The campground contains several primitive cabins that you can rent to spend the night in.

🔺 **Zane Shawnee Caverns**   ☎ 937-592-9592
7092 State Rte. 540 · Bellefontaine

CAMPING OUT AT THE LAKE

The caves are not too far from Indian Lake State Park, where you can also have a lot of fun with the family. There is a nearly 6,000-acre lake with boating, swimming, and fishing. The state has a campground with more than 400 campsites, including some with cabins you can rent for the night. They also offer the RV rent-a-camp program, where you get a fully equipped 30-foot-long RV complete with air conditioning and color television. These facilities are very popular, and it's a good idea to make reservations as soon as you have a vacation date in mind.

🔺 **Indian Lake State Park**
☎ 937-843-2717 office; 937-843-3553 campground
12774 State Rte. 235 N · Lakeview

SOUTHWEST
OHIO

The Man in the Moon and Little Sure-Shot

Fort Recovery, Greenville, Leo, Lima, New Bremen, Piqua, Troy, Wapakoneta

The moon-shaped Armstrong Air & Space Museum

THE BIRTHPLACE OF MOONWALKING

The man who made the "one small step for man, one giant leap for mankind," Neil Armstrong, first man to walk on the moon, was raised in Wapakoneta. Today, a moon-shaped building that seems to be rising from a mound along Interstate 75 is a museum dedicated to Armstrong's history-making voyage. Inside you'll find the small airplane in which he learned to fly. There are pictures and memorabilia that trace his life from small-town Ohio to outer space. Also on display are personal items that he took with him to the moon, and there is a theater where a film of the most-watched event in history is played over and over. There is also a gallery of news headlines from around the world and copies of awards and presentations given to Armstrong on his return to earth. A dramatic place to take a photo of the family is at the end of the sidewalk leading to the museum entrance. It resembles an airport runway leading to a rising moon.

▲ **Armstrong Air & Space Museum**   ☎ 800-860-0142
500 Apollo Dr. · Wapakoneta
I-75 and Bellefontaine Rd.

OHIO'S OWN BATTLE OF THE LITTLE BIG HORN

Ohio's version of General Custer at the battle of the Little Big Horn was General Arthur St. Clair. In 1791, St. Clair went into Northwest Ohio to punish the Native Americans for the earlier defeat of General Josiah Harmar, who had been sent by George Washington to quell some of the Indians on the Ohio frontier. Washington warned St. Clair to be careful and watch for surprise attacks, but St. Clair walked into a trap and his force was decimated by Chief Little Turtle and his braves. St. Clair lost more than 700 soldiers, and the defeat sent him running back towards Pittsburgh. (Custer lost fewer than 200 soldiers in the better-known battle of Little Big Horn.)

It was a humiliation for the young United States Army, and George Washington wasn't going to take it. A year later, with a rebuilt army, he dispatched one of his most-feared generals, "Mad" Anthony Wayne, to northwestern Ohio to reclaim the territory and make it payback time for the Indians. Wayne built a fort near the site of St. Clair's defeat and called it Fort Recovery. The Indians, 2,000 strong under Little Turtle and the famed Shawnee War Chief Blue Jacket, attacked the fort. But this time they were fighting a different kind of general who was ready for them and had a better-trained force. The Indians were sent fleeing, with Anthony Wayne in pursuit. The chase ended months later with the Battle of Fallen Timbers near Toledo, which proved to be the pivotal battle of the Ohio frontier. (See "The two graves of Mad Anthony Wayne" in my book, *Strange Tales From Ohio*.) The reconstructed fort is open to tourists from May to September. It features two blockhouses, a monument, and a museum that displays artifacts found in the area from the time of the battle. *[SEASONAL]*

   ▲ **Fort Recovery Historical Site**   ☎ 800-283-8920
      One Fort Site St. · Fort Recovery

ANNIE OAKLEY WAS A BUCKEYE

For a tiny town, Greenville has had more than its share of famous people and events.

For starters, the historic Greenville Treaty between Native Americans and General "Mad" Anthony Wayne, which opened the Ohio frontier to settlement, was signed here. Coincidentally, it was at the same time that two of Wayne's officers, Meriwether Lewis and William Clark first met and began a friendship that culminated in the Lewis and Clark discoveries in the American West.

Some famous citizens who were born or lived here include Commander Zachary Lansdowne, skipper of the ill-fated *Shenandoah*, at the time the largest dirigible in the world when it crashed in 1925 in southeastern Ohio. (See "The Mystery of the Ring" in my book *Strange Tales*

From Ohio.) One of the world's foremost journalists and adventurers, Lowell Thomas, also called this home.

But Greenville's most famous daughter was a woman born Phoebe Moses. (Some historians claim it was Mozee.) The world remembers her as Annie Oakley. Legend has it that Sitting Bull called her "Little Sure-Shot." She was one of the world's top woman marksman with a rifle. She gained fame with the Buffalo Bill Wild West Show and travelled the world giving shooting demonstrations. Her life has been dramatized on stage, screen, radio and TV in the show *Annie Get Your Gun.* In her last years, she came home to Greenville, and she died there in 1926. She, and her husband, Frank Butler, are buried in a small country cemetery just outside of town.

The Garst Museum has one of the largest collections of Annie's weapons and personal effects on display, as well as exhibits honoring Lowell Thomas, Commander Lansdowne, and the Greenville Treaty. A lot of American history is crammed into this small museum.

▲ **Garst Museum**   ☎ 937-548-5250
205 N. Broadway · Greenville

ANCIENT INSCRIPTIONS

An ancient culture in Ohio left a message that has survived for thousands of years, and we are still trying to decipher it.

In Leo, near Jackson, a slab of sandstone contains 37 drawings of animals, humans and some footprints. The inscriptions, named for the small village near where it was found, are believed to have been left behind by the Fort Ancient Native Americans who were responsible for some mounds and Fort Ancient north of Cincinnati, in the Miami and Ohio Valleys. They occupied the area between 1000 and 1650 A.D.

No one is quite sure whether it is some kind of message or perhaps the very first example of graffiti in Ohio. Free and open year-round.

▲ **Leo Petroglyph**   ☎ 800-686-1535
Township Rd. 24 · Leo
About 5 miles northwest of Jackson; take U.S. Rte. 35 to County Rd. 28 in Leo, turn left on Township Rd. 24

WATCH WHAT YOU PUT IN YOUR MOUTH

Ohio has many small-town museums, but there is one in western Ohio that you really don't want to miss: the Allen County Museum in Lima. For openers, the museum is the only county museum in the state of Ohio that is accredited by the American Association of Museums. It's that good.

They have everything here from a Conestoga wagon to the jail cell from which famed gangster John Dillinger escaped. There is a wonder-

Bicycle Museum of America

ful display of art and a children's museum that allows a lot of hands-on activities. But my favorite attraction in the museum is one that they don't really publicize very much. It's the collection donated by two doctors, a father and son, of things that they had recovered out of people's throats and stomachs. You know, things like coins, screws, and hairpins. (See "Hard to Swallow" in my book, *Ohio Oddities*.) It's almost worth the trip just to see this exhibit.

▲ **Allen County Museum**   ☎ 419-222-9426
   620 W. Market St. · Lima

VINTAGE BICYCLES

A local industrialist in west central Ohio who was a bicycle collector decided that his little community should have a first-rate museum. So when the owners of the famed Schwinn bicycle company decided to auction off their personal collection of vintage bicycles, he went to Chicago and bought the entire collection. Bringing it back to New Bremen, he added it to his personal collection to create perhaps the finest bicycle museum in the country. You'll see the very first wooden bicycle, designed for troops in the Spanish-American War, and there are bicycles made to look and act like children's giant pedal cars. In this two-story museum, chances are you'll spot a look-alike for the first bicycle that you ever owned.

If you ride a bicycle or ever rode one, you'll enjoy visiting the Bicycle Museum of America.

▲ **Bicycle Museum of America**   ☎ 419-629-9249
   7 W. Monroe St. · New Bremen

A HORSE-DRAWN BOAT RIDE

The *General Harrison* is a 70-foot-long replica of the type of canal boat that once plied the Miami Canal in southwestern Ohio. The Piqua Historical Area is a collection of original homes and a restored section of the old canal that ran nearby. Rides are available on the canal boat, which is pulled by mules. The attraction is closed on Monday, Tuesday, and Wednesday. *[SEASONAL]*

▲ **Piqua Historical Area**   ☎ 800-752-2619
9845 N. Hardin Rd. · Piqua

SLEEP IN A MALL

If you are headed for the Air Force Museum in Dayton, you might want to consider an overnight stay in Piqua, where you can literally sleep in a shopping mall. That means that you have 50 stores to shop in, a multiplex theater at your doorstep, and a food court, an indoor swimming pool, and a fitness center. That should be enough to keep the whole family busy and tire out some restless kids. The Comfort Inn is attached to one end of the Miami Valley Centre Mall. It has all the amenities you usually expect from Comfort Inn, like free movie channels, and some suites are equipped with whirlpool baths to help ease those long-drive kinks.

▲ **Comfort Inn**   ☎ 800-228-5150
987 E. Ash St. · Piqua

SMELL THE FLOWERS

You can smell the flowers as well as walk among some great beauty at this nature center north of Dayton.

The center is located on land purchased by Clayton Bruckner, once owner of the WACO Aircraft Corporation. He bought 146 acres along the Stillwater River in 1933. The land has a great variety of trees, shrubs streams and springs. The original land has been increased to 165 acres, and is now open to the public as a nature preserve. It includes a wildlife rehabilitation center, where injured wildlife are nurtured back to health and returned to the wild, or, in some cases, given a permanent home for the rest of their lives. The center has six miles of trails through wetlands, forest, and prairie grasses.

▲ **Brukner Nature Center**   ☎ 937-698-6493
5995 Horseshoe Bend Rd. · Troy

Antiquing in the Miami Valley

Clifton, Springfield, Urbana

ANTIQUE HUNTER PARADISE

Heart of Ohio Antique Center in Springfield claims to be one of the largest antique dealers in America. They offer 116,000 square feet of display area. The place, carpeted and air-conditioned, has offerings from more than 700 dealers representing 20 states. From furniture to glassware, there are literally thousands of one-of-a-kind antiques to be found here. There are also many other large antique malls nearby and in downtown Springfield.

▲ **Heart of Ohio Antique Center** ☎ 937-324-2188
4785 E. National Rd. · Springfield
I-70 at U.S. 42, Exit 62

OHIO'S LARGEST ANTIQUE MALL (THEY CLAIM)

This place bills itself as "Ohio's Largest Antique Mall." I don't know about that, but it is very big. The building contains upward of 200 individual dealers who have rented space to display their specialties. The owner is physically challenged and has made sure that the place is wheelchair accessible. There are nice wide aisles, good lighting, and handicapped-accessible bathrooms. There is also a lobby with a huge chandelier and fireplace where members of the family who are not into antiques can sit by the fire and relax or read and a small snack area with vending machines.

As for the antiques, there is a good selection of everything from silver and glass to big items like architectural antiques and furniture. You can also bargain. Management has the right to wheel and deal to a certain extent, but if you insist, they will pass along any offers that they refuse to the dealers and let them make the final decision.

▲ **Springfield Antique Mall** ☎ 937-322-8868
1735 Titus Rd. · Springfield
Just outside of Springfield on I-70 (you can see it from the highway)

A WORKING GRISTMILL

One of Southwest Ohio's hidden gems is the historic Clifton Mill in Clifton. It's one of the largest water-powered gristmills in the world still

Clifton Mill, one of the largest water-powered gristmills still operating

in operation. The waters of the Little Miami River are diverted through the base of the mill, powering the grinding wheel much as they have done for almost 200 years.

In addition to fresh-ground flour and meal, the mill also offers a gift shop that sells its product and other souvenirs.

There is a small restaurant where the breakfast fare is legendary. They make pancakes here—I mean they make real pancakes here. Pancakes that are almost the size of manhole covers. They boast that rarely can anyone finish a stack of three of their flapjacks. For dessert, if you are still hungry, they offer their signature oatmeal pie.

The mill really shines during the Christmas season. The day before Thanksgiving, they turn on more than two million lights that outline the mill, mill wheel, and adjoining valley. There is also a display of 3,000 animated Santa Claus figures and a miniature model of the village of Clifton that has electric trains and even an animated Christmas parade. There is also a Santa Claus workshop, where a real Santa practices for the big night every 15 minutes by running up and down his chimney and waving to appreciative families below.

Not surprisingly, at Christmas time the mill attracts thousands of people each evening. A sizable staff is required to serve the crowd and to keep people from wandering too close to the illuminated mill wheel or from falling into the valley of the Little Miami River, which runs through the grounds.

The lights are on at the mill each evening, except Tuesdays, until New Year's Day. On Tuesdays, the lights are out, and the mill is closed. It says so in all their advertising. There are signs posted all around the front of the mill saying, "Closed on Tuesdays."

The first year that they lit the mill, Tony Santariano, the owner, put

The giagantic pancakes at Clifton Mill

the lighting display on a timer so the lights came on promptly each evening at 6:00 P.M. and off at 9:30 P.M. On Tuesdays, he would just turn off the timer so the lights would not come on.

That year, Christmas happened to fall on a Tuesday, and so the mill was closed. Christmas night, Tony and two of his daughters were moving a canoe that they had received as a gift from their home to a storeroom in the darkened mill. However, when they pulled up to the street the mill is on, they found it choked with cars and people. It was about 5:45 P.M. Darkness had just fallen, and people were waiting to see the lights come on.

Tony tried to explain to the crowd that there would be no lights tonight, that the mill was closed on Tuesdays, and, for safety reasons, he could not turn on the lights because he had no staff. The crowd was not happy about this. In fact they became downright surly. They started to shout at Tony and his daughters. The trio, with their canoe, beat a hasty retreat inside the mill.

"Don't turn on any lights!" Tony warned his daughters. "If they see a light on, they'll think I changed my mind and that we're open."

He told one of his daughters to toss him the mill keys. He wanted to be sure the door was locked.

She tossed the keys, which went sliding under a counter. The three were searching the floor trying to find the keys in the blacked-out room when suddenly:

WHAM!

The night was flooded with lights. Tony had forgotten to turn off the timer, and all the thousands of lights outside had sprung to life.

The crowd of nearly 200 outside cheered and surged forward onto the grounds.

Realizing that the three of them could not control so large a crowd, Tony ran to the light switch and turned it off, plunging the mill into darkness again.

For the next half-hour Tony and his daughters huddled on the floor of the darkened mill as people pounded on the door, and they occasionally peeked out windows to see if the angry crowd had left.

Realizing that people wanted to see the lights every night of the week, Tony and his family now light the mill each evening from November 26 until the first of the New Year, except on nights when the weather makes viewing dangerous, such as heavy rain or ice storms. They have only had to close a couple of times in the years since that Christmas, but it would be a good idea to call the evening you plan to visit, just so you won't be disappointed. *[SEASONAL]*

▲ **The Clifton Mill** ☎ 937-767-5501
75 Water St. · Clifton

OHIO, 10,000 YEARS AGO

"This is Ohio 10,000 years ago," a guide told me as we walked a boardwalk back into the Cedar Bog, operated by the Ohio Historical Society near Urbana.

You almost expect to see a woolly mammoth come strolling through the aged conifer trees that border the swamp-like bog. The ecosystem here was probably created by the glaciers as they advanced south carrying soil and seeds from forests far to the north of Ohio.

The almost mile-long boardwalk carries you into the heart of Ohio's largest boreal fen. This was a gathering spot for the Native American tribes that once passed through this ancient piece of land. Cedar Bog is a hauntingly beautiful place in any season of the year. From the cries of the tree-frogs in the early spring to the honk of geese flying overhead as winter approaches, the sounds are the musical accompaniment to a journey into a very special place in Ohio.

▲ **Cedar Bog Nature Preserve** ☎ 800-860-0147
980 Woodburn Rd. · Urbana

Dayton Aviation

Clifton, Dayton, Jeffersonville, Wilburforce, Wright-Patterson Air Force Base, Yellow Springs

THE LARGEST MILITARY AVIATION MUSEUM IN THE WORLD

The largest military aviation museum in the world, this is perhaps one of Ohio's best year-round attractions. It offers a spectrum of aviation history, from the Wright brothers through today's stealth technology, and includes exhibits on space exploration. An IMAX movie theater puts you right in the pilot's seat. In the 17 acres of exhibits, there are more than 400 aircraft on display. My favorite spot at the museum is in the annex, located on the other side of the runway and reachable by bus from the main building. It houses many additional aircraft, including those once used by U.S. presidents. Here you will find Harry Truman's *Independence*, the *Columbine* used by Dwight Eisenhower, and planes once used by John F. Kennedy, Lyndon Johnson, and others. Several of the presidential aircraft are open, and you can walk through them and see what presidential travel was like.

One of the nicest things about the museum is that admission is free. There is a charge for the IMAX theater. Open seven days a week. Closed: Thanksgiving, Christmas, and New Year's Day.

▲ **The National Museum of the United States Air Force**
☎ 937-255-3286
1100 Spatz St. · Wright-Patterson Air Force Base
Gate 28 B

SLEEP AT BOB HOPE'S HOTEL

You can sleep here at America's only commercial hotel located on an active military base. The hotel, named after famed Ohioan Bob Hope, is located on the Wright-Patterson Air Force Base. It took a special act of Congress to build the hotel there. The real purpose of the structure is to provide housing for servicemen and families who come to Dayton to attend some of the Air Force schools there, but when extra rooms are available they are open to the public. The rooms are spartan but clean, with amenities like private bath, TV, desk, and computer ports and wireless Internet service. The hotel also has a restaurant and bar.

▲ **Hope Hotel and Conference Center** ☎ 937-879-2696
Bldg 823, Area A · Wright-Patterson Air Force Base
Contact hotel for directions onto the base.

The National Museum of the United States Air Force has a huge display

WHERE THE WORLD LEARNED TO FLY

North Carolina may be able to boast that mankind made its first flight in their state, but the Ohioans who made that flight really learned how to fly back in the Buckeye State. You can see the actual spot and learn how it was under Ohio skies that Wilbur and Orville Wright learned how to do more than just take off and fly in a straight line. It was on this former cattle farm, which today is part of the giant Wright-Patterson Air Force Base in Dayton, that they taught themselves how to turn, climb, and dive an airplane. You can see a rebuilt hanger that they used, as well as the first propulsion system that they built to launch their kite-like airplanes.

Admission is free, but since the site is now on a military air base, always check first to see if it is open to the public. They sometimes close down when security levels are elevated.

▲ **Huffman Prairie Flying Field and Interpretive Center**
☎ 937-425-0008
1828 S. County Rd. 25A · Wright-Patterson Air Force Base

CLIFTON GORGE STATE NATURE PRESERVE

You can find more than 300 kinds of wildflowers growing here, and more than 100 species of trees. The Little Miami River has cut a 22-foot gorge through this park. Legend has it that Daniel Boone once leaped across the gorge in a bid for freedom after being captured by Native Americans. If you like to hike, there are four miles of challenging trails. The preserve is right next to John Bryan State Park.

▲ **Clifton Gorge State Nature Preserve**   ☎ 937-767-7947
State Rte. 343 · Clifton
¼ mile west of Clifton

OHIO'S LARGEST OUTLET MALL

There are more than 95 stores in this outlet mall, and more are on the way. You'll find everything from name-brand jeans to fine china. As with all outlet malls, not everything is a bargain. Watch for closeouts, discontinued stock, and seconds for the best prices.

⏶ **Prime Outlets at Jeffersonville I & II**   ☎ 740-948-9090
8000 Factory Shops Blvd. · Jeffersonville
I-71 at Jeffersonville exit

THE STORY OF THE CIVIL RIGHTS MOVEMENT

At nearby Wilburforce, you can see the story of the civil rights movement of the 1960s unfold in photos, exhibits, films, and recordings. Housed here is the Afro-American Cultural Center, which, besides the permanent exhibit on the civil rights movement, offers constantly changing exhibits of paintings and other cultural activities.

⏶ **National Afro-American Museum and Cultural Center**
☎ 937-376-4944
1350 Brush Rd. · Wilburforce

THE LAST REAL DAIRY

Just a short distance from Clifton is a farm that has become a major tourist attraction in the Miami Valley. This is a true dairy. All you have to do is walk out the door and look to your left. Chances are you will be looking at their giant herd of Jersey cows and some of their goats and other animals that love to be fed and given attention by visitors. Their dairy farm is next door to the store, and the barns are open to visitors. Kids can pet baby cows and goats, climb on tractors, and watch the milking operation.

Next door in the dairy they serve dozens of flavors of rich Jersey ice cream. There is also a bakery and a gift shop. But wait, there's more. They also have two miniature golf courses, batting cages, a driving range, and a large restaurant on the property.

⏶ **Young's Jersey Dairy**   ☎ 937-325-0629
6880 Springfield-Xenia Rd. · Yellow Springs

A COLLEGE TOWN BED AND BREAKFAST

This lovely old home near Antioch College is also within walking distance of downtown Yellow Springs. It has been made into a bed and breakfast that attracts many academics visiting the college.

⏶ **Morgan House Bed and Breakfast**   ☎ 937-767-1761
120 W. Limestone St. · Yellow Springs

Dayton Area

Dayton, Fairborn, Huber Heights, Miamisburg, Vandalia

DAYTON'S EARLIEST RESIDENTS

A part of early American history was almost turned into a sewage treatment plant for the city of Dayton. It was the early 1970s when, thanks to the work of the folks at the Dayton Museum of Natural History, the remains of an ancient Native American village were uncovered on the site. Work was stopped on the sewage treatment plant, and construction was moved to another location. Over the years, the museum workers have been able to partially rebuild the thatched roof huts and buildings that made up the village, which was believed to have been built by the Fort Ancient culture some time between the years 1000 and 1600 A.D. The scientists have been able to discern that the small town was only lived in for about 20 years, then abandoned. The layout of the village also included apparent astronomical alignments. While it is believed the Fort Ancient people were farmers, the mystery is why they suddenly abandoned this town.

The site is open to the public and includes an interpretive center and museum. It's a chance to walk through a village that was here long before Ohio became a state.

▲ **SunWatch Indian Village**   ☎ 937-268-8199
2301 W. River Rd. · Dayton

SunWatch Indian Village, a reconstructed village of early Native Americans

A HANDS-ON MUSEUM

This is a sort of combination of Dayton's Natural History Museum, a small zoo, and a children's discovery museum, all rolled into one. That Kid's Playce has a host of things for small fry to discover and play with, including a neat tree house that goes out through the roof of the building and a spiral slide you can take from the roof back to the ground floor. The zoo contains many animals indigenous to Ohio, and two galleries hold temporary exhibits that often mix in some of the real specimens and artifacts from the museum's collection. This is a regular stop for my grandkids when they are in downtown Dayton.

▲ **Boonshoft Museum of Discovery**   ☎ 937-275-7431
2600 DeWeese Pkwy. · Dayton
Between two parks on the northwest side of downtown Dayton.

CARILLON HISTORICAL PARK

This may be one of the least-known attractions in Dayton. It is a 65-acre park hidden away near the river. Here, the Deeds Carillon, a huge bell tower that overlooks the park, is the site of concerts at various times during the year. There is also a small historical village that includes a 1905 Wright brothers plane, a replica of their bicycle shop, an 1896 schoolhouse, and a number of other interesting buildings and displays. The park is closed November through March. There is an admission charge.

▲ **Carillon Historical Park**   ☎ 937-293-2841
1000 Carillon Blvd. · Dayton

A POET LIVED HERE

Paul Laurence Dunbar of Dayton was born to two former slaves. He grew up to become the poet laureate of African-Americans. While he lived only 34 years in a time of racial prejudice, he accomplished much, publishing a dozen books of poetry, five novels, four books of short stories, and a play. Two of his supporters were boyhood friends, Wilbur and Orville Wright (see "The Poet From Dayton" in my book, *Strange Tales From Ohio*).

Dunbar died of tuberculosis in 1906. In 1936, the state of Ohio honored Dunbar by making the home where he lived and died a state memorial. It was the first state memorial to honor an African-American.

Today the home is much as it was when Dunbar lived there, you can see the study where he did his writing and examples of his work. There is a visitors' center at the rear of the home. The memorial is also part of the Dayton Aviation Heritage Trail that honors the Wright Brothers and Paul Laurence Dunbar for their work in the Miami Valley.

▲ **Dunbar House**   ☎ 800-860-0148
219 Paul Laurence Dunbar St. · Dayton

CLASSIC PACKARDS

This is one of the finest privately owned museums in the state. They have taken a Packard dealership from the 1930s and restored it—right down to the service department, where the mechanic's white coat still hangs beside his personal tool chest. They have dozens of classic Packards on display, from the showroom to the service center. Get this: You can even rent one of their classic limousines for special events. Call them for the details.

▲ **Citizens Motorcar Company** ☎ 937-226-1710
420 S. Ludlow St. · Dayton

WORLD'S LARGEST SURPLUS STORE

If it's surplus, any kind of surplus, Mendelson's Liquidation Outlet in Dayton probably has it. They buy literally anything that is surplus, from an old radar site from Wright-Patterson Air Force Base to more than one million books from the Time-Life Corporation. You can find restaurant equipment, safes, department store mannequins, every conceivable kind of electronic item, and wire in various forms, colors, and shapes—enough to wire a whole city. The merchandise is always arriving, and what they may have on display this week will be gone next week, replaced by something else. If you are a do-it-yourself person or a crafter, this is a regular stop. Open to the public Monday through Saturday.

▲ **Mendelson's Liquidation Outlet** ☎ 800-422-3525
340 E. First St. · Dayton

SOME SAY PIZZA, SOME SAY PIAZZA

At least that's what happens in the Dayton area. Many of the local folks think the best pizza (or piazza) comes from a local chain of restaurants called Marion's Piazza. They specialize in a very thin, hard crust, and they cut the pizza (or piazza) in little squares. Great when you have a table full of kids who are finicky eaters. One other thing to bear in mind: they take no credit cards here, only cash, but they have an ATM machine in the lobby in case you forget. It's a kid-friendly place and is usually very crowded after soccer or football games. There are several locations around town. The one we tried is below:

▲ **Marion's Piazza** ☎ 937-429-3393
1320 N. Fairfield Rd. · Dayton

A HALLOWEEN MUSEUM

Another little-known Dayton-area attraction, Foy's, really comes to life each September and October when this year-round costume shop expands over much of downtown Fairborn's two main city blocks. Here you will find costumes for adults and children, items you can use to make your own costumes, haunted house exhibits—mechanical or just plain scary—and even a museum dedicated to the best of the haunted house exhibits they sell. (There is a small charge to visit the museum.) You can't miss it; larger-than-life Halloween figures adorn the tops of many downtown buildings. *[SEASONAL]*

▲ **Foy's Variety, Halloween, and Costume Stores**   ☎ 937-878-0671
20 E. Main St. · Fairborn

A GREAT PARK

Another of the Five Rivers Metroparks in Montgomery County is the wonderful Carriage Hill Farm, north of Dayton. The park covers a whopping 900 acres and includes a historical farm, where time is frozen in the 1880s. You can watch farmers plowing, cultivating, and harvesting with horses and hand-operated equipment. Inside the farmhouse you can see how farmers' wives operated a home over a century ago.

The park also offers horseback riding, hiking, fishing, and picnic areas. Group camping is available.

▲ **Carriage Hill Farm Museum**   ☎ 937-278-2609
7800 Shull Rd. · Huber Heights
At Rte. 201

FLY THE WRIGHT WAY

Ohio's contribution to aviation is unparalleled in the world. Not only were the Wright brothers, who first proved man could fly with a powered aircraft, born here; the Buckeye State is also the birthplace of John Glenn, the first American to orbit the earth, and Neil Armstrong, the first human to walk on the moon. If a group of Dayton-area enthusiasts had their way, the motto, "Ohio, the heart of it all" would be replaced by the slogan, "Ohio, birthplace of aviation."

If you would like to see and experience what it was like to fly in the days of the Wright brothers, head down to Miamisburg and sign up for a flight in the "Wright B Flyer." This is as close a replica of the original Wright brothers' Model "B" aircraft as modern aviation regulations will allow. You sit on an open wing, just as the first army pilots did. The two propellers are each driven by a single heavy-duty bicycle-like chain. The contraption looks more like a box kite than an airplane.

The plane was built by a group of aviation professionals who wanted to re-create the army's first aircraft in such a way that they could actually fly it. While they have substituted some modern steel rigging for the original piano wire and added a transponder and radio to keep federal officials happy, the craft still looks and flies like the original.

This is the way it works: If you purchase a Wright B Flyer Honorary Aviator Membership for $100, you will be invited to take a flight in the

Wright B Flyer—as close a working replica of the original as aviation regulations allow

Wright B Flyer. Upon signing a release you are escorted to the aircraft and helped to a seat on the wing beside the pilot. You are offered a pair of goggles and a headset to communicate with the pilot, since there is no cabin and no windshield on the plane. The two propellers are behind you. Once they fire up, conversation is very difficult. You taxi to the end of the runway and start your takeoff roll. It hardly seems that you are going fast enough when the plane gently drifts into the air.

Flying the plane, as one pilot put it, is "like driving a tractor across a freshly plowed field." The flight consists of a straight-ahead course at an altitude of about 50 to 75 feet for a distance of roughly 1,000 feet (higher and farther than the Wright brothers flew on their first flight). Then you land and are taxied back to the hangar, where you can pose for pictures in the plane and receive a certificate that tells the world you flew in the same aircraft that taught the world to fly.

Weather permitting, the flights are scheduled on Tuesdays, Thursdays, and Saturdays. Reservations are requested. The hangar, which is a replica of the Wright brothers' early hangar, serves a multiple of purposes: storage space for the aircraft, construction of a new airplane, and a museum (with gift shop of early flight memorabilia).

▲ **Wright B Flyer, Inc.** ☎ 937-885-2327
10550 Springboro Pike · Miamisburg

THE BIGGEST MOUND

It's another of those mysterious mounds that dot Ohio, but this is the biggest. The Miamisburg Mound is not only believed to be the tallest mound in Ohio, but also in the eastern United States. The mound, thought to have been built by the Adena culture of Native Americans may have been constructed as early as 800 B.C. It is more than 877 feet in circumference and originally stood over 70 feet high. The Adenas apparently used it as a burial mound for members of their culture.

Today visitors can climb 116 steps to the summit of the mound for a great view of the surrounding park and playground that make up the state park where the mound is located.

Open year-round; admission is free.

▲ **Miamisburg Mound**   ☎ 937-866-4532
  101 N. First St. · Miamisburg
  One mile south of exit 44 (State Rte. 725) and three miles west of exit
  42 off I-75

HAMBURGER WAGON

This is a Miamisburg institution. Since 1913, this tiny horse-drawn hamburger wagon has parked each day on Market Square. It's a very simple business. They cook small hamburgers made from a secret recipe in big iron skillets. That's all they sell: hamburgers. No cheeseburgers, no hot dogs, no soda pop or french fries. (They do sell potato chips.) The main reason they are here is to just sell hamburgers, usually by the bagful. And don't ask for catsup or mustard. They offer their hamburgers just four ways: with pickle, with pickle and onion, with onion, or with nothing. That's it. The lack of side dishes or drinks doesn't seem to deter customers, who start lining up as soon as the wagon's wooden awning is lifted. The Hamburger Wagon is open every day from 10:30 A.M. until 7:00 P.M. On Sunday they open at 11 A.M. They have no phone. By the way, just across the street is a small potato chip factory, where you can get a can of pop, as well as some fresh kettle-cooked chips.

▲ **Hamburger Wagon**   ☎ 937-847-2442
  Market Square · Miamisburg

TRAPSHOOTERS HALL OF FAME

Ohio may have more halls of fame than any other state in the nation. We celebrate the very best in football, inventors, broadcasters, rock musicians—even trapshooters. This national exhibit preserves the memory of such trapshooters as Annie Oakley and famed composer John Philip Sousa, among many others. Here you can see the guns used by the enshrinees, as well as photos of trapshooting championships. The hall is open Monday through Friday.

▲ **Trapshooters Hall of Fame**   ☎ 937-898-4638
  601 W. National Rd. · Vandalia

Antique Capital of the Midwest

Harveysburg, Lebanon, Morrow, Oregonia, Waynesville, Wilmington

The tiny community of Waynesville, in Warren County, is only five city blocks long and has only one main street. Yet in those five blocks are packed nearly 40 antique shops with hundreds of antique dealers and their wares, making this community the "Antique Capital of the Midwest."

There was a Waynesville even before there was a state of Ohio. The village was founded in 1796, and many of the town's older buildings have been preserved.

The town also sponsors one of the stranger, but quite popular festivals in the state: the Ohio Sauerkraut Festival. Held since 1970, this festival is one of the few places you'll find candy made from sauerkraut and even ice cream with a sauerkraut base!

What makes the festival stranger still is that the town is not known for raising cabbage, nor are many people here of German heritage. In fact, the idea for the festival grew out of a meeting by town merchants over ideas for a festival, and one merchant made the chance remark that he had just had sauerkraut for lunch and had enjoyed it. Why not sponsor a sauerkraut festival? They did, and the rest is pungent history.

▲ **The Village of Waynesville** ☎ 513-897-8855
Waynesville Area Chamber of Commerce
108 N. Main St. · Waynesville

ONE OF OHIO'S OLDEST INNS

It is possibly Ohio's best known and oldest hostelry. No one is quite certain how it got its name, but in the early days of the nineteenth century, when Ohio was still on the frontier and literacy was a sometime thing, shop owners used pictures to advertise their wares. A sign depicting a gold lamb was hung over the combination stagecoach stop and tavern, thus its name. It was recognized in 1940 as the oldest hotel in the Buckeye State by the Daughters of the American Revolution. The inn today has 18 guest rooms with four dining rooms downstairs and five upstairs.

While presidents of the United States from John Quincy Adams to George W. Bush have visited the Golden Lamb, you don't have to be

The Golden Lamb in Lebanon is one of Ohio's oldest inns

a president to stay or eat there. The Lamb is most famous for family-style chicken and turkey dinners. The menu is a simple one: vegetable, mashed potatoes, several salad selections, turkey or chicken, and homemade rolls with fruit preserves.

▲ **The Golden Lamb** ☎ 513-932-5065
27 S. Broadway · Lebanon

SEASONAL TRAIN RIDES

If you're looking for an unusual way to get your Halloween pumpkins, how about a train ride to the pumpkin patch? This tour train north of Cincinnati has open gondola cars as well as passenger cars so that the kids can really see what it's like to ride on a train. In the spring, there is a trip to see the Easter Bunny; in the fall there's a trip to a pumpkin farm where kids can pick out a pumpkin to take back with them on the train. Trips originate at the old railroad station in historic Lebanon. *[SEASONAL]*

▲ **Cincinnati Railway Company** ☎ 513-933-8022
198 S. Broadway · Lebanon

ONE OF THE MOST BEAUTIFUL HOMES IN OHIO

It stands on a slight hill, overlooking what is today Ohio Route 42 on the south side of Lebanon. It has been called "One of the finest examples of Greek Revival architecture in the Middle West."

Glendower is a mansion built before the Civil War by one of our state's founders, John Milton Williams. It has 13 rooms, but the real beauty is outside where its classic cornices and porticoes, its fluted Ionic and unfluted Doric columns, and low roof topped off with a captain's walk seem to attract the attention of every passing motorist.

A sixteenth-century English country fair comes alive at the Ohio Renaissance Festival

Now operated by the Ohio Historical Society, the building is open for tours from June to December. Call for hours of operation. *[SEASONAL]*

▲ **Glendower** ☎ 800-283-8927
105 Cincinnati Ave. · Lebanon

WHEN KNIGHTS WERE BOLD

If you have ever fantasized about living in a time of knights and dragons, lords and ladies, you can live out your fantasy here in southwest Ohio. For nine weekends each autumn (from late August into October), a sixteenth-century English country fair comes to life in the rolling hills of Warren County, complete with a 30-acre village where armored knights on horseback joust with spears and swords. There are court dancers and jesters, strolling minstrels, jugglers, and even serving wenches.

Craftspeople from around the country come to the festival to sell their wares, including swords, clothing, blown-glass items, and traditional foods of the period are served. *[SEASONAL]*

▲ **The Ohio Renaissance Festival** ☎ 513-897-7000
State Rte. 73 · Harveysburg
Two miles west of I-71

ANOTHER OHIO MYSTERY

Fort Ancient, north of Cincinnati, is big: a total of 18,000 feet of earthen walls—more than three miles' worth. They were built 2,000 years ago by the Fort Ancient Culture of Native Americans. Why did they build it? What was its purpose? Who were the Fort Ancient people, and what happened to them? Those are mysteries.

We do know that it was built by hand, the natives using animal bones

as plows and scoops, and clam shell hoes, carrying the dirt by the bas-
ketful to create the walls. We also know that the position of some of the
walls used the sun and the moon to provide the natives with a calendar
system.

Be sure to visit the museum at the site. More than 9,000 square feet
of exhibits tell the story, or at least as much as we know, about the Native Americans in this part of Ohio. When you see the size of the fort
and consider how long ago it was constructed, you will gain new appreciation for a culture that we really know very little about.

   ▲ **Fort Ancient** ☎ 800-283-8904
     6123 State Rte. 350 · Oregonia

A REALLY BIG FLEA MARKET

On a nice summer weekend, nearly 1,000 vendors can be found set
up indoors and outdoors here at the intersection of I-71 and State Route
73. The permanent buildings can hold 500 dealers; hundreds more
set up in the surrounding parking lots during the summer when the
weather permits. This market has everything from furniture to fresh
produce. Open year-round on Saturday and Sunday.

   ▲ **Caesar Creek Flea Market** ☎ 937-382-1669
     7763 State Rte. 73 W · Wilmington
     State Rte. 73 and I-71, exit 45

BIRTHPLACE OF THE BANANA SPLIT

Wilmington lays claim to being the birthplace of the banana split
sundae. You know. You take a banana, split it long-ways, put it in a dish,
top it with three dips of ice cream (chocolate, vanilla, and strawberry),
then put some chocolate topping on the chocolate ice cream, crushed
strawberries on the strawberry ice cream, and crushed pineapple on
the vanilla ice cream. Add a liberal shot of fresh whipped cream, then
sprinkle some nuts across the top of the creation. Crown it with a cherry, and you have a banana split.

Local legend is that a restaurant operator by the name of Ernest Haz-
ard created the first banana split here in Wilmington in 1907. (See "The
First Banana Split" in my book *Ohio Oddities*). Today, they even have a
Banana Split Festival each year to celebrate the sweet ice cream delicacy.
Gibson's Goodies, an ice cream shop in downtown Wilmington, is the
place to sample an authentic banana split made just the way that Ernest
Hazard first made them. During the festival each year, Gibson's turns
out over 2,000 banana splits.

   ▲ **Gibson's Goodies** ☎ 937-383-2373
     718 Ohio Ave. · Wilmington

Cincinnati

Cincinnati, North Bend, Covington (KY), Newport (KY)

The Cincinnati Museum Center houses three museums

A NEW USE FOR OLD TRAIN STATIONS

Cincinnati turned its beautiful but abandoned old Union Terminal into an outstanding tourist attraction. Today it houses three museums and a huge state-of-the-art OMNIMAX movie theater.

In the Museum of Natural History & Science, you can walk through a cave and a glacier.

In the Cincinnati History Museum, you can stroll through Cincinnati's riverboat era; the life-size paddlewheel boat tied at a wharf is a popular display.

The Cinergy Children's Museum has more than 35,000 square feet of displays on three floors, and it has options on two more floors in the giant building. There are displays that will entertain and educate preschoolers—everything from a fishing exhibit with real water, where kids fish with magnets to reel in metal fish, to a place where they can roll balls down a hill and see the difference in speed when the hill is straight or curved. Older youngsters can have fun with television special effects, learn about assembly lines, try their hands at making things, and turn giant gears by walking on a treadmill.

The OMNIMAX theater offers a 72-foot-high domed screen that wraps above and around the viewers.

The huge rotunda of the building has been maintained much as it was in its glory days. Massive murals still cover the walls. The old information center in the center of the rotunda today serves as a visitor relations booth for the three museums and theater. With its shops, theaters, and restaurants, the museum center has something for everyone in the family.

▲ **Cincinnati Museum Center** ☎ 800-733-2077
1301 Western Ave. · Cincinnati

A HIGHBROW HALL OF FAME

While Cleveland is home to the Rock and Roll Hall of Fame, Cincinnati is the site of the American Classical Music Hall of Fame. Located in Memorial Hall on Elm Street, the hall is located right in the heart of downtown Cincinnati. While you won't find the Beatles or the Temptations here, you will find names like Duke Ellington, Scott Joplin, and John Philip Sousa alongside Toscanini and George Szell—all composers, conductors, or musicians who left their mark on American music. The hall has plaques that spell out the accomplishments of the enshrinees. You will also find music and artwork along with other exhibits that celebrate the world of American classical music.

▲ **American Classical Music Hall of Fame** ☎ 513-621-3263
1225 Elm St. · Cincinnati

A SPECTACULAR VIEW

I may have been born and raised in northern Ohio, but I love Cincinnati, with its hills and a river flowing by the front door.

You have to love a town that celebrates things like flying pigs. Just check out the statues on top of four columns at the entrance to Sawyer Point Park on the river. They resemble a set of steamboat stacks, but on top of the stacks are four flying porkers that celebrate the city's hog-processing history.

There's another landmark you're sure to recognize at Fountain Square in downtown. It's the "Genius of the Waters" the beautiful water fountain sculpture that was always featured on the opening of the TV show *WKRP in Cincinnati*. The fountain is 35 feet high and has been around since 1871. It's right next door to the tallest building in town.

That would be Carew Tower, the real landmark that you can spot for miles around. The 49-story-high building was constructed in 1929, and it very much resembles the Empire State Building in New York, although only about half as tall. An observation deck on the top floor allows you to see all the way to Kentucky. (OK, that's actually just across the river.) Seriously, the view is quite spectacular, and it's a favorite tourist destination.

There is an admission fee to the observation deck.

▲ **Carew Tower** ☎ 513-241-3888
441 Vine St. · Cincinnati

BIG CATS AND MANATEES

The Cincinnati Zoo is considered one of the nation's top five zoos. It has one of the largest collections of rare animals in America, including 21 types of rare and endangered wild cats. They also offer a "Jungle Trails" exhibit, which is a naturalized rain forest where exotic animals from Asia and Africa live.

It became one of the first zoos in Ohio authorized by the U.S. Fish and Wildlife Service to give a home to injured manatees. The manatees at the zoo have either been orphaned or injured and need care before they can be released back into the wild. None will be permanent residents there: the mission is to get them back to their natural habitat as quickly as possible. In the meantime they have become a major attraction, pulling in long lines of visitors during the summer months. Since their pool is enclosed and climate controlled, visitors can see the huge animals, also known as sea cows, any time of year.

USA Today once tagged the annual Cincinnati Zoo Festival of Lights as one of the "10 best in the nation." I won't argue. It's a true fairyland at night when there's snow on the ground. Besides hundreds of thousands of lights, there are many other attractions, from ice skating to a camel rides to train and tram rides. This family event has become a holiday tradition.

▲ **Cincinnati Zoo and Botanical Garden** ☎ 800-944-4776
3400 Vine St. · Cincinnati

A BLENDING OF ART AND WINE

The building that houses the Cincinnati Taft Museum of Art has quite a history that blends art, politics, and wine. The Baum-Longworth-Taft house was built in 1820. Down through the years, it has served as home to Nicholas Longworth, who brought the wine industry to America (See "The Grapes of Ohio" in my book, *Strange Tales From Ohio*) and Charles Taft, who was the brother of President William Howard Taft, and grand uncle of Governor Robert Taft. Charles and his wife, Anna, left their home and their extensive art collection to the city of Cincinnati. It is now considered one of the finest small art museums in America, containing more than 650 works of art, including pieces from Europe and America, as well as Chinese porcelains.

▲ **Taft Museum of Art** ☎ 513-241-0343
316 Pike St. · Cincinnati

National Underground Railroad Freedom Center

A MUSEUM DEDICATED TO FREEDOM

While the main focus of this museum is the Underground Railroad—the network of abolitionist groups that helped African-American slaves in their bid for freedom—it also commemorates the fight for freedom around the world. Cincinnati was selected as the home for this national museum because it was a hub of the Underground Railroad in the 1800s. Often, when slaves escaped from the south and crossed the Ohio River, this was the first large city that they came to that offered them assistance in fleeing north to Canada and freedom.

The center's three buildings are supposed to represent courage, co-operation, and perseverance. The curving architecture represents the winding Ohio River and the frequently changing path to freedom for the slaves.

▲ **National Underground Railroad Freedom Center** ☎ 513-333-7500
50 E. Freedom Way · Cincinnati

A LOVE BOAT WITH WINGS

"Your own little *Love Boat* with wings" is what Captain Dave McDonald calls the single-engine plane, capable of carrying up to six people, that is the sole aircraft of his Cincinnati-based Flamingo Airlines.

McDonald's niche is day trips on specialty flights. For example, he offers a quick down-in-the-morning, back-in-the-afternoon shopping flight to Gatlinburg, Tennessee, and an afternoon shopping flight to Cleveland. For something a little more colorful, he offers a quick flight to Chicago, where you are met at the airport by a limousine that whisks you on a whirlwind tour of spots once frequented by Al Capone and other infamous Chicago mobsters.

But Dave's real claim to fame and most successful flight so far is called

"Flights of Fancy." Dave says this flight is for romantics. The plane carries only a pilot and two passengers: you and your significant other. The middle row of seats has been removed, replaced by large satin pillows. There is a rose, a box of chocolates, a bottle of champagne, and a curtain that blocks the pilot's view of the back of the aircraft. There is also, according to Dave, a "very, very, discreet pilot." The plane takes off and climbs over a mile in the sky, circling over the Ohio River for an hour before returning to its home base at Lunken Airport.

McDonald says that while his pilots are the epitome of discretion, some things do draw their attention. Like the evening one pilot was flying a couple on a Flight of Fancy and the curtain suddenly fell or was accidentally kicked down, landing in the empty passenger seat next to the pilot. A long, naked leg stretched between the seats and retrieved the curtain and, moments later, it was back in place.

There was also the time Dave was flying along at about 5,500 feet over the river, when he was kicked in the back of the head by a couple in the back of the plane who had become a bit rambunctious. Also, more than one champagne cork has bounced off the pilot's head during flight.

"They really do have a lot of privacy back there," Dave McDonald says. "Besides, I'm so busy flying the plane, I don't have time to think about what's happening." As for eavesdropping on his passengers, Dave points out that the roar of the motor covers most sounds, and he is also wearing a pair of earphones and listening to air traffic controllers in the Cincinnati area.

⚠️ **Flamingo Airlines**   ☎ 513-321-7465
Lunken Airport, 358 Wilmer Ave. · Cincinnati
About five miles east of downtown, along the Ohio River.

A PRESIDENT WAS BORN HERE

William Howard Taft, the twenty-seventh president of the United States, was born in Cincinnati. He was the only man ever to serve as both president of the U.S. and chief justice of the U.S. Supreme Court.

His birthplace has been restored by the National Park Service, and it is open to the public. The home had for many years been an apartment house, and little was left of the original floor plan. The Park Service was able to restore it by using Taft's mother's letters to friends, in which she described the rooms, the wallpaper, and the furniture.

⚠️ **William Howard Taft National Historic Site**   ☎ 513-684-3262
2038 Auburn Ave. · Cincinnati

A ROMANTIC DINING SPOT

How about a restaurant that will remind you of a night in, say, San Francisco? Perched high atop Mount Adams in downtown Cincinnati is the Celestial Restaurant, which offers diners day and night a superb

Newport Aquarium, just across the river in Kentucky

view of the downtown skyline, the Ohio River, and the towns and hills of northern Kentucky. Local folks give this place raves for both its view and the food.

▲ **Celestial Restaurant and Lounge**   ☎ 513-241-4455
1071 Celestial St. · Cincinnati

OHIO, THE CEMETERY FOR PRESIDENTS

Ohio vies for the honor of producing the most presidents of the United States (we claim eight), and many of them thought enough of their native state to want to spend eternity here. The first was William Henry Harrison. (OK, he was born in Virginia, but always claimed Ohio as his home.) Harrison holds quite a few distinctions. He was a military hero who commanded the western army during the War of 1812. He spent most of his life in politics in Ohio and Indiana. His main distinction was that he became the first U.S. president to die while in office (and also the president with the shortest term of office) when he died just 30 days after being inaugurated in 1841.

Harrison is buried not far from where his home stood, just west of Cincinnati, along the banks of the Ohio River at North Bend. An obelisk of limestone with a marble entranceway rises 60 feet above the tomb, which is inscribed with the many offices that Harrison held. From the terrace is a spectacular view of the Ohio River valley.

The tomb also contains the remains of William Henry Harrison's son, John Scott Harrison, who was the father of another U.S. president, Benjamin Harrison. John Scott Harrison's body was stolen from a nearby cemetery shortly after his death and was later recovered in a Cincinnati Medical School, (See "The Missing Body" in my book *Ohio Oddities*). To discourage any further grave-robbing, the recovered body was

B.B. Riverboats offers mealtime trips and full-day excursions

sealed in William Henry Harrison's tomb, where, presumably, it has since rested in peace.

⚠ **Harrison Tomb** ☎ 800-686-1535
Cliff Rd. W · North Bend
About 15 miles west of Cincinnati off U.S. Rte. 50

OCEANIC ADVENTURE

Mix 350,000 gallons of water with 25 sharks and you have one of the great attractions in the Midwest. This aquarium located just across the Ohio River in Newport, Kentucky, offers a lot to see, but the main attraction is an 85-foot-long clear plastic tunnel that you walk through at the bottom of a huge tank filled with man-sized sharks. You feel like you're right in there with them. In fact, you can go nose-to-nose with a shark and walk away without a scratch. The aquarium is open daily, year-round, and is well worth the visit.

⚠ **Newport Aquarium** ☎ 859-261-7444
1 Aquarium Way · Newport, Kentucky

A HISTORIC CINCINNATI BED AND BREAKFAST

This grand old home is located on a street of historic homes just across the Ohio River from downtown Cincinnati. It's especially appreciated by executives visiting Cincinnati who don't want to stay in a big hotel, with all the hassles of parking and tipping. The home has been beautifully restored, with high ceilings and chandeliers that look like something out of a movie. There is a bridal suite with gas fireplace and whirlpool tub, but all the regular rooms are nice, too, including several in an old carriage house, where you sleep in a former horse stall. Each room has its own phone, television, and private bath. They also serve a full breakfast, not a skimpy continental thing with juice and toast. Reservations are a must here almost any time of year.

▲ **Amos Shinkle Townhouse Bed and Breakfast**   ☎ 800-972-7012
  215 Garrard St. · Covington, Kentucky
  Just across the river from Cincinnati

A RIVERBOAT CRUISE

If you can't afford a cruise for a week or two on the *Delta Queen*, perhaps you can afford an afternoon on the *Belle of Cincinnati* or the *Mark Twain*, two of Cincinnati's paddlewheel tour boats.

It's a great way to see the Cincinnati skyline and learn a bit about the history of this famous river port. They offer lunch, dinner, and Sunday brunch cruises, and full-day trips.

▲ **B.B. Riverboats**   ☎ 859-261-8500
  1 Madison Ave. · Covington, Kentucky

Cincinnati Area, North

Cincinnati, Fairfield, Hamilton, Kings Island, Mason

Jungle Jim's Grocery is anything but ordinary shopping

JUNGLE JIM

No one will accuse Jim Bonaminio of being conservative in his approach to the grocery business. Take the entrance to his store in Fairfield, just outside of Cincinnati: There is a jungle lake filled with life-sized, fiberglass, pink and blue hippopotami, an elephant spouting water, giraffes, and other creatures of the jungle. There is even a waterfall.

Along the walk to the front door are giant replicas of strawberries, bananas, and an orange.

Welcome to Jungle Jim's Grocery. One of the first things you spot upon walking into the store is a giant ear of corn and a stick of butter. This is a big store! The produce section alone covers nearly an acre and represents fresh fruit and vegetables from every corner of the earth. High overhead is a giant-sized can of Campbell's soup swinging on a child's playset. A stuffed animal that looks like Elvis breaks into song every few minutes in the bakery. If you see a man dressed like someone on a jungle safari rolling up and down the aisles on a Segway, that futuristic two-wheeled scooter, and stopping to help someone choose the freshest vegetables, you have just met "Jungle" Jim Bonaminio, the owner.

Jim Bonaminio grew up in Lorain County and began his career sell-

ing fruit and vegetables out of the back of his pickup truck at busy in-
tersections. Today he is considered one of the top independent grocers
in America, as well as one of the most innovative. He even built an
"Event Center" on the upper stories of his neighborhood grocery colos-
sus and installed a monorail from his parking lot to transport people
from the lot to the upper deck. From bathrooms that have won awards
for "America's best bathroom" to a real fire truck suspended over a giant
display of hot sauce, this is a very different experience when it comes to
grocery shopping.

Why all the weirdness? Bonaminio points out that kids love to come
to his grocery store—and that children often influence where parents
shop. He also notes that the giant fiberglass animals and the waterfall
help people remember and talk about his store. While some of his com-
petitors may call Jim Bonaminio crazy, he's laughing all the way to the
bank.

Open seven days a week.

▲ **Jungle Jim's Grocery**   ☎ 513-674-6000
5440 Dixie Hwy. · Fairfield

ABOUT THAT CINCINNATI CHILI

You can't come to Cincinnati without trying the chili for which the
city is famous. Whether you have it three-way or four-way, it is a gas-
tronomic experience. The chili, more like spaghetti with a cinnamon-
flavored tomato sauce, is served with optional cheese, onions, and red
beans. There are chili shops all over Cincinnati. The one we tried is
perhaps the best known.

▲ **Skyline Chili**   ☎ 513-874-1188
4180 Thunderbird Ln. · Fairfield
79 restaurants in Ohio, Kentucky, Indiana, and Florida; contact the
main office for location information

WAKEBOARDING IN SOUTHWEST OHIO

Want to enjoy the sport of wakeboarding (sort of a cross between a
snowboard and water skis) but don't own a boat? You might visit Ohio's
first cable-wakeboard park near near Cincinnati.

It works this way: There is a 10-acre lake with a cable system running
overhead. Riders sit on a pier along one side of the water as the cable
system circles the lake; when it reaches the last rider, it hooks his or her
cable and tugs them onto the lake at speeds of up to 20 mph.

According to first-time riders, it looks easier than it actually is. In
fact, they recommend that beginners launch themselves on their knees
and ride that way until they are comfortable with the cable speed. Basi-
cally, when they are not too busy, riders can stay on the cable until they

Ride a wake board without a boat at Wake Nation

fall off; then they swim to shore and get back in line for the next available cable. Six people can ride the lake at one time.

For more experienced riders who can stand all the way around the course, there are ramps and other obstacles to navigate through and over.

According to one skilled rider, the advantage of the cable system versus a boat is cost. But the drawback is you keep going around the same circle time after time, unlike a boat where you can move up and down the shoreline to change the scenery.

▲ **Wake Nation** ☎ 513-887-9253
201 Joe Nuxhall Way · Fairfield

GIANT SCULPTURES

This unusual outdoor cultural center features more than three dozen enormous works of art placed on hills and in valleys.

Harry Wilks wanted to build a special home along the Great Miami River in Butler County. He had a large art collection that he planned to house in his new home. But when it was finished, the location was so beautiful that many other people also wanted to build along the same area of the river. Wilks, in an effort to protect the environment, started buying up the property and invited sculptors to bring their works to his growing hillside property. He eventually created a sculpture park and donated his land, his home, and his collection to a non-profit corporation that today operates this outdoor sculpture park and museum. Some of the sculptures are so huge that passing airplanes can spot them from the air. (The largest, Abracadabra, by Alexander Liberman, is two-and-a-half stories tall and nearly four stories wide.)

Art is big—really big—at Pyramid Hill Sculpture Park

Today the park is a year-round tourist attraction, from summer concerts to holiday lighting displays in the winter. There are more than 40 monumental works of art scattered over 250 acres of hillside. Contact the park for a calendar of special events.

▲ **Pyramid Hill Sculpture Park and Museum**   ☎ 513-887-9514
1763 Hamiltion-Cleves Rd. · Hamilton

KINGS ISLAND AMUSEMENT PARK

One of America's most famous theme parks, Kings Island has more than 350 acres of thrill rides, a water park, shops, and restaurants. It is home of The Beast, the world's longest wooden roller coaster; and The Racer, a double-track wooden coaster with one train running forward and one running backward.

Boomerang Bay is a 15-acre water park with an Australian flavor; its 15 water slides, including inner tube rides, are guaranteed to get you very wet and cool you off on a hot Ohio summer day.

▲ **Kings Island**   ☎ 800-288-0808
6300 Kings Island Dr. · Kings Island

A DIVE-IN MOVIE THEATER

No, that's not a typo; there really is a "Dive"-in movie theater in southwestern Ohio. It's at one of my favorite aquatic parks, the Beach Waterpark in Mason, just across from Kings Island Amusement Park.

I got acquainted with the Beach many years ago. My son Craig, then about 10 years old, and I went to do a story for television on the park. We were floating on inner tubes down the Lazy Miami River (actually, a man-made shallow stream that runs 1,200 feet throughout the park). It was a cold day, and when I reached to adjust the inner tube I was riding in my wedding ring slipped off my finger and into the water. I tried to grab it, but the current swept it away. We climbed out and searched the entire length of the ride, but no ring. With hundreds of people in the water and dozens of drains and catch basins along the route, I just figured I had seen the last of my wedding ring. I did alert park personnel, and they assured me they would alert maintenance people to watch for the ring, but I really felt the ring was gone. We spent the rest of the day finishing our story and, toward evening, we started to leave. As we crossed a bridge over the "river," I saw a lifeguard and thought I might as well mention the loss to her. As I was standing on the bridge telling her about the loss of the ring, she continued to watch the riders in the water. Suddenly she said, "Look!" and leaped over the bridge into the water, which is only about thigh-deep throughout the course. She bent over and scooped up my ring, which was tumbling along the bottom on the current. I guess that is the day I should have also gone out and bought a lottery ticket.

So you can understand why I feel fond of the Beach and its personnel. But fondness has nothing to do with the fact that this is one of the major water parks in Ohio, and, perhaps, the only one that has a Dive-in Movie Theater. At the Kahuna Beach section of the park on Saturday nights they offer family films on a big screen. You can either watch from a lounge chair on the sand of the beach or dive in and float in an inner tube while enjoying the movie. With about 50 different water rides and even a water roller coaster this is a perfect place to spend a hot Ohio summer day or weekend.

▲ **The Beach Waterpark**   ☎ 800-886-7946
2590 Waterpark Dr. · Mason

The Beach Waterpark, home of the dive-in movie

SOME BARGAIN SHOPPING

Just outside of Cincinnati is a place that manufactures down-filled comforters for some of the major department and specialty stores in America. They have an outlet store at the factory, where you can buy not only the comforters but down-filled clothing, as well. The best buys are the comforter seconds, which may have been rejected by the department stores because of a crooked stitch or mismatched fabric. You can usually save up to 50 percent on these items, but you have to ask for them.

▲ **Down-Lite International**   ☎ 513-489-3696
7818 Palace Dr. · Cincinnati

HOMEMADE POTATO CHIPS

One of my favorite stops just on the north side of Cincinnati is a former drive-in restaurant that has made chicken their specialty. They marinate fresh Amish-raised chickens in citrus juices before cooking. It's their biggest seller, and they also make fresh, homemade potato chips to go with their meals. It's a great place to take kids.

▲ **Silver Spring House Restaurant**   ☎ 513-489-7044
8322 E. Kemper Rd. · Cincinnati

Ohio's Early Capitol City

Bainbridge, Chillicothe, Georgetown, New Richmond, Peebles, West Union

OHIO'S MOUNT VERNON

Adena could rightfully be called Ohio's Mount Vernon. This was the home of one of our founding fathers, Thomas Worthington, who was our first senator and our sixth governor. The mountaintop estate, which originally consisted of 2,000 acres of land, was designed by Benjamin Latrobe, noted for his work on the White House in Washington, D.C., and the Capitol building. It was the view of Mount Logan, across the Scioto River, that is depicted on our state seal, a view that can still be seen from the lawn of Adena. If you are interested in Ohio history, this is a great place to start.

▲ **Adena State Memorial**   ☎ 800-319-7248
846 Adena Rd. · Chillicothe

MOUND CITY

Near Chillicothe you can see one of the great mysteries of the past: Mound City. This was one of the centers of the Hopewell Culture of pre-historic Americans. The Hopewells left behind earthworks in the form of squares, circles, and other geometric shapes more than 1,000 feet across. Some of the mounds were up to 30 feet in height, and some were used as burial sites. Researchers believe that the mounds and earth-works were used in the social, ceremonial, political, and even the economic life of these people, but no written record has been found.

What you see today is a recreation of some of the original grouping of mounds and earthworks. Most of the originals were destroyed by early farmers, and further damage was done to the site during World War I when the government leveled the mounds to build Camp Sherman Army Training Base. A portion of the historic location was rescued in the early 1920s by the efforts of a local archeological group that campaigned to have the mound area declared a national monument. It was during this time that original mound and enclosure sites were recreated. The National Park Service took over care of the site in the 1940s.

▲ **Hopewell Culture National Historical Park**   ☎ 740-774-1125
16062 State Rte. 104 · Chillicothe

Tecumseh Outdoor Drama celebrates a Native American hero

STORY OF A NATIVE AMERICAN HERO

Each summer night in Sugarloaf Mountain Amphitheatre near Chillicothe, the story of a Native American hero is told.

Tecumseh, the great chief of the Shawnee Tribe, was born not far from where his story is presented by actors using the words of Pulitzer Prize nominee Allan W. Eckert. The show has run every summer since it was first presented in 1972. The outdoor drama is one of Ohio's best, with over 100 cast members, horses, cannons and blazing forts. It bring history alive. It gives us a chance to see why Tecumseh fought the advance of the white settlers as they attempted to move the Indians from the Ohio frontier and why he said, "We are determined to defend our lands and, if it be the Great Spirit's will, we wish to leave our bones upon them."

It is a moving story, and one the entire family can enjoy. *[SEASONAL]*

▲ **Tecumseh Outdoor Drama**   ☎ 866-775-0700
   Sugarloaf Mountain Amphitheatre, 5968 Marietta Rd. · Chillicothe

THE PHONE-IN DRIVE-IN

Chillicothe is home to a drive-in restaurant that hasn't changed much since the 1950s. The Sumburger Drive-In still has curb service as well as indoor dining. They have an unusual way to order: you use a telephone at the table to call in your order to the kitchen. The burgers are large and are served with crinkle-cut fries. They also have Kool-Aid on the menu, offering a flavor of the day. That alone was enough to get me to stop for lunch.

▲ **Sumburger Drive-In**   ☎ 740-772-1055
   1487 N. Bridge St. · Chillicothe

A BED AND BREAKFAST FIT FOR A PRESIDENT

The area around Atwood Lake Resort is called "the edge of Paradise." You will understand why when you visit here. The 1,540-acre lake is the largest inland sailing lake in Ohio. The resort offers 104 guest rooms, a restaurant, indoor and outdoor pools, two golf courses, tennis courts, camping, cottages, swimming, and a marina where you can rent everything from a canoe to a float boat.

▲ **Atwood House**   ☎ 740-774-1606
68 S. Paint St. · Chillicothe

THE HOUSE GRANT CALLED HOME

The eighteenth president of the United States, Ulysses S. Grant, grew up and lived in this home in Georgetown longer than in any other. The home was saved from destruction in 1977 by nationally known wildlife artist John Ruthven and his wife Judy. They restored the home to the appearance that it had when Grant lived there. Furnished rooms inside are dedicated to Grant and contain other local memorabilia. In 2002 the property was turned over to the Ohio Historical Society.

There are other sites in Georgetown associated with President Grant, such as the school he attended and the site of his father's tannery, a business the family operated for many years. It was from here that Grant received his appointment to West Point. When he left, he entered the pages of history. The home is open from Memorial Day to Labor Day. *[SEASONAL]*

▲ **Grant Boyhood Home**   ☎ 937-378-4222
219 E. Grant Ave. · Georgetown

BIRTHPLACE OF A PRESIDENT

It's sometimes hard to believe as you approach the tiny three-bedroom cottage not far from the banks of the Ohio River, that a president of the United States was born here. Not only a president, but also a commander of the United States Army during the Civil War.

This small white house was where Ulysses S. Grant was born in 1822. The family lived here for less than a year before they moved down the road to Georgetown, where Grant grew to manhood. However, the Grant birthplace has had almost as interesting a history as its former occupant. It actually moved all over the country before finally returning to a permanent foundation here in the 1930s. (See "General Grant's Wandering Home" in my book, *Ohio Oddities*)

The birthplace is now operated by the Ohio Historical Society, and it is open to the public from April through October. *[SEASONAL]*

▲ **Grant Birthplace**   ☎ 513-553-4911
U.S. Rte. 52 · New Richmond

In Point Pleasant, in Clermont County, just off of U.S. Rte. 52 about five miles east of New Richmond

A FUNERAL HOME MUSEUM

This museum may not be for everyone, but it certainly is unusual! It collects and displays hundreds of tools used by undertakers since 1848, including embalming kits, shrouds, burial clothing, funeral home ledgers, old wooden caskets, and more. Of particular interest are the nine horse-drawn funeral vehicles.

This collection came about because funeral home operator William Lafferty just couldn't bear to part with his old equipment, especially antique horse-drawn hearses that had been used by his family to conduct funerals for four generations. It's like the saying goes: "You have two or three things and the next thing you know you have a collection." Lafferty started buying and collecting additional funeral vehicles down through the years. By the time he died in 1987, he had amassed a sizeable collection of both horse-drawn and motorized vehicles used in the funeral trade. His family has built a special building to house the collection that is open to the public, as they say, by chance or appointment.

▲ **William Lafferty Memorial Funeral and Carriage Collection**
☎ 937-544-2121
205 S. Cherry St. · West Union

THE CRADLE OF DENTAL EDUCATION

The Paint Valley, located near Chillicothe, is one of my personal favorite areas of the state in the autumn. It's an area of hills and streams and small towns. One of those towns is Bainbridge, which has an unusual claim to fame: it's called the "Cradle of Dental Education" because it's considered the place where dentistry truly became established as a profession. Dr. John M. Harris was a medical doctor who settled in Bainbridge in the 1820s. He began teaching medical students the practice of dentistry and in 1828 started the world's first dental school. Today the school is a dental museum where visitors can see a variety of antique dental instruments and sets of false teeth. I must admit that on my visit, my teeth hurt just looking at some of the primitive tools used in the practice of dentistry.

▲ **Dr. John Harris Dental Museum**   ☎ 740-634-2246
208 W. Main St. · Bainbridge

MOUND OF MYSTERY

This is probably the most mysterious of Ohio's mounds. It is believed to have been built by Native Americans of the Fort Ancient culture around 1000 A.D., though some say it may have been built as recently as 1300 A.D. The mound depicts what appears to be a huge snake about

The mysterious mound at Serpent Mound State Memorial

to devour an egg as it winds its way a quarter of a mile up a hilltop. It is not a burial mound, although burial mounds have been found nearby. No one is quite sure of the significance of the Serpent Mound. Perhaps it had religious significance; maybe it was used as some sort of calendar by early people. No writings about the mound have ever been found, nor any explanation of why it was built. An observation tower nearby provides a better view of the enormous serpent. The property is owned today by the Ohio Historical Society. The grounds are open year-round. There is a parking fee.

▲ **Serpent Mound State Memorial**   ☎ 800-752-2757
3850 State Rte. 73 · Peebles
Near Hillsboro; six miles north of State Rte. 32 and 20 miles south of Bainbridge

SOUTHEAST
OHIO

Rural Attractions

Bidwell, Hocking Hills, Jackson, Logan, Nelsonville, New Plymouth, Rockbridge

The real Bob Evans farm

DOWN ON THE FARM

You may have eaten in the restaurants bearing his name or purchased some of the sausage his company sells without knowing that Bob Evans was a real person. But he was, and you can visit the farm near Gallopolis where his sausage empire started.

The thousand-acre Evans farm, located in Rio Grande, is where Bob and his wife, Jewell, lived for many years. Today it's home to a museum that features the counter from the first Bob Evans restaurant, where it was not unusual to find Bob Evans sitting at the counter having a cup of coffee and chatting with the regulars.

The craft barn sells all kinds of hand-made items from the area, there are hiking trails and self-guided tours around the farm buildings, where you can see many kinds of farm animals and possibly some of the quarter horses that Bob has raised over the years. There is also a nearby campground where festivals and events are held, including the Bob Evans Farm Festival, which attracts thousands.

▲ **Bob Evans Farm** ☎ 800-994-3276
791 Farmview Dr. · Bidwell

HOME TO NINE STATE PARKS

The state park capitol of Ohio is the Hocking Hills region, where there are nine, count 'em, nine state parks, a state forest, and one of the largest metroparks in Ohio. Probably the best known of all the parks is Old Man's Cave. The most accessible park is Ash Cave, which also is the largest and most impressive cave in the state. Conckle's Hollow has the deepest gorge in Ohio. Cantwell Cliffs, though not easy to reach because of its remote location, has what hikers say is one of the most beautiful views in the county. There are also Rock House, Cedar Falls, Lake Logan, and Clear Creek Metroparks. What's really great about all these parks is that they are just a few miles apart, and you can spend weeks seeing all the sights. For detailed information and maps of the parks, contact the Hocking Hills Tourism Association.

▲ **Hocking Hills Tourism Association**   ☎ 800-462-5464
Hocking Hills Regional Welcome Center
13178 State Rte. 664 S · Logan

FLOATING DOWN THE RIVER

Some years back, we stopped at this popular canoe livery to do a news story on canoeing the Hocking River. Since I have a terrible sense of balance, we decided to take along an inflatable rubber raft that I would use instead of a canoe. We were getting ready to head upstream and I was madly pumping our little handpump to inflate my boat when one of the folks from the canoe livery saw the veins in my head starting to protrude, my face turning bright red, and perspiration making a river down my back. He kindly offered to help, pointing out that they had an air compressor nearby and could quickly handle my small inflation job. Without giving it much thought I handed them the deflated boat. But when they hooked up the powerful air compressor, the air shot into the boat with such force that it ripped apart with a huge bang! "Never saw one do that before" the man said. We discovered that only one air chamber had burst, so we carefully inflated the rest of them and the boat looked pretty good. I declined their offer to take a canoe and slapped my sagging but inflated boat into the river and jumped in. Fortunately the river was only about 12 inches deep at that point, because the deflated air chamber sagged to the bottom of the river, taking my posterior with it. The only thing sticking out of the water was my head and my feet. Everything else was very wet. But damp as I was, we finished the story.

I do recall the beauty of the Hocking River that you can only see from the water, especially the natural rock bridge located in the Rockbridge State Nature Preserve, which is right along the river. Also, if you like to fish, the Hocking is well-stocked with small mouth bass and pan fish. You can get in a canoe and float without doing much paddling downstream. The Hocking River is considered to be a medium-difficulty river by experienced canoers. It has an average gradient of about four-and-a-half feet each mile, making for an easy ride, even for beginners. Rent a canoe and leave the work to the river; it's a great way to get acquainted with one of Ohio's most scenic areas. *[SEASONAL]*

▲ **Hocking Valley Canoe Livery and Fun Center**   ☎ 800-686-0386
31251 Chieftain Dr. · Logan

A GATHERING SPOT

This mini-mall on the outskirts of Logan has a long history with the town. Folks in the 1840s used to pay 15 cents to ride a canal boat from Logan out to this rural picnic grove. After the Civil War, it was a gathering spot for Union veterans, including President William McKinley, to hold reunions. Today it still attracts tourists with a petting farm, an Amish-style restaurant, antique stores, an ice cream parlor, a miniature golf range, a motel, and craft stores. This is also home to the Hocking Hills Canoe Livery, where you can rent canoes, kayaks, and rafts for trips down the Hocking River.

▲ **Rempel's Grove**   ☎ 800-634-6820
12819 State Rte. 664 S · Logan

WORTH THE WAIT

If you are looking for luxury and primitive at the same time, you can't do better than the Inn at Cedar Falls. Innkeeper Ellen Grinsfelder, one of my favorite people, and her staff make every visit here something that becomes a lifetime memory. The inn is surrounded on three sides by Hocking Hills State Park, yet it is only three miles to other attractions, like Ash Cave, Old Man's Cave, and the historic town of Logan. While the rooms in the old barn, cozy cottages, and the luxury cabins offer all the amenities, as well as privacy and a chance to experience the solitude of the Hocking area, be sure to make a reservation for dinner in the historic log cabin where the inn started. The gourmet kitchen is in the middle of the dining room, so you can watch each course as it's being prepared and chat with the chef. How's this for breakfast: French toast, stuffed with cream cheese and raspberry preserves, served with warm maple syrup and fresh raspberries? That was just one of the dishes we were served the morning after we spent the night in the inn.

▲ **The Inn & Spa at Cedar Falls**   ☎ 800-653-2557
21190 State Rte. 374 · Logan

A STEAM TRAIN RIDE

One of Ohio's first excursion trains is located in nearby Nelsonville. The railroad, operated by volunteers, uses diesel-powered engines to give tourists a slow ride through the Hocking Valley. Tickets can be obtained at the depot in Nelsonville. The train usually runs on week-ends seasonally, but it does make special runs on holidays. Call for the schedule. *[SEASONAL]*

   ▲ **Hocking Valley Scenic Railway**   ☎ 800-967-7834
     33 E. Canal St. · Nelsonville

ROCKY BOOTS

For more than 70 years, some of the finest outdoor boots in the world were made right here in Ohio. Rocky Boots no longer makes the boots here, but the old factory has been turned into an outlet center, where you can find bargains on discontinued styles as well as overruns and even first-quality boots and clothing that bear the Rocky label.

   ▲ **Rocky Outdoor Gear Store and Clearance Center**   ☎ 740-753-3130
     45 E. Canal St. · Nelsonville

COLLEGE FOR HOTEL MANAGERS

This otherwise ordinary inn is operated by Hocking College, and it is an essential part of the hospitality program that the college offers students who would someday like to be chefs, innkeepers, or food and beverage managers. The hotel is mostly staffed by advanced students and instructors. There are two restaurants, a swimming pool, and some rooms offer whirlpool tubs. During our visit, we found the food to be wonderful. Several of the senior cooking students had prepared the dinner menu that evening.

   ▲ **Inn at Hocking College**   ☎ Reservations: 800-272-6232;
     Local: 740-753-3531
     15770 State Rte. 691 · Nelsonville

A LUNCH BOX MUSEUM

Sometimes the simplest things can become a tourist attraction. Take a small country store in the Hocking Hills. Owner LeDora Ousley collects lunch buckets. You know, those stamped metal things we used to carry to school each day with our PB&J sandwiches crammed inside. The outside probably had a picture of our favorite TV show like *The Brady Bunch* or *Roy Rogers*.

Well LeDora has them filling shelves throughout the store. None of the collection is for sale: it's just to look at and enjoy, except for a few duplicates that she might be willing to part with. The store's main function is as a café, hence the name: Etta's General Store and Lunchbox Café. It's mostly sandwiches and pizza, but they do offer a couple of neat items like their hobo ham steak, which is really a fried bologna ring cut one inch thick and cooked with some onions on the grill. It will bring back memories of when bologna was a staple on many menus. You can also get a really good PB&J sandwich here. By the way, if you don't have

Etta's Lunchbox Café and General Store

time to sit at the lunch counter and eat, LeDora and her crew will be glad to pack up your lunch so you can go for a hike and eat it later, but it will be packed in a paper bag, not in one of her lunchboxes.

▲ **Etta's Lunchbox Café and General Store**   ☎ 740-380-0736
35960 State Rte. 56 · New Plymouth

BED AND BREAKFAST IN A CASTLE

This is a real castle, built in the late twentieth century on a hill in Vinton County not far from Hocking State Park. Copied from castles in Scotland, the building offers luxury rooms with king or queen beds and private bathrooms, and some with whirlpool baths. They also have an assortment of cottages on the castle grounds and even some gypsy wagons for those who like to camp out in the woods. Breakfast is served in the great room, and, for an additional cost, dinner can also be arranged. This is a very popular spot for special events, romantic getaways, and honeymoons.

▲ **Ravenwood Castle Bed and Breakfast**   ☎ 800-477-1541
65666 Bethel Rd. · New Plymouth
South of Hocking Hills and Old Man's Cave area, south of Lancaster

A SCOTTISH COUNTRY INN

This modern structure built in the style of a sixteenth-century Scottish manor is tucked away in the woods near the Hocking Hills Cave area. Besides the manor, the owner also has built 13 cottages and crofts in the woods, each located to ensure privacy, and all equipped with a fireplace, living room–kitchen, bedroom, and private bath. Sit and watch the stars from a large hot tub, located on a your cabin's deck facing the woods. Rooms in the manor and carriage houses have fireplaces

Glenlaurel has 13 cottages for rent

and whirlpool baths. Available at extra cost is a six- or seven-course dinner for two; the host for the evening recites poetry before dinner. On many Saturday evenings a bagpiper pipes you to dinner. No accommodations for children; the inn, they say, is "for lovers only." Special note: the inn and the grounds are non-smoking.

▲ **Glenlaurel, a Scottish Country Inn**   ☎ 800-809-7378
14940 Mount Olive Rd. · Hocking Hills

Really Big Things

Ava, Caldwell, Cumberland, McConnelsville

Big Muskie's bucket at Coal Miners' Memorial Park

BIG MUSKIE'S BUCKET

This is coal-mining country, and here you'll find a memorial to the miners who once worked this land. It's the bucket that once belonged to Big Muskie, the largest dragline on earth. It was so big that it had to be assembled on the work site. When finished, it stood 13 stories high. The bucket, which weighed an incredible 460,000 pounds, was capable of picking up 320,000 tons in one bite. That's a volume equal to a 12-car garage. Sadly, the Big Muskie was dismantled and sold for scrap in the 1990s, but you can still see the enormous bucket at the Coal Miners' Memorial on Ohio Route 78. There is a small park there with picnic shelters and restrooms. Be sure to bring along your camera.

▲ **Coal Miners' Memorial Park** ☏ (no phone)
   State Rte. 78 · Caldwell (16 miles west of Caldwell)

LOCAL CUISINE

When it comes to food, if you are looking for fine dining, you may want to drive south to Marietta. However, if you are looking for just something more than the usual assortment of national chains ranging from pizza to burgers, they also have several good alternatives that serve typical meat-and-potatoes fare.

The Archwood Family Restaurant took over one of my favorite places, the Sandwich Shoppe on the Square. Under the new name it still attracts the folks downtown for lunch.

Another spot that locals claim is a favorite is Lori's Family Restaurant on nearby Route 78. If you are tired of mass-produced chain food then you might want to experiment with some local cuisine. Both of these places offer local flavor in food as well as clientele.

△ **Archwood Family Restaurant**　☎ 740-732-2090
426 Cumberland St. · Caldwell

△ **Lori's Family Restaurant**　☎ 740-732-4711
17020 Route 78 · Caldwell

A CALDWELL BED AND BREAKFAST

One of the things that Noble County likes to promote is that most of its attractions are free. If you are planning a trip to this part of Ohio, it won't break the bank. One of the nice bed and breakfasts located in downtown Caldwell offers convenience: a quiet, pleasant place to spend the night and a sumptuous breakfast of whatever you like the next morning for less than a night at many chain motels along the interstate. The Harkins House Inn is a nicely restored Queene Anne colonial home that has been taken back to its original appearance from when it was built in 1905, with the addition of some modern amenities inside. The two guest rooms are bright and roomy, and one offers a gas fireplace.

△ **Harkins House Inn**　☎ 740-732-7347
715 West St. · Caldwell

AN OHIO CONSERVATION CENTER FOR ENDANGERED SPECIES

This major tourist attraction is a center where endangered exotic animals from all over the world are allowed to run free on seven square miles of reclaimed strip-mined land. Over 400 different animals, some already extinct in their native lands, are housed here. (Some animals from tropical areas are sheltered in barns during the winter months.)

Visitors are allowed inside the fenced-in pasture only on special buses with guides. Touching or feeding the animals is not allowed. The animals roam free, so there is no guarantee what you will see. If they're near the roads, you can get an up-close look. However, many of the animals here were born in captivity and are accustomed to, if not downright curious of people; it's a rare visit when you don't see most of the endangered species.

Among the animals in the center are giraffes, white rhinos, eland, camels, and some rare Przewalski's horses. The animals chosen are of species that are rare or endangered, and the purpose is to keep the breed going by offering them shelter here in Ohio at The Wilds. There is

Endangered species run free at The Wilds

also a carnivore conservation center with cheetahs, African wild dogs, and dholes.

There is an admission charge. Open from May to October.

▲ **The Wilds**   ☎ 740-638-5030
14000 International Rd. · Cumberland
South of Cambridge; call for directions

OHIO POWER LANDS

Ohio Power Lands is a good example of what can be done with some land that was once strip mined. Today, 350 lakes stocked with fish dot 30,000 acres of reclaimed land. Picnic areas in shaded groves overlook meadows of wildflowers. There are hiking trails and primitive camping areas open to the public. The area is also open for hunting and trapping. All of this is free; just write for information on how to obtain the free-use pass: American Electric Power Company, P.O. Box 328, McConnelsville, OH 43756, or you can visit them online and obtain a permit at www.aep.com.

▲ **American Electric Power ReCreation Land**   ☎ 740-962-1208
McConnelsville

THE WRECK OF THE SHENANDOAH

In the early part of the twentieth century, Ohio was the scene of a great tragedy. The U.S. navy airship *Shenandoah*, America's first dirigible and the first to use helium, crashed into a southeastern Ohio hillside, killing 14 crew members. At better than 600 feet in length, the airship was as big as some of the ore freighters on the Great Lakes. The ship was torn apart in a September thunderstorm in 1925, near Ava.

You can see a memorial marker in the center of the small community of Ava, not far from where the ship broke up. There is also a small museum, located in a former camper-trailer, with artifacts from the crash and other memorabilia.

▲ *Shenandoah* **Memorial and Museum**   ☎ 740-732-2624
50495 State Rte. 821 · Ava

Wreckage Site Number 3 of the Shenandoah *dirigible disaster*

The Northwest Territory Started Here

Marietta

The Valley Gem *sternwheeler on the Muskingum River*

LIFE ON THE RIVER

Marietta, located at the confluence of the Muskingum and Ohio Rivers and steeped in history, is where the Northwest Territory began. Today it wears its age like a badge, proudly—still a small river city, though a favorite with tourists for years.

One man who helped put Marietta on the tourist maps was Captain Jim Sands of the *Valley Gem* sternwheeler. For many years he operated one of the last of the paddlewheel boats that operated on this part of the Ohio River. His son, Captain Jason Sands, and Jason's wife, Katie, now run the boat.

The *Valley Gem* gives visitors a chance to experience the slow, regal travel of the great sternwheelers. The boat goes up the Muskingum and through the century-old hand-operated locks at the Muskingum River dam. It's a wonderful trip on an autumn day, with both sides of the river painted in fall colors. *[SEASONAL]*

▲ *Valley Gem* **Sternwheeler** ☎ 740-373-7862
601 Front St. · Marietta
Docked at Washington St. Landing

TWO HISTORY CENTERS

The Campus Martius Museum is on the site of the first organized American settlement in the Northwest Territory. It contains the restored home of Rufus Putnam, one of the founders of Marietta. It also has a good collection of exhibits on the early history of Native Americans and later migrations of people into and within Ohio.

The Ohio River Museum, a block away, is a treasure trove of Ohio River steamboat history in three buildings. Outside, you can tour the *W.P. Snyder Jr.*—the last intact steam-powered, stern-wheeled towboat in the United States

Both facilities are run by the Ohio Historical Society. *[SEASONAL]*

▲ **Campus Martius Museum** ☎ 800-860-0145
601 Second St. · Marietta

▲ **Ohio River Museum** ☎ 800-860-0145
601 Front St. · Marietta

A TRIBUTE TO COKE

This museum mainly commemorates Coca-Cola. It even has a soda fountain, which, of course, sells Coke. You can find early soft-drink advertising, soft-drink machines, and a gift shop, where not only can you buy some of your favorite soft drink to take home, but you can also buy replicas, and in some cases originals, of advertising signs and products.

▲ **Marietta Soda and Fountain Museum** ☎ 740-376-2653
109 Maple St. · Marietta

FLAGS AND POLES

Here's a business you've just got to salute: a shop that sells nothing but flags and flagpoles. You can buy anything from a miniature American flag for a parade all the way up to a 40-foot aluminum pole and all the hardware to get Old Glory flying in front of your home or business.

▲ **American Flags and Poles** ☎ 800-262-3524
276 Front St. · Marietta

LEVEE HOUSE CAFÉ AND RESTAURANT

This former dry goods store, the first in the Northwest Territory, has stood for more than 170 years facing the Ohio River. The current owner renovated it and made it into a restaurant specializing in gourmet cuisine. The expanded lunchtime menu offers gourmet pizza and wraps. Also, in good weather, the tables on the patio are a great place to have a glass of wine and watch a sunset on the Ohio River. You can also catch the trolley here that offers guided tours of this historic river city.

▲ **Levee House Café and Restaurant** ☎ 740-374-2233
127 Ohio St. · Marietta

LAFAYETTE HOTEL

The Lafayette Hotel, one of the last of the riverboat-era hotels, was built in 1918 on the point where the Muskingum River empties into the Ohio. From the rooms guests can look out at the rivers and see tugs pushing huge barges toward Pittsburgh or New Orleans.

Named for the Marquis de Lafayette, who once visited the city in the 19th century, the historic building has been renovated and modernized but still keeps much of its riverboat charm. It has 77 rooms, including suites. The Gun Room is their restaurant famous for its collection of antique firearms.

The Lafayette's triangular building, located in the heart of downtown Marietta, is within walking distance of many of the city's attractions.

▲ **Lafayette Hotel**   ☎ 740-373-5522
102 Front St. · Marietta

IT'S NOT JUST A STUMP—IT'S PUBLIC ART

In most towns a wind storm that knocks down ancient trees means a pain in the you-know-where to local officials. It means a costly cleanup and the loss of beautiful shade trees. But in Marietta, Ohio, following a big wind storm back in 1998, city officials came up with a new variation of the old expression, "If life gives you a lemon, make some lemonade."

Chainsaw artist David Ferguson was commissioned to turn the stumps of the downed trees, some of them more than 100 years old, into works of art. The local convention and visitors bureau has a map showing the location of all of the trees.

▲ **Marietta-Washington County CVB**   ☎ 740-373-5178
121 Putnam St. · Marietta

Pottery and Glassware

Cambridge, Lore City, Norwich, Roseville, Zanesville

A LEGENDARY GLASS COMPANY

One of the legendary Cambridge glass companies is still in business, turning out all kinds of glassware, and they invite tourists to drop in and see how they do it.

Mosser Glass makes all kinds of pressed glass items, from Victorian glass cake stands to glass kerosene lamps to ornate glass lampshades, as well as dishes and decorative articles. It's educational, and it can be a fun break while traveling to watch the workers heat glass to a molten glow, then pour it into molds to make some of their products. Tours are usually available Monday through Friday during working hours.

> ▲ **Mosser Glass Factory Tour**   ☎ 740-439-1827
> 9279 Cadiz Rd. · Cambridge
> About ¼ mile west of I-77 (Exit 47)

A TOWN MADE OF GLASS

A museum in Cambridge celebrates the world famous Cambridge glassware that was commercially manufactured in this city from 1902 until the mid 1950s. Located in an old utility company building, high on a hill (the first museum was the victim of a flood in 1998), the museum offers a look at the Cambridge glassware that was once manufactured in several plants nearby. Using mannequins, the museum exhibits show how the furnaces, molds, and other items for the making of glassware were used.

This is a great place for collectors of glassware to learn how to distinguish originals from reproductions and to see some of the items that once made this little town known all over the country.

> ▲ **National Museum of Cambridge Glass**   ☎ 740-432-4245
> 136 S. Ninth St. · Cambridge

A GLASS FACTORY

Cambridge has always been known for its glass industry and, in recent decades, its decorative glass. Perhaps its most famous product was Degenhart glass. The manufacturer, now known as Boyd's Crystal Art Glass, continues to turn out many famous products and develops new ones each year. They also offer tours of their glass-making plant, where you can watch artisans at work molding glass. There is a factory outlet store where you can buy their products.

▲ **Boyd's Crystal Art Glass**   ☎ 740-439-2077
1203 Morton Ave. · Cambridge

OUTDOOR DRAMA

One of Ohio's pioneer outdoor dramas is performed here. *The Living Word*, the story of Christ and his crucifixion, is staged in an outdoor amphitheater that creates a feeling of realism as the story unfolds. While most of the cast is made up of local volunteers, the performance has been well received down through the years. The play is shown only on Friday and Saturday evenings during the summer months. Call for times and dates.

▲ **The Living Word Outdoor Drama**   ☎ 740-439-2761
6010 College Hill Rd. · Cambridge

OHIO'S BIGGEST BAKERY

This bakery claims to have the largest single store in Ohio. If it's baked, you can probably find it here, along with some of their award-winning trail bread. Their monster cookies are as big as pizza pies, and a birthday cake department features two portrait artists who can duplicate a photograph with cake icing to create a birthday cake portrait of the person being honored.

▲ **Kennedy's Cakes and Donuts, Inc.**   ☎ 740-439-2800
875 Southgate Pkwy. · Cambridge

CONEY ISLAND DOGS

This place started out in life as a hot dog stand, but that was long ago, before a fire destroyed the original place. The current restaurant still sells the famous Coney Island dogs, but they have also turned it into a full-scale family restaurant that has become a favorite stop for tour groups. The place is also known for its pies, made fresh every day. While they don't offer tablecloths or six forks and four knives at every place setting, this is a good place to take the kids for some home-cooked, plentiful servings.

▲ **Theo's Restaurant**   ☎ 740-432-3878
632 Wheeling Ave. · Cambridge

A PLACE TO PLAY AND SLEEP

The largest (and probably most popular) state park in Ohio is Salt Fork, near Cambridge. The massive park encompasses more than 17,000 acres sprawling across much of Guernsey County. Named for a salt well by Native Americans, the park is located near what was once Zane's Trace, which became part of the National Road, today known as U.S. Route 40, one of the first major east-west transportation routes.

The park and lodge were built in the 1960s and early 1970s. Rolling hills surrounding the lodge and cabins are filled with streams and lakes. The modern lodge with 148 rooms is complemented by 54 cabins that are family-friendly, with heat and running water. The lodge also offers both indoor and outdoor swimming pools. There is an 18-hole golf course and nearby marinas where you can rent just about any kind of boat that floats on the lake. This is a great place for a getaway with the entire family. If you like wildlife, just take a drive through the grounds on a warm night. Deer wander in herds everywhere here. It's not unusual to find several standing on the front porch of the lodge.

▲ **Salt Fork State Park**　☎ 800-282-7275
14755 Cadiz Rd. · Lore City
Just north and east of I-77 and I-70 at Cambridge

THE MAIN STREET OF AMERICA

U.S. Route 40 was originally known as the National Road because it stretched from Cumberland, Maryland, to Vandalia, Illinois. The highway was begun in 1806, long before there were cars and trucks. In fact, the National Road in Ohio holds the distinction of being the location of the first recorded traffic fatality when a stagecoach overturned near Zanesville in 1835 (See "Ohio's First Traffic Fatality" in my book, *Ohio Oddities*).

Today you can see what this road meant to the rest of the United States at the National Road/Zane Grey Museum, near Zanesville. There is a 136-foot-long diorama that shows how the highway developed from a crude trail to a modern highway for trucks and automobiles. U.S. 40 was truly the "Main Street of America."

The other half of the museum is dedicated to Zanesville native Zane Grey, considered to be the father of the adult western novel. His book *Riders of the Purple Sage*, published in 1912, became a classic. In all, he wrote more than 80 books. Many of his manuscripts and other memorabilia are on display here. *[SEASONAL]*

▲ **National Road / Zane Grey Museum**　☎ 800-752-2602
8850 East Pike · Norwich

OHIO-MADE LAWN ORNAMENTS

This is a good spot to pick up some Ohio-made pottery and cement lawn ornaments. You can find lots of seconds from some of the famous Ohio pottery names and save up to 50 percent (or more) on things like birdbaths, garden globes, and huge crocks or even cement cows, pigs, and geese that can be dressed in clothes. You could probably save a few more cents by going direct to the factories to buy some of these things, but here you can get a good variety, save a lot of money in gas and wear-and-tear on your car, and save time.

▲ **Ohio Pottery** ☎ 740-872-3137
8540 East Pike · Norwich
Exit 164 off I-70, west of Cambridge.

PADDLING DOWN THE RIVER

One of the first sternwheeler boats I ever got to ride on was the *Lorena,* which still sails out of downtown Zanesville each summer.

The 104-foot-long sternwheel tour boat can carry 90 passengers and is named after a popular Civil War song that told of a lonely man missing his sweetheart, Lorena. The song was written by Henry Webster, pastor of a Zanesville church in 1840. The song was supposedly based on a broken relationship between Webster and a local woman. During the Civil War, the haunting melody became a favorite of soldiers, both blue and gray.

The first *Lorena* that sailed the river in 1895 was a floating palace capable of carrying 700 passengers. It was destroyed by a fire in 1916 near Parkersburg, West Virginia. The present-day *Lorena* was built in the 1940s originally as a riverboat; it was renovated in 1975 and renamed *Lorena* for the U.S. bicentennial celebration in 1976. It has been a fixture on the Muskingum waterfront in Zanesville ever since.

With both tourist and dinner cruises, the boat is a popular destination. Its season runs from June until September. *[SEASONAL]*

▲ **The *Lorena* Sternwheeler** ☎ 800-246-6303
Zane's Landing Park, Market St. · Zanesville
Off Market Street at the River

BLOOMER'S CANDY

This is one of the big names in candy in central Ohio. Bloomer's chocolates are sold at many small markets and specialty stores. While tours of their factory are not available, there is a quaint factory store in the local railroad station. The advantage of going to a factory store is obvious: you get a choice of all of the many varieties they make. The candy is usually fresher, too, and sometimes seconds are available at discounted prices.

▲ **The Sweet Station (Bloomer's Candy)** ☎ 740-455-2314
231 Market St. · Zanesville

THE RIGHT STUFF'S FAVORITE

Tom was the original owner; Bill Sullivan, who used to work for Tom, bought the place many years ago but never changed the name. This has been a very busy spot since *USA Today* newspaper named Tom's as one

White paper hats and bow ties are still worn at Tom's Ice Cream Bowl

of the best places to eat ice cream in the country. Since then, little has changed as far as Tom's goes. The place still looks like time stopped here in the 1940s. The help still wear those little white paper hats and bow ties. The ice cream is made right behind the counter, fresh every day, and they still put so much sauce on their sundaes that it drips right off the plate. They claim that former astronaut and U.S. Senator John Glenn is a regular customer.

▲ **Tom's Ice Cream Bowl**   ☎ 740-452-5267
  532 McIntire Ave. · Zanesville

The Old West Comes to Ohio

Barnesville, Belmont, Cadiz, Flushing, St. Clairsville

Dickinson Cattle Company is a real longhorn steer range right here in Ohio

RIDE THE RANGE

Believe it or not, one of the country's largest longhorn steer ranches is right here in Ohio. The Dickinson Cattle Company of Barnesville took over thousands of acres of strip-mined property in Belmont County and turned it into a ranch where they raise not only champion longhorn steers, but also Watusi and BueLingo cattle. So many curious folks stopped by to see what was going on that the Dickinson finally bought an old school bus and they now give guided tours of the ranch during the summer months. They also have a store where you can buy meat from the cattle and other longhorn products. *[SEASONAL]*

▲ **Dickinson Cattle Company**   ☎ 719-683-2655
35000 Muskrat Rd. · Barnesville

RENT-A-CAMP

At this state park you can try camping without spending much money. Barkcamp State Park's rent-a-camp program provides a family with a walled tent for the night, along with cots, lantern, cooler, cook stove, picnic table, and even a broom to clean up with. All you have to bring along is your blankets and food. It costs $30 a night. The rent-a-camp program is available at several state parks throughout Ohio.

You can rent a complete camp setup at Barkcamp State Park (or bring your own)

Barkcamp State Park contains more than 1,000 acres of land and has a 117-acre stocked fishing lake. There are 150 campsites on the property available to campers on a first-come, first-served basis. There is also a 700-foot-long public beach with picnic shelters.

▲ **Barkcamp State Park**   ☎ 866-644-6272
65330 Barkcamp Park Rd. · Belmont

OHIO'S FOREST PRIMEVAL

If you would like to see what Ohio must have looked like to the early settlers, I have just the place. It's one of my personal favorite spots in all of the Buckeye State: Dysart Woods, located in Belmont County in southeast Ohio.

Dysart Woods covers a bit over 50 acres and contains trees that are 300 to 400 years old. It's said to be the largest known unglaciated primeval oak forest in this part of the state. That means some of the trees are over four feet in diameter and stand at least 140 feet tall!

The woods today are studied by Ohio University programs and are open to the public.

▲ **Dysart Woods**   ☎
State Rte. 147 · Belmont
Take the Belmont exit from I-70; South on State Rte. 149 to State Rte.
147 about 5 miles; watch for sign on the right

HOME OF THE "KING OF HOLLYWOOD"

He was known as the "King of Hollywood," but Clark Gable was born in the middle of the Ohio coalfields in Cadiz. A small, two-story frame home is an exact replica of Gable's original home, which stood near downtown Cadiz but was torn down many years ago. Pictures of Gable and his family adorn the walls. You can see the small upstairs bedroom where the future star was born. In a nearby bedroom is a pair of pajamas from his Hollywood days, as well as correspondence between Gable and former president Dwight D. Eisenhower. Outside, Gable's 1954 Cadillac sits in the driveway. It is said that he was driving this very car when he had his first heart attack.

In the basement is a small theater where a short film is shown about Gable's life in Cadiz and his career in Hollywood.

At present there is no elevator to take handicapped visitors to the second-floor museum or the basement theater area, but officials for the museum said one is planned.

▲ **Clark Gable Birthplace Gift Shop and Museum**   ☎ 740-942-4989
138 Charleston St. · Cadiz

ANOTHER BIG ICE-CREAM CONE

This one is in an out-of-the-way spot in Southeast Ohio, near Tappan Lake. Deersville is just a tiny little community, but everyone in the area knows the Deersville General Store. That's the place of giant ice-cream cones. They make their own ice cream here. At present they make eight different flavors, some of which are only seasonal, like peach or fresh strawberry, because they require the availability of fresh fruit. The cones are an ice cream eater's dream. For example, a single is actually about two-and-a-half large dips of ice cream, and a double amounts to nearly five dips!

Legend has it that famous Americans like Harvey Firestone and even Thomas A. Edison have stopped at the Deersville General Store, probably seeking out a really big ice-cream cone.

▲ **Deersville General Store**   ☎ 740-922-0831
212 W. Main St. · Deersville

A PLACE FOR A FAMILY REUNION

If you are looking for a big old home in which to hold a real family reunion or just a bed and breakfast for a night that is not far from lots of activities in southeast Ohio, this is it. Stratton House Inn was once home to the family who operated the Stratton Mill, where one of the first self-rising pancake flours was created. The old mill, now being rehabilitated, is just down the road. The Inn sits atop eleven sprawling hilly acres. It has five bedrooms and four baths and can accommodate up to 25 people. The three-story, century-old home has been updated and modernized, but still retains much of the flavor of its beginnings. And, unlike many bed and breakfasts, children are welcome.

▲ **Stratton House Inn**   ☎ 800-678-2435
100 Stratton Ln. · Flushing

A POPULAR EATING PLACE

They come from three states to eat at this cafeteria on U.S. Route 40, just outside St. Clairsville. Mehlman's has been in business for more than three decades. Everything they serve is made daily from scratch: fresh soups, breads, pies. They offer dozens of entrées ranging from meat loaf to baked steak.

Lines of hungry customers usually stretch out the front door on weekends. But the line moves surprisingly fast, and usually customers wait no more than 20 or 30 minutes to reach the serving tables. Prices are moderate, and because everything is priced á la carte, you can order just what you want.

▲ **Mehlman Cafeteria**　☎ 740-695-1000
　51800 National Rd. · St. Clairsville

The Edge of Paradise

Bolivar, Dellroy, East Sparta, Zoar

Atwood Lake Resort

LARGEST INLAND SAILING LAKE IN OHIO

The area around Atwood Lake Resort is called "the edge of Paradise." You will understand why when you visit here. The 1,540-acre lake is the largest inland sailing lake in Ohio. The resort offers 104 guest rooms, a restaurant, indoor and outdoor pools, two golf courses, tennis courts, camping, cottages, swimming, and a marina where you can rent everything from a canoe to a floatboat.

▲ **Atwood Lake Resort**   ☎ 800-362-6406
2650 Lodge Rd. · Sherrodsville

A MODERNIZED VICTORIAN

This 1880 Victorian home has been modernized: all rooms have private baths, and some have whirlpools, gas fireplaces, and balconies. The big selling point here is the location—just across the street from Atwood Lake in southeast Ohio with lake views. It's also not far from New Philadelphia and the outdoor drama *Trumpet in the Land*. The owners also offer gourmet breakfasts. The house is filled with antique glassware and furnishings.

▲ **Whispering Pines Bed and Breakfast**   ☎ 866-452-5388
1268 Magnolia Rd. (State Rte. 542) · Dellroy

Canoeing on the Tuscarawas River

A QUIET CANOE EXPERIENCE

If you've ever taken the family canoeing on a hot summer day and found the river looking like I-71 at rush hour, you may just want to consider this canoe livery near Bolivar on the Tuscarawas River. They have only about 50 canoes. That's all they rent, so they don't crowd the river like many other canoe liveries do. This does mean waiting for a canoe at times, but the experience you and the family have and the peace and quiet of the river will be well worth it. By the way, the initials stand for Nature Trails Rental. They offer some special events, like Halloween haunted trails and a Christmas decoration tour of area homes when it's too cold to go canoeing. *[SEASONAL]*

▲ **NTR Canoe Livery**   ☎ 330-874-2002
State Rte. 212 · Bolivar
Just east of I-77

A ROMANTIC BARN

The Enchanted Pines Retreat Bed and Breakfast in Bolivar is located in a barn-like structure. The home is built like a Yankee barn, and that means that this post-and-beam construction has cathedral ceilings that soar 30 feet above you. The inn has more than 5,000 square feet of space, with large, airy rooms in this modern building and an in-ground swimming pool for summer visitors. There is a tea room and shop connected with the business, where you can buy the one-of-a-kind decorations you see throughout the home. Bedrooms have private baths and whirlpool tubs. The building, which is set on a ridge overlooking six wooded acres and beautiful gardens, offers much privacy to visitors.

▲ **Enchanted Pines Retreat Bed and Breakfast**   ☎ 877-536-7508
1862 Old Trail Rd. NE · Bolivar

OHIO'S UNKNOWN SOLDIER

Even though Ohio was just rugged frontier at the time, the state did play a role in the American Revolution. Fort Laurens, in the small community of Bolivar, near Zoar, is the site of the only Revolutionary War fort in Ohio. Named in honor of the president of the Continental Congress, Henry Laurens, it was built in 1778 during a campaign to attack the British at Detroit. The problem was that it was located so far out in the wilderness that it made supplying the troops almost impossible, and the fort's American forces nearly starved to death while withstanding a month-long British-led Indian siege of the fort. Today, only the outline of the fort remains. There is a memorial building where some of the defenders of the outpost are buried in the wall, and on the grounds is the tomb of the supposedly unknown American soldier whose body was recovered in the 1970s when archeological work was done on the fort grounds. The fort is open to the public Wednesday through Sunday from May to September.

▲ **Fort Laurens State Memorial**   ☎ 800-283-8914
County Rd. 102 · Zoar
Exit 43 off I-77; ½ mile south of State Rte. 212.

HOME OF THE ZOARITES

This area was founded as a communal society in 1817 by a German religious group called the Society of Separatists of Zoar. The Zoarites built sturdy German-type buildings for their community, and while the buildings survived for centuries, the community did not, and disbanded in 1898. Today, several of the surviving buildings are owned by the Ohio Historical Society, which has restored them, and the area is now known as the Zoar Village State Memorial. The focal point of the community is a large public garden that attracts tourists every summer, as well as a host of other restored buildings depicting what life was like in the nineteenth century, with costumed guides. While many attractions in the village are open year-round, the state-operated buildings are open on a seasonal basis. Call for hours. *[SEASONAL]*

▲ **Zoar Village**   ☎ 800-874-4336
State Rte. 212 · Zoar

Acknowledgments

It is always difficult to remember everyone who has contributed something to a book. No matter how many names I list, I am sure that I will inadvertently leave out someone who made my life easier by their suggestion or assistance in the writing of this book. So, to those I forgot I sincerely apologize. Blame it on an aging memory and know that your help was greatly appreciated.

I do want to publicly thank many of my dear friends like Ted and Karen Driscol, Jim and Barb Pijor, Kevin and Cindy Ruic. My daughter, Melissa Luttmann and her husband, Peter as well as my other daughter, Melody McCallister and her husband, Ernest McCallister for their help in suggestions, researching and encouragement when I started this book. My son, Craig Zurcher, who inspired many of the trips and spent 10 summers traveling with me and appearing on TV when he was young. There were other friends like Char Lautzenheiser and Gary and Bob Rice who were never too busy to answer a question or to help track down some arcane fact.

I am indebted to many of the county travel and tourist agencies in Ohio. They have let me draw on their expertise and helped me to find some of the most interesting places in Ohio down through the years.

Some of the destinations in this book I first reported on in my monthly column in the *Ohio Motorist* magazine, published by the Ohio Motorist Association. My deep thanks to Managing Editor Phil Hartman for his many suggestions over the years.

I also can't forget the contribution of my former boss, and friend, Virgil Dominic who created the "One Tank Trips" series on WJW-TV and gave me the best assignment of my career, one that lasted 25 years as producer, writer and host of the travel segment.

Other former colleagues at WJW-TV deserve a mention: The beautiful and talented Tomi Toyama-Ambrose who helped produce many of my television shows and who has continued to be so helpful over the years. The many talented photographers I worked with: including, Bill West, Bill Wolfe, Bob Wilkinson, Ron Mounts, Jimmy Holloway, Mark Saksa, Ali Ghanbari, Herb Thomas, Ted Pikturna, Ralph Tarsitano, Gary Korb, Cragg Eichman, Roger Powell, Greg Lockhart, Ron Strah, the late Bob Begany, John Paustian, Dave Almond and Peter Miller.

And finally, David Gray, who has published all of my books and continues to challenge me with new ideas each year, Rob Lucas who helped with the update of this edition, Chris Andrikanich who keeps me busy with book signings, and Jane Lassar who makes sure I get my 15 minutes of fame each time a book is published.

To all of you my deepest thanks.

Photo Credits

Page 3, Neil Zurcher; p. 5, Dutchman Hospitality; p. 7, Heini's Cheese Chalet; p. 9, Donna's Premier Lodging; p. 10, Wendell August Forge; p. 13, Guggisberg Cheese; p. 15, Inn at Honey Run; p. 18, Neil Zurcher; p. 19, Jamie Curio; p. 20, Experience Columbus; p. 21, A. D. Farrow Harley-Davidson; p. 23, Franklin Park Conservatory and Botanical Garden; p. 24, Experience Columbus; p. 25, E. Terry Clark; p. 26, Ohio Historical Society; p. 29, G. Jones (courtesy of the Columbus Zoo and Aquarium); p. 33, American Motorcyclist Association; p. 34, Longaberger Company; p. 36, Great Circle Earthworks; p. 39, Roscoe Village Foundation; p. 43, Neil Zurcher; p. 48, Neil Zurcher; p. 50, Hyatt Regency Cleveland at the Arcade; p. 51, Thom Sivo (courtesy of Cleveland Botanical Garden); p. 52 (right), Western Reserve Historical Society; p. 52 (left), Cleveland Museum of Natural History; p. 54, Heidi Adams Cool; p. 55, Julio Ganzalez; p. 56, David Valencic; p. 58, Neil Zurcher; p. 59, Kent State University Museum; p. 60, Walden Country Inn and Stables; p. 62, Cuyahoga Valley Scenic Railroad; p. 63, Shoenfelt Photography; p. 65, Ashley Leonard (courtesy of the Akron Aeros); p. 66, Stan Hywet Hall & Gardens; p. 67, Quaker Square Inn at the University of Akron; p. 73, Military Air Preservation Society; p. 75, National First Ladies' Library; p. 76, William McKinley Presidential Library and Museum; p. 79, Tom Bower; p. 83, Neil Zurcher; p. 88, Neil Zurcher; p. 90, Neil Zurcher; p. 91, Discover Ohio; p. 92, Daniel Snyder; p. 96, Century Village; p. 98, Geauga Park District; p. 100, End of the Commons; p. 102, Neil Zurcher; p. 103, National Packard Museum; p. 111, Neil Zurcher; p. 114, Landoll's Mohican Castle; p. 115, Neil Zurcher; p. 116, Adrienne Wallace; p. 119, Richland Carousel Park; p. 123, Lehman's; p. 125, Neil Zurcher; p. 129, Harry Hunt; p. 131, African Safari Wildlife Park; p. 133, Jet Express; p. 135, Cleveland Press Collection, Cleveland State University Archives; p. 137, Kelleys Island State Park; p. 138, Waters Edge Retreat; p. 140, Perry Victory and International Peace Memorial; p. 142, Cedar Point; p. 144, Robert Myer; p. 145, Great Wolf Lodge; p. 147, Neil Zurcher; p. 149, Neil Zurcher; p. 150, Neil Zurcher; p. 153, Milan Historical Museum; p. 156, Discover Ohio; p. 157, Tony Packo's; p. 158, B&B Railroad Depot Bed and Breakfast; p. 159, Xanterra Parks and Resorts; p. 161, Neil Zurcher; p. 162, Sauder Village; 165, Rutherford B. Hayes Presidential Center; p. 170, Barn at Walnut Glen Bed and Breakfast; p. 173, Piatt Castles; p. 177, Armstrong Air and Space Museum; p. 180, Bicycle Museum of America; p. 183, Neil Zurcher; p. 184, Neil Zurcher; p. 187, National Museum of the United States Air Force; p. 189, Dayton Society of Natural History; p. 193, Neil Zurcher; p. 196, John Hartsock; p. 197, Ohio Renaissance Festival; p. 199, Cincinnati Museum Center; p. 202, National Underground Railroad Freedom Center; p. 204, Newport Aquarium; p. 205, B. B. Riverboats; p. 207, Jungle Jim's Grocery; p. 209, Neil Zurcher; p. 210, Pyramid Hill Sculpture Park and Museum; p. 211, Beach Waterpark, The; p. 214, Joe E. Murray (courtesy of Tecumseh Outdoor Drama); p. 217, Discover Ohio; p. 221, Bob Evan's Farm; p. 225, Etta's Lunchbox Café and General Store; p. 226, Glenlaurel; p. 227, Neil Zurcher; p. 229, The Wilds; p. 230, Neil Zurcher; p. 231, Valley Gem; p. 238, Jarrod Bates; p. 239, Dickinson Cattle Company; p. 240, Neil Zurcher; p. 243, Atwood Lake Resort and Conference Center; p. 244, NTR Canoe Livery.

Index